CATHOLIC REVIVALISM:
THE AMERICAN EXPERIENCE
1830–1900

Catholic Revivalism
The American Experience 1830–1900

Jay P. Dolan

UNIVERSITY OF NOTRE DAME PRESS
NOTRE DAME   LONDON

Library of Congress Cataloging in Publication Data

Dolan, Jay P. 1936–
    Catholic revivalism: The American Experience, 1830–1900.

    Bibliography: p.
    Includes index.
    1. Catholic Church in the United States—History.
2. Parish missions—United States. 3. Revivals—United
States. I. Title.
BX1406.2.D64   282'.73   77-89755
ISBN 0-268-00722-5

To Patricia

Contents |

Acknowledgments |

One of the most meaningful phrases in the language of man is "thank you." For someone writing a book it is a most appropriate sentiment since authors, historians especially, accumulate a lot of professional debts. My debts are many, but first and foremost I must thank those scholars whose works I have consulted. They taught me many things I did not know and enabled me to build on what they had done. Their names are too numerous to mention, but their works are cited in the footnotes.

I have a special debt to Timothy L. Smith who first encouraged me to pursue this project. On several occasions I had the opportunity to discuss certain aspects of the manuscript with him and I benefitted from his advice. He also read the entire manuscript, and I profited from both his dissenting comments and his constructive criticism.

Other colleagues who read the manuscript in one form or another were Martin E. Marty, Jerald C. Brauer, William R. Hutchison, John F. Wilson, James J. Hennesey, S.J., Robert F. McNamara, Nathan A. Hatch and Philip Gleason. My thanks to them for their willingness to assist my work and refine my thinking. Harry Grile, C.SS.R., shared his research on the Redemptorists with me and Thomas J. Schlereth pointed me to important material concerning the history of another order of preachers, the Congregation of Holy Cross. My thanks also to Henry Regnet, S.J., of St. Louis University who let me consult his personal collection of material relating to the life of Francis X. Weninger, S.J.

Sections of this work were first presented at the Shelby Cullom Davis Center for Historical Studies at Princeton University in 1974, at the Johns Hopkins-Harwichport

Seminar in American Religious History in 1975, and in a seminar at the University of Chicago in 1976. My thanks to the participants in these seminars for their helpful criticisms.

A note of special thanks must go to the Shelby Cullom Davis Center for Historical Studies at Princeton University and its director, Professor Lawrence Stone, for providing a fellowship in 1973-74 which enabled me to begin the research on this book. Working at the Center and sharing the camaraderie of its fellows and the history faculty of the university was a very pleasant and rewarding experience. The Word of God Institute in Washington, D.C., directed by John Burke, O.P., also provided a generous grant which allowed me to take time off from teaching in order to complete the book. The University of Notre Dame also provided a research grant that permitted me to travel and gather material used in the study. During the time I was engaged in this study, the chairmen of my department at Notre Dame, Philip Gleason and Marvin R. O'Connell, were especially understanding and supportive of my work.

The graduate students with whom I worked over the past few years contributed to this book more than they might have imagined by helping me to clarify my thinking about Catholic revivalism. I also owe a special "thank you" to Peter Lombardo, assistant archivist at the University of Notre Dame, who competently and graciously assisted me in a variety of ways during the past few years.

I am greatly indebted to Barnabas D. Hipkins, C.SS.R., the Redemptorist provincial archivist, and Lawrence McDonnell, archivist for the Paulist Fathers, for their cooperation. Without their assistance I could never have written this book. Other archivists who were especially helpful were Clement Buckley, C.P., the Passionist provincial archivist, Thomas E. Blantz, C.S.C., archivist for the University of Notre Dame, and Anthony Zito, assistant archivist at Catholic University.

The library staff at the University of Notre Dame also provided generous assistance, and the faculty typing pool at Notre Dame promptly and efficiently typed the final draft of the manuscript.

My wife, Patricia, was a big help throughout the entire project. Pouring over baptismal registers, confirmation lists and city directories she did much of the basic research on which chapter five is based. She read the manuscript at various stages along the way and offered valuable advice. The dedication of the book to my wife inadequately expresses my gratitude to her for her understanding, cooperation, and support of my work.

Jay P. Dolan
University of Notre Dame
August, 1977

Introduction |

When Charles G. Finney, one of the premier Protestant revivalists of the nineteenth century, was writing his memoirs, he included a brief passage about a convert at his 1842 revival in Rochester:

> Several of the lawyers that were at this time converted in Rochester, gave up their profession and went into the ministry. Among these was one of Chancellor W——'s sons, at that time a young lawyer in Rochester, and who appeared at the time to be soundly converted. For some reason, with which I am not acquainted, he went to Europe and to Rome, and finally became a Roman Catholic priest. He has been for years laboring zealously to promote revivals of religion among them, holding protracted meetings; and, as he told me himself, when I met him in England, trying to accomplish in the Roman Catholic church what I was endeavoring to accomplish in the Protestant church. . . . When I was in England, he was there, and sought me out, and came very affectionately to see me; and we had just as pleasant an interview, so far as I know, as we should have had, if we had both been Protestants. He said nothing of his peculiar views, but only that he was laboring among the Roman Catholics to promote revivals of religion.[1]

The person to whom Finney referred was Clarence Walworth, lawyer, convert, Roman Catholic priest and one of the foremost parish mission preachers in nineteenth-century Catholic America.[2]

The connection between Walworth's apostolate as a parish mission preacher and Finney's revival ministry very poignantly illustrates the main thesis of this study. The religion of revivalism was not exclusively a Protestant enterprise, but it also swept through Catholic America in the second half of the nineteenth century and, in the process, shaped the piety of the people and strengthened the institutional church.

Most Catholics are familiar with the parish mission. It was a time when a religious order preacher was invited to the parish to revive the religious vitality of the people. For a week or more the preacher would hammer home the saving truths of Christianity, urging people to repent and do penance for their sins. Then, his work done, the preacher would leave, not to return again for another two or three years. The nineteenth-century version of this phenomenon was basically the same: Groups of religious order preachers toured Catholic America conducting parish missions in an effort to revive the religion of the people.

In this study the terms *parish mission* and *Catholic revival meeting* are used interchangeably. The reasons for this are twofold. Nineteenth-century observers, Finney included, were quick to see the similarity between the two phenomena and described the parish mission as a revival. In addition, the parish mission fostered a type of religion, evangelicalism, that has long been associated with the technique of mass evangelism known as revivalism.

Religious order preachers traditionally conducted the parish mission. Nor was the work confined to any particular order engaged in the pastoral ministry. In this study, however, I have concentrated on three groups: the Jesuits, the Redemptorists, and the Paulists. Other groups are considered but only in a general manner. The selected groups provide an accurate representation of the parish mission phenomenon and adequately reflect its historical development in the nineteenth century. To have included a broader representation of religious orders and of mission preachers would have been redundant. Catholic preachers were remarkably similar in what they said in their sermons; this similarity was due in large part to the uniformity of doctrine fostered in nineteenth-century Roman Catholicism. It was also based on the evangelical nature of revivalism, a theme common to all Catholic mission preachers.

This study ends in 1900. And the reason is not entirely arbitrary. Even though the parish mission continued well into the twentieth century, it had achieved a definite form and style by the end of the 1800s and consequently underwent little change in subsequent decades. In speaking with people who had experienced parish missions in the twentieth century this point became self-evident. Joseph Fichter's study of a southern parish in the late 1940s also supports this assessment.[3]

The first two chapters trace the origin and growth of Catholic revivalism during the nineteenth century. In seeking to explain its emergence, the European tradition of the parish mission is studied along with the causes indigenous to the American experience. With this historical background in place, the study then focuses on the revival meeting itself and the preachers who made it work, describing what actually went on when Catholics gathered together for a parish mission. The fourth chapter analyzes the sermons of a representative group of preachers. The central message of their preaching was clearly evangelical and the Catholic emphasis on the reception of the sacraments imparted to this a special dimension; thus the phrase *sacramental evangelicalism*, which best describes the type of religion promoted at the Catholic revival meeting. The term *evangelical* obviously has a variety of meanings depending on the theological perspective or tradition from which one is writing.[4] In this study I have used the term in a very generic way as a religious motif or mood which can be found in many different Protestant denominations as well as in the Catholic tradition.

After studying the religion of revivalism I then sought to determine who the people were that listened to this gospel and what impact it had on their lives. Evangelicalism placed a great deal of emphasis on the personal experience of conversion, and from this point of view it encouraged a type of piety that was not only experiential, but also very individualistic. According to the revivalist, salvation was a personal goal to be pursued by all God's children, and the pursuit of this goal was achieved by following a code of conduct that was primarily individualistic in tone. A major indicator of this was the emphasis given to the temperance pledge during the parish mission.

In addition to the personal or individual effects of revival preaching there was also a very evident communal aspect. Catholic evangelicalism not only changed the lives of individuals by offering them a unique experience of saving grace, it also served to strengthen the community and promote the consolidation of the institutional church. Like Janus, the Roman god, evangelical Catholicism had two faces. It was both individual and communal. At certain moments one theme was dominant, then the other would come into focus. The emphasis on individual conversion did not exclude the need of the community in the pursuit of piety and vice versa. Chapter six focuses on the personal, individual effects of revival religion; the following chapter explains how revivalism transformed the church by organizing and strengthening the community of believers. For the sake of analysis, these two effects of revival religion are examined separately, but in order to understand the fullness of this phenomenon they must be viewed as two sides of the same coin.

The final chapter seeks to point out the similarities between Catholic and Protestant revivalism. Although they were clearly not identical phenomena, the similarities were too striking to be ignored. Charles Finney realized this when he commented on the work of Clarence Walworth, and Walworth himself sensed it as well. Such similarities indicate how widespread and popular the religion of evangelicalism was in nineteenth-century America. Yet, the opportunities for comparison do not end there. Catholic revivalism also bears striking resemblances to the contemporary charismatic movement in the Catholic church. Moreover, the religion of revivalism goes a long way toward explaining why twentieth-century Catholics behaved in the manner they did. The similarities between revivalism and pentecostalism reflect the popularity of experiential religion among Catholics and its impact on the culture of Catholicism suggests that the parish mission movement exercised a very formative influence on the development of the American Catholic community.

Historians have always considered revivalism as a major force in American religious history. Yet, they have consistently limited their vision to the Protestant phase of this phenomenon, believing that Roman Catholics were not so evangelically oriented. This study corrects that limited view and suggests that the religion of revivalism not only found a home among Catholics, but indeed was a major force in forming their piety and building up their church. To tell the story of revivalism in America the Catholic phase of this history must be included. Moreover, for anyone writing the history of American Catholicism the revival phenomenon cannot be omitted. To the person in the pew the revival experience meant a great deal more than ecclesiastical politics and institutional development. It touched their lives and spoke to them in a very personal and meaningful way—"repent and be saved, or else." History is necessarily more than the study of politics and institutional growth; it also is the story of people—how they lived, thought, worked, played, and prayed. To tell the story of American Catholicism and not include what was perhaps the most popular religious movement in the nineteenth century does not do justice to the richness of the American Catholic experience. This study attempts to balance the scales of American

Catholic historiography by focusing on the people as well as the institution. It is an account of a social and religious movement that permeated Catholic America and transformed the religion of the people. It offers a new insight into a two-hundred-year-old tradition and to the extent that it succeeds, it is a reinterpretation of that experience.

The Origins of
Catholic Revivalism | **1**

In the early decades of the nineteenth century,
Catholicism in the United States was still very much
a missionary church struggling for survival in an
unfriendly environment. This is perhaps difficult to appreciate for anyone viewing the church in the last quarter of
the twentieth century. The American Catholic church is
generally perceived as a richly endowed, politically powerful
organization that claims the allegiance of one-quarter of the
national population and boasts of an educational system
surpassed only by the public school bureaucracy. Across the
urban landscape the spires of Catholic churches line the
nation's freeways, continually reminding people of the
church's pervasive and influential presence in the city. At
election time, politicians court the Catholic vote and church
prelates possess a measure of clout in the statehouse and city
hall. As one of the nation's largest real estate holders, the
church seems to possess unlimited financial resources. As
part of an international organization headquartered in Rome,
its influence even extends around the globe.

But whatever power, wealth, and influence the church
enjoys at home or abroad is an achievement gained only in
the twentieth century. Indeed, as far as the Vatican was
concerned, it was only in 1908 that the United States ceased
to be missionary territory. Only then was the American
church judged to have reached a level of maturity compara-
ble with the ancient churches of France, Italy, and Germany. A hundred years earlier the Catholic church in the
United States possessed neither power, wealth, nor prestige.

1

It was an outpost of Roman Catholicism, equal in significance to a small diocese in Europe and surpassed in importance by the church in Canada as well as Cuba.[1]

As a missionary territory the United States held a peculiar attraction among Europeans. Ever since the days of the Jesuit missionaries in the seventeenth century this fascination was centered on "the savages," the "pagan Indian population" who appeared so ripe for conversion. Even as Andrew Jackson was pushing the Indians west of the Mississippi in the hope that somehow they would disappear from view, European priests were caught up in the spirit of the noble savage and romantically dreamed of sailing to the far distant shores of America to convert "the poor Indian."[2] In 1829, Austrian Catholics founded a missionary society, the Leopoldinen Stiftung, to support the American church and "in their enthusiasm they gave the Verein a more specific object; namely, the conversion of the pagan Indians."[3]

This zeal for the Indian population underscored a peculiar European view of the United States. It was a land of cowboys and Indians, a mission country, and priests dreamed about the great things they would do in this exotic and "strange land." Much like their confreres who sailed to Turkey and China they came as missionaries to the New World. They set out to preach "the gospel to the Indian and to the citizens of the New World";[4] not knowing what to expect they brought with them books, mass vestments, crucifixes, rosaries, and boxes of other religious paraphernalia. As one missionary put it, "America was a land of savages, where a missionary might expect at every step to have to make extraordinary sacrifices."[5] Knowing "nothing about America and its language," they were ill-prepared for such a mission.[6] Upon their arrival the missionaries were amazed at what they found. New York was a special eye-opener. The French missionary, Edward F. Sorin, landed in New York in 1841 and observed that "generally one is surprised on arriving from Europe to find in a land not long since inhabited by savages, a city whose streets and stores might compare, sometimes even favorably, with those of Paris and London"; its harbor, he noted, was "probably one of the most beautiful in the world."[7]

Despite their naiveté about American life, the missionaries were correct in describing Catholic America as mission country. Compared to the church in France or Germany, American Catholicism was insignificant. In 1815, 28.5 million Catholics lived in France and 24 million in the Habsburg empire; the United States numbered only one hundred and fifty thousand Catholics, equal to the Catholic population of India, and like India it was mission country.[8] The American church was in its infancy, lacking organization and its institutions clearly suffering in comparison with those of the Protestants. Catholics claimed fewer churches than any other religious denomination in 1815, and most of those they did own were either abandoned Protestant churches or small log chapels. They were a minority group wherever they lived, and the foreign character of both the laity and the clergy set them off from the mainstream of American society.[9]

Missionary priests noted the primitive condition of the church and continually bemoaned the loss of faith among Catholics in the New World. The popular belief was that thousands had abandoned the religion of their ancestors. Dispersed widely across the countryside and totally deprived of any religious ministry they had either drifted into indifference or joined a Protestant church. To combat the problem, mission societies were organized in Austria, Germany, and France. They encouraged priests to join the mission in America and sent large amounts of money to support them in their work and aid in the building of churches.

In the 1830s the religious situation of American Catholics

3

was not much different from what it had been in 1815. "Everything is beginning from scratch," wrote one priest, and "everything is just beginning to be built, raised, arranged, and maintained."[10] The establishment of new dioceses had given the church a measure of organization, but Catholicism was still struggling with the problem of a mission church—too few priests and too many abandoned souls. The apostolate to the Indian continued to attract missionaries from Europe, but many soon discovered that their work was not with the Indians who were being removed beyond the settled frontier. Rather their immigrant countrymen became their special concern. Since the end of the War of 1812 thousands of immigrants had come to the New World, and the most pressing need of the church in the 1830s was not the Indian mission, but the immigrant apostolate.

In the 1830s the showplace of American Catholicism was Baltimore, Maryland. The Catholic cathedral was a prominent feature of the city's skyline, and according to one visitor, it was "considered by all Americans as a magnificent church."[11] Baltimore Catholics could also boast of five other churches, one college, and a seminary. The religious situation of the city was rather favorable, but beyond the city limits the landscape was quite different. St. Mary's County was the site of the original colonial Catholic settlement, and in the early nineteenth century half of the population in the area was still Catholic. In contrast to the magnificence of the Baltimore cathedral, however, they worshiped when they could, in "miserable wooden chapels," and many of them only occasionally saw a priest. Neighboring Charles County was even worse off in terms of available priests and churches.[12] The same pattern was noticeable in the diocese of New York. New York City numbered about thirty-five thousand Catholics with four churches and only a few clergymen to care for their needs. North of the city the religious situation was much more bleak. In upper New York state "endless numbers of neglected souls" were scattered far and wide. In a tour of the diocese Bishop John Dubois discovered that wherever he visited he found "ten times as many Catholics as I expected; seven hundred are found where I understood there were but fifty or sixty; eleven hundred, where I was told to look for two hundred."[13] Along the northern boundary of the state two thousand Irish and French Catholics lived scattered across an area of one thousand square miles and rarely, if ever, did they see a priest.[14]

In 1830 the six states of New England had a population of almost two million people. Only fifteen thousand of this number were known to be Catholic and half of them lived in Boston. The others were dispersed throughout the rest of New England. Some one thousand lived in Burlington, Vermont, and another thousand lived nearby in the small villages along Lake Champlain; there was no church in the area and a priest came by only two or three times a year.[15] Speaking about New England a missionary noted that in many places Catholics were rarely visited by a priest and so, whole families were in danger of losing the faith.[16]

After the War of 1812 a great frontier movement had swept across the Appalachians heading toward the Mississippi. "Whole caravans of emigrating families, having sometimes a dozen wagons in company, passed along the streets of Louisville, Cincinnati, Brownsville, Pittsburgh, or Wheeling." Across the summits of the Alleghenies passed "wagon after wagon, the women and children sometimes riding and often walking after in an irregular line, and the men driving the teams, or urging on the livestock." They made their way "across these lofty mountains, seeking a new residence, in an almost unknown land." Nothing could slow the advance of population and "what had been wild Indian country now swarmed with new settlers."[17] They came from the eastern states and most of the countries of western Europe. The old frontier was moving westward, and pioneer settlers in Kentucky and Tennessee sold their homesteads, loaded their wagons and headed for the fertile soil of Indiana and Illinois. The church followed the migration west and slowly began to establish itself in the old Northwest. But the problems it confronted were reminiscent of the situation it had to contend with along the Atlantic seaboard.

Kentucky had a Catholic presence by the end of the eighteenth century, but it was never very large. By 1815 "not less than 10,000" Catholics lived in the state.[18] About nineteen churches, most of them log chapels, were scattered across the countryside. Less than ten priests spent their time traveling from one settlement to another ministering to the people. Fifteen years later Kentucky Catholics numbered about eighteen thousand, but formal religion along the frontier was still an infrequent experience. Bardstown was the center of the Catholic colony, and like other cities along the frontier it was well supplied with churches, priests, and schools. In the backwoods country the situation was less favorable with priests on horseback being able to visit the widely dispersed settlements only once or twice a year.

Many Kentucky Catholics had migrated to Indiana, settling down in the southern counties that bordered the road between Louisville and Vincennes. By 1836 an estimated forty-five thousand Catholics lived in Indiana and four priests had the impossible task of trying to keep the fires of religion burning. Vincennes was better off than most towns, but even this settlement struggled "under a decline of piety and religious instruction," the people having been "long neglected."[19] In the region around South Bend "the Catholic religion was very little known." As late as 1842 only three hundred Catholic families lived within a hundred mile radius of South Bend, "dispersed, disunited, dissolute, with hardly a sentiment of Catholicity remaining."[20] Half of the population "was composed of savages, and the other half of

Catholics who could almost all be placed in the same category."[21]

Even though Ohio was the most populated state west of the Alleghenies in the 1830s, it numbered little more than thirty thousand Catholics.[22] Cincinnati was home for a large number of them; as in other urban centers, religion was in a comparatively good condition as far as institutional development was concerned. The cathedral was an imposing sight, able to accomodate one thousand people, and residents of the Queen City boasted of its elegance.[23] Leave the city and it was a different, but familiar scene. Crude log chapels, with "rough blocks of wood, covered with dust to serve as seats" were more the order of the day.[24]

St. Louis was the center of Catholicism in the Mississippi Valley. Half of the city's population was Catholic, and the cathedral was the pride of St. Louis. One booster claimed that "it can boast of having no rival in the United States for the magnificence, the value and elegance of her sacred vases, ornaments and paintings; and indeed few churches in Europe possess anything superior to it."[25] Close to half of Missouri's Catholics lived in or around St. Louis in the 1830s. The rest had homes in towns and villages along the Mississippi and Missouri rivers. One priest was responsible for some two thousand Catholics scattered across parts of Missouri, Illinois, and the Wisconsin Territory. The Mississippi was his highway in summer and winter as he visited the tiny clusters of Catholics.[26]

In the Deep South the Catholic presence was not very strong. New Orleans had long been a center of Catholicism during the reign of the Spanish and French. But after the Louisiana Purchase the church in New Orleans underwent a long period of neglect. As late as 1830 there was only one church in the city and it was tailored to the needs of the French-speaking.[27] A contemporary estimated that one hundred and fifty thousand Catholics lived in Louisiana and

Mississippi in 1835, and the ratio of priest to people was one of the worst in the country (1 for every 5,555 people).[28] No one really knew for sure how many Catholics lived in the southern states, but the implications were clear. Catholicism was in a sorry state, and the complaint most frequently heard in these parts was the scarcity of priests and the neglect of religion.[29] Alabama and Florida had a combined population of 344,257 in 1830 and only eight thousand Catholics. Mobile was the center of the church in Alabama with two thousand Catholics. Church services were held in a private home![30] In the outlying regions religion was in an even worse condition; one missionary described the Catholics as a people who "deprived of instruction and the help of religion, preserve only the name of Catholic and an empty shadow of their belief."[31] Close to two million people lived in the Carolinas and Georgia, a region where only ten thousand Catholics were accounted for. The bishop of the area claimed that "there are almost close to 100,000 who being dispersed here and there are deprived of all religious assistance."[32]

Catholicism was indeed in a sorry condition throughout the United States and the most frequent reason given for this situation was the inadequate number of priests. Missionaries had come from France, Ireland, Belgium, and the German-speaking states, but their number was still insufficient to meet the needs of a population that was steadily increasing in number and continually dispersing itself across the continent. One bishop confessed that half of the Catholics in the country "do not have any priests—especially if we include those visited rarely and only by chance."[33] The consequences were obvious; religion was being neglected and scores of people were being lost to the church. "Deprived of all religious assistance, almost never seeing the missionaries, a very large number of Catholic émigrés from Europe end up by entirely forgetting all practice of religion and fall into a mortal indifference," noted one report. "Their children," it went on to observe, "raised in ignorance or drawn into the Protestant schools, then enter by marriage into Protestant families whose errors they adopt."[34]

To remedy the problem bishops turned to Europe for help. Yet, European Catholicism did not have a surplus of clergy either, and though the flow of missionaries was steady, it was never sufficient to meet the needs of the missionary church and its people.[35] Indiana had a ratio of one priest for every ten thousand Catholics and the dispersal of the population was such that most people rarely saw a priest. The situation on the rural frontier was certainly extreme, but conditions were not good in the city either where the church was in comparatively better shape. St. Louis had one parish for twelve thousand people; the Cincinnati Cathedral had at least eight thousand parishioners; in New York it was common to have a congregation numbering more than ten thousand people. Too few parishes, not enough priests and a population either scattered across the frontier or densely concentrated in the city were not conditions favorable to the consolidation of a missionary church. Coupled with this was the obvious pattern of religious neglect among Catholic Americans.

This neglect of religion was manifested in different ways. Foremost was the obviously low level of religious practice. Attending mass, receiving the sacraments of penance and the eucharist at least annually and having their children baptized by a priest were major responsibilities for a church Catholic. These were the things that counted and a practicing Catholic was expected to fulfill these duties. In the United States the performance of such duties was at an ebb during these early years and mission reports continually commented on this fact. But people were not just negligent in observing the traditional practices of religion, their enthusiasm for religion itself was waning. Although the evidence is sketchy, it was consistent and widespread enough to support such a generalization. How pervasive it was is impossible to measure in exact terms but missionaries continually wrote about "a decline in piety," "indifference" toward religion, and people preserving "only the name of Catholic and an empty shadow of their belief." Finally, there was the "loss of faith." This too is difficult to quantify, but the fear was so widespread that there had to be some basis to it. Catholics did drop out of the church and many joined Protestant denominations. The clergy knew it and continually debated over how great this "loss of faith" was.

To revitalize the religion of the people something extraordinary was needed. The hierarchy believed that a major solution to the problem would be the calling of a national council and the consolidation of the church on a national basis. No bishop could go it alone and "be able to effect other than partial good in his own diocese," wrote Bishop Benedict Fenwick of Boston to his episcopal colleague in Baltimore, James Whitfield; but, "were we to unite in one settled plan of operations, assist one another and pull together, what a happy difference would it not make in the general result."[36] In 1829 the hierarchy finally met and attempted to bring some measure of organization to the mission church. The legislation focused primarily on ecclesiastical discipline and the enactment of policies that would harmonize administrative and pastoral practices. As a result of the council the church did achieve a measure of national unity in its organizational policies, but the conditions of religious malaise persisted. During the decade of the 1830s the hierarchy gathered together two more times to strengthen the organizational unit of the church. Further policy decisions were made about ecclesiastical discipline, and bishops were urged to establish seminaries to train candidates for the priesthood. But this was a long-range goal that could not meet the immediate needs of a population that would double in size by 1840 and triple its numbers by 1850.[37]

What was needed was a popular revival of religion; ecclesiastical discipline focused on legislative reform, but the church was in dire need of religious reform. This was no easy task, but the 1830s were to usher in the first stirrings of a religious revival that would eventually sweep across Catholic America. The key to this revitalization was the parish mission, or what may be more aptly labeled the Catholic revival meeting.

Revival meetings were common events in antebellum America, so frequent in fact that one contemporary historian believed that revivals were "a constituent part of the religious system."[38] According to Perry Miller, "the dominant theme in America from 1800 to 1860 is the invincible presence of the revival technique."[39] Catholics were not immune to this influence and eventually they too became caught up in the religion of revivalism. But it was not the pervasive Protestant revival that provided the model for American Catholics. They looked upon Protestant revival meetings as "heathenish" assemblies.[40] Martin J. Spalding discussed frontier revivalism at great length in his book on Kentucky Catholicism, and his assessment was decidedly negative. "The whole matter," he wrote, "furnishes one conclusive evidence of the weakness of the human mind when left to itself; and one more sad commentary on the Protestant rule of faith."[41]

In a lengthy discussion of Catholic missions and Protestant revivals, Orestes Brownson explicitly took up the question of the connection between the two phenomena. In his opinion, Methodist-style camp meetings represented the degeneration of Protestant revivalism and were not worthy of "civilized beings." Other "more refined" revivals did bear some resemblance to Catholic missions, but if there was any imitation involved, it was on the part of Protestants. In Brownson's opinion, parish missions were "purely Catholic" and their origins were not to be found in Protestant America but in the distant past of Catholic Europe.[42] Brownson as well as other apologists consistently took this position in explaining the origins of the parish mission. Although such an explanation was predictable, given the hostility of Catholics toward anything Protestant, in this instance history was on the side of the apologists. Rather than imitate American Protestants, Catholics were following a centuries-old European tradition.

This was not unusual for nineteenth-century Americans, especially as regards religion. "There is scarcely anything in the whole gamut of religious life in America," Winthrop Hudson observed, "that does not have its equivalent and usually its antecedent in Europe, and most often in the British Isles."[43] Protestant revivalism, most clearly in the eighteenth century but also in the nineteenth, exhibited a direct transatlantic connection with German Pietism and English Methodism. There were differences of spirit and emphasis in revivalism as it developed in the Atlantic communities, but such differences did not preclude a common bond in the transatlantic revival movement. For Catholic revivalists the European influence was much more pronounced in the nineteenth century than it was for Protestants. For a missionary church whose lifeline reached into the heart of Europe this was to be expected. This was a common experience in American religious history; Catholics, like Protestants, were borrowing from Europe. What they imported was a form of pastoral ministry that traced its roots back to sixteenth-century Europe.

The sixteenth century was a critical period for Roman Catholicism. Weakened by widespread religious malaise among clergy and people and threatened by the Protestant reform movement, the church underwent a complete spiritual overhaul. "The success of this reform movement," wrote one historian, "must be attributed in large part to a special form of pastoral ministry, the parish mission, which was born at this time."[44]

The parish mission was a new form of preaching that was

first developed among the religious orders founded during the Catholic reform period. The most important religious order both for the reform of the church in general and the development of the parish mission in particular was the Society of Jesus. Since their founding in 1534 by Ignatius of Loyola, the Jesuits, as they are commonly known, had considered "the parish mission as one of [their] essential tasks."[45] As these missionaries crisscrossed the highways of Europe, the parish mission began to take on a recognizable form. By the 1590s elaborate instructions outlined the method and program of the mission so that it could "bring help to so large a number of souls who, by ignorance of the things necessary for their salvation, live in a state of sin and are exposed to eternal damnation."[46] The seventeenth century witnessed an expansion of the parish mission and a more elaborate systematization of this special ministry that aimed at the religious revival of Catholic Europe. In Italy the Jesuit preacher, Paul Segneri (1624–1694), effectively incorporated the traditions of the preceding century into a mission program that would have an important influence during and after his lifetime. In France, Vincent de Paul (1580–1660) founded the Congregation of the Mission (the Vincentians) to preach parish missions among the country folk.

By the eighteenth century the parish mission had entered its heyday of popularity; "in Germany," according to the historian of the movement, "there did not remain one locale of any importance which did not have its mission."[47] Alphonsus de Liguori (1696–1787) founded the Congregation of the Most Holy Redeemer (the Redemptorists) in Italy in 1732 to preach missions, and his influence in this work of renewal became so important that church councils authoritatively cited his writings on parish missions. In France the tradition of Vincent de Paul continued into the eighteenth century, and a vigorous mission movement became ingrained in French Catholicism.

Toward the end of the eighteenth century the parish

mission suffered a severe paralysis. Popular opinion began to turn against the exaggerated expressions of piety that had developed during the Baroque period. The terrifying scenes of hell painted by the preachers, severe public flagellations, sermons seemingly without end, and grotesque exhibitions of dead bodies harmed the appeal of the mission. The intellectual currents of the enlightenment reinforced this reaction and also sought to embarrass the work of the missionaries. Then, in 1773, the political suppression of the Jesuits who had been in the forefront of the movement dealt a death blow to parish missions. The French Revolution and the wars that followed "halted the work nearly completely."[48] Politically the parish mission had been identified with the interests of the papacy, and this ultramontane association was a serious liability in countries ruled by independent-minded monarchs. The mission was also viewed as an important agency of the church in its support of conservative political authority against the emerging tide of liberal, often revolutionary, politics. As a result, the people's mission was outlawed in many countries.

In most German-speaking countries civil authorities banned the *volksmission*; thus, "Germany scarcely knew the missions before 1848."[49] In France the revolution had dealt a fatal blow to the church and the parish mission; Napoleon permitted the resumption of the mission in 1802, but seven years later they were again outlawed when the emperor sought the subjugation of the pope and the church. The restoration of the monarchy allowed the resumption of the parish mission, and from 1815 to 1830 it played a major role in the effort to renew Catholic life in France. Enjoying the favor of the Bourbon king, the mission movement flourished. People sang the praises of Jesus and the king at mission ceremonies. "*Vive Jesus, vive la croix, vive le Roi,*" they shouted. "*Vive la France! Vive le Roi! Toujours en France, les Bourbons et la foi.*"[50] The church's close identification with the monarchy in its attempt to recreate a Catholic France eventually spelled the doom of the mission. In 1830 when the Bourbons fell from power, the mission was again outlawed.

In other countries the mission began to reappear with new vigor after 1815. When the new pope, Leo XII, proclaimed a jubilee year in 1825, it became the occasion for spectacular parish missions in Alsace, Switzerland, and Italy. During the 1830s the tempo of the movement increased and the Redemptorists held numerous missions in Belgium. Some of these took place in towns close to the German border, and many Germans crossed over into Belgium to attend. Catholics from Baden also crossed the frontier to attend missions in Alsace border towns. By 1840 the parish mission was beginning to recapture the popularity it had enjoyed a century earlier. Even in those countries where it was still outlawed, France and Germany in particular, missions occasionally reappeared, camouflaged under the name of a retreat.[51]

In the United States the religious situation was ideally suited for the parish mission. The scarcity of priests encouraged an itinerant ministry that reached out to scattered settlements of Catholics. The priest's visit did not last very long, and during his stay some type of brief but intense evangelization was necessary. Since it might be years before a priest returned to the rural communities, something extraordinary was needed to rekindle the fires of religion among churchless, priestless Catholics. Even in the more populated settlements where priests visited regularly three or four times a year something special was needed to keep the people's religion alive. The mission was suited to such circumstances. It could be lengthened or shortened depending on the size of the community; but whatever its duration it provided a period of intense preaching, the possibility of receiving the sacraments of penance and the eucharist and the opportunity of getting religion and setting oneself

15

straight with God as the church had traditionally instructed. For more than two hundred years the mission was the accepted type of ministry in such circumstances. It was an extraordinary event aimed at reviving the religion of a community that manifested little enthusiasm for or obvious neglect of the spiritual life. It was not surprising then, given the religious situation in the United States and the two-hundred-year-old tradition of the parish mission, that it did appear in the New World. In fact, the Catholic revival became a standard event in mission countries throughout the world in the nineteenth century.

The first missions or revivals in the new nation most likely took place in Maryland toward the end of the eighteenth century. The preacher who adopted this practice was Father John Baptist M. David, an émigré from the French Revolution. Not much is known about his mission preaching other than the description given in 1844 by Martin J. Spalding in his *Sketches of the Early Catholic Missions of Kentucky*. According to Spalding, David began preaching missions shortly after his arrival in the United States in 1792 and continued this work in Maryland until his assignment to Georgetown College in 1804. These missions were described as retreats, a pseudonym for parish missions at this time because of the unfavorable reputation that they had acquired in many European countries—in some places even the very use of the word was prohibited. During the early years of the nineteenth century missionaries in the United States often used the words retreat, exercises, or mission interchangeably. Even though each traditionally had its own specific purpose and one was theoretically distinct from the other, it is clear from Spalding's description that the retreats David preached "every year to each of his congregations" exhibited many of the features of a parish mission. They sought to revive religion in "congregations cold and neglectful of their Christian duties"; conversion and instruction were the goals of his preaching and adopting a traditional feature of the mission, he divided his audience according to sex and their state of life, that is, married or single men and women. Like many preachers, David based his retreats on the *Spiritual Exercises* of Ignatius of Loyola. In commenting on David's mission preaching, Spalding noted that "as far as our information extends, he seems to have been the first clergyman in the United States who adopted a practice, which has since proved so beneficial to religion."[52]

Another European missionary, the Jesuit Anthony Kohlmann, held missions in the German parishes of Philadelphia and Baltimore in 1807 shortly after his arrival in the country. The following year found Kohlmann in New York City as pastor of the Catholic parish. To remedy the poor and "neglected" conditions of religion he preached at least one mission in the parish in 1809. In commenting on his work Kohlmann used the phrase *mission* as well as *Exercises* to describe his ministry.[53]

Although few references to parish missions can be found prior to 1825, most likely additional ones did take place. European priests who came to this country confronted conditions that were ideally suited for revival preaching, and it would not be surprising to find them inaugurating a ministry that years of tradition had designed specifically for such circumstances. Moreover, many of these missionaries came from France where parish missions were enjoying a brief period of popularity under Napoleon; after 1815 they entered an even more prolonged and more flourishing era. For these early years the link between parish missions in France and the United States is unclear, but it is reasonable to suspect that such a ministry was part of the missionary's cultural baggage. One thing is clear, however, and that is the widespread appearance of Catholic revivals held in conjunction with the jubilee year of 1825.

Pope Leo XII had announced a jubilee, or holy year, for

1825 as a major step in a crusade for spiritual renewal. When the holy year came to a close in Rome, the jubilee was extended to all the countries of the Catholic world.[54] In the United States, as in many European countries, the jubilee provided the occasion for holding parish missions and for the next few years jubilee missions were preached in many parts of the country. Missionary bishops, aided by other priests, generally took this occasion to visit the Catholic settlements of their dioceses. At each stop they held a mission and announced the spiritual indulgences connected with the jubilee.

In Ohio, Bishop Edward Fenwick began his missionary tour with an eight-day revival in the Cincinnati cathedral in December 1826. Then, in the next eight months Fenwick and two other priests traveled to every corner of Ohio holding revivals along the way.[55] Other priests preached the mission in Michigan during the following year. For almost two years, 1826–28, Kentucky was the setting for more than twenty different revivals. Bishop Benedict J. Flaget opened the tour with an eight-day mission in the Bardstown cathedral. At each successive stop the bishop and two or three other preachers generally followed the same plan: an eight-day mission with a sermon in the morning, a conference in the afternoon, and a second sermon in the evening. A reading of Flaget's account of the mission clearly implied that what they were doing was not something new. They were adapting an old tradition to a new environment and were delighted with their success. People came from great distances to attend the revival, and they spent the entire day in church waiting to hear the sermon and confess their sins. "All hearts appeared to be truly moved," wrote one priest. "This was seen in the vividness of the sorrow and in the abundance of tears which accompanied the confession of their sins. Sinners of the most inveterate habits were seen weeping over their past wanderings and prepared to make the greatest sacrifices to amend their lives."[56]

In 1829, Flaget toured Indiana, and in June he preached an eight-day mission in Vincennes. An observer noted that "the deportment of the Catholic body was such as to be called by our separated brethren 'a revival.'"[57]

By 1829 the mission had become an accepted feature of Catholic evangelization. The national council of bishops alluded to it in their 1829 deliberations and made special exceptions for priests who celebrated the eucharist during the course of a mission.[58] As the legislation suggests and the correspondence of the priests confirms, missions were held anywhere a group of Catholics could be gathered. In recounting his itinerant ministry one missionary stated that "when time permits and there is neither a house or barn large enough, he preaches in the open air and mounts the trunk of a tree or a palisade and harangues the people until he is fatigued."[59] Priests preached in court houses, in Protestant churches and in private homes, wherever they could gather an audience. The rationale was always the same, to revive the religion of the people who had long been without the consolations of the word and the sacraments.

During the 1830s missions continued to reappear, often in some of the most destitute areas of Catholic America, where, the hierarchy noted, "many Catholics . . . were condemned to wander in spiritual desolation until becoming estranged from their religion they were indifferent to its concerns or its practices; and they and thousands of their children have been themselves lost to the church."[60] Illinois, Missouri, Louisiana, Alabama, Michigan, and Kentucky were just some of the areas where mission preachers sought to revive the religion of Catholics. A major impetus to the spread of the missions in this decade was the arrival in 1832 of the Redemptorists.

One member of this small band of three priests and three brothers was Father Francis Haetscher. He had seventeen years of experience in preaching missions in Europe and within a month after his arrival in America he resumed this ministry.[61] The first Redemptorist missions were in northern Ohio; later some were held in the Detroit area. A confrere of Haetscher, Francis Tschenhens, also gave missions in Ohio. He noted that for many of the German immigrants this was the first time in America that they had thought about their conversion.[62]

The Jesuits had been on the scene in America for numerous years, but during the 1830s their numbers were increased when a group of French Jesuits journeyed to Kentucky. Expelled from France where the Jesuits had actively participated in the 1815–30 revival of religion, this small band of three priests and one brother arrived in the United States in 1831. Their number soon increased as more recruits joined the Kentucky Jesuits. During the 1830s "the Jesuits began to give parish missions in Bardstown." Then they expanded their work "to cover the towns and cities of the dioceses of Vincennes, Nashville, and Cincinnati."[63] Another group of Jesuits also held a few missions in Catholic settlements in Missouri. An important stimulus to the development of Jesuit missions at this time was the election of Father John Roothan as their superior general in 1829. Roothan had encouraged parish missions while he was the superior in Switzerland; as head of the Society throughout the world he continued to foster this apostolate among the Jesuits.[64]

The decade of the forties witnessed a substantial increase in the number of Catholic revivals. New recruits bolstered the number of Redemptorists and Jesuits, and the arrival of additional religious orders also increased the manpower supply. By 1849 the number of Jesuits had increased to 188, a good number of whom were on the road preaching missions. Father John McElroy traveled the circuit along the East coast; in the West Jesuit preachers held missions in Ohio, Kentucky, and Indiana.[65] But the biggest boost for Jesuit missions occurred in 1848 with the arrival of the Austrian preacher, Francis X. Weninger.

"I had come to America to give missions," Weninger wrote and in December 1848 his wish was fulfilled when he gave his first mission in Oldenburg, Indiana.[66] Two thousand German Catholics attended the revival, some traveling "from a distance of fifteen, eighteen and twenty miles and even farther." A newspaper account noted that Weninger's sermons "drew tears of repentance and consolation from the eyes of his hearers. Often there was general sobbing and weeping throughout the church."[67] In the next year Weninger continued his itinerant ministry traveling throughout the Midwest preaching nine more missions to German-speaking settlements.

The Redemptorists also increased their manpower during this decade; by 1849 they numbered forty-seven priests. The new recruits from Europe enabled the Redemptorists to step up their revival work so that by 1850 they had held a total of thirty-six missions in French, German, and English-speaking settlements in Michigan, New York, Maryland, Pennsylvania, and Louisiana.[68]

Franciscan and Holy Cross priests arrived in the United States in the 1840s and both groups preached missions in the Midwest. But the major work of Catholic revivalism at this time fell to the Jesuits and Redemptorists. Together they held about seventy missions during the 1840s, more than three times the total known number of the previous decade.[69]

The identification of the Jesuits and Redemptorists with the Catholic revival was not unexpected. Both societies had a long tradition of preaching missions in Europe, and they carried this with them to the United States. In some instances the link was very explicit. Both Weninger and Haetscher resumed a practice which they had found successful in Europe. As Weninger put it, "I learned the immense value of these spiritual exercises [in Austria], an experience which I found eminently useful in my subsequent career as a missioner in the New World."[70] For others the link was not so explicit, but it was clear that they were following a practice in the United States that was a tradition in their order and was fast becoming a trademark in the renewal of nineteenth-century European Catholicism. In the 1850s and 1860s the transatlantic connection would become even clearer as parish missions increased in popularity in both the United States and Europe.

Despite the obvious transatlantic link, the parish mission in America was different from its European counterpart. It lacked the obvious political overtones that the mission had in France, Germany, Italy, and other countries. In addition, the American version of the mission, despite its close resemblance to the traditional parish mission, served a different function in the New World. In Europe the mission sought to restore the religion of established congregations; in the United States it aimed at the revival of religion among a group of newcomers who had only recently planted their roots. Established parishes were few and far between in such places as Alabama, Louisiana, and Illinois. The task of the mission was to reach out to Catholics dispersed across an expanding landscape and gather them together, often for the first time, in the hope of preserving their Catholic heritage in a land where being Roman Catholic was not very fashionable. In those areas where a parish had been recently established the itinerant missionary was frequently called upon to preach a mission to aid in the organization of the new congregation. Very often, as in Weninger's mission at Oldenburg and the 1826 missions in Kentucky, the revival was the occasion for a religious roundup of Catholics living within a day's journey of the church. In the city it served a similar function of aiding the organization of new parishes and reaching out to gather in the lukewarm living in the anonymity of crowded urban neighborhoods.

As the tide of Catholic immigration swelled in the 1840s something extraordinary had to be done to channel the newcomers into the church lest they drift away from the religion of their ancestors. People had to be gathered together and the fires of religion had to be stoked, if not rekindled anew. The revival was an apt means to achieve these goals, and priests were quick to see its usefulness on the American mission.

Compounding the problem was the state of religion among the newcomers. Irish and German immigrants were coming from countries where the practice of religion was at an ebb. The habit of regular church-going was not a practice that many immigrants carried with them, and people "for years," noted one priest, "had been estranged from the sacraments."[71] The situation was even more critical given the Catholic fear of Protestant proselytization. One report noted that the 1830 Catholic population was around five hundred thousand, but "the number of Catholics should have been several millions had not innumerable defections taken place." During the 1840s the number of priests and churches doubled, but the fear remained. "The widespread heresy of our land, and its vast efforts of propagandism, the mixture of Catholics with Protestants especially in parts seldom visited by a priest, the growing materialism of the age . . . are causes that still operate largely to the disadvantage of religion, and call for the most vigorous measures to oppose their influence."[72]

Underlying this fear of Protestant encroachment was the free church tradition in the United States that had made religious denominations "primarily purposive, voluntary associations engaged in the free society in the propagandization of the Gospel."[73] Reverend Albert Barnes, a Presbyterian preacher, underscored this point when he wrote:

> There is a spirit in this land which requires that the gospel shall depend for its success not on solemn processions and imposing rites; not on the idea of superior sanctity in the

23

> priesthood in virtue of their office; not on genuflections and ablutions; not on any virtue conveyed by the imposition of holy hands, and not on union with any particular church, but on solemn appeals to the reason, the conscience, the immortal hopes and fears of men, attended by the holy influences of the Spirit of God.[74]

Since religion relied on persuasion, Catholics were legitimate targets for conversion and could be persuaded to become Protestants without fear of society's reprisal. To counteract this, priests could not look to support from the state. Since the prevailing culture in the United States, unlike many European countries, was not Catholic, priests had to rely on persuasion more than on the influence of a cultural tradition to move the hearts of their audiences. They had to save them not just from the snares of the devil but also from the clutches of Protestant preachers. Thus, the religious situation in America encouraged the development of the parish mission. It was ideally suited for an environment where religious declension was widespread, Protestant competition was real, the free church tradition was normative, and persuasion rather than coercion was demanded.

By mid-century, revivalism was the mainstream of American Protestant religion. This was not yet the case for Catholics. They were caught up in the spirit of revivalism, but at first the involvement was sporadic, limited to individual itinerant priests. With the jubilee revivals of 1826 the tempo increased. By the 1840s it was clear that the parish mission had become "so effectual in renovating the life of the soul."[75] But before revivalism could be a major current in the mainstream of American Catholic religion the parish mission would have to become an "invincible presence" in Catholic America. This would take place during the second half of the nineteenth century.

The Revival Crusade | 2

Historians are often inclined to single out certain periods in a community's history which they believe to be critical. As far as the Catholic community in the United States is concerned, one such period emerged in the middle decades of the nineteenth century. It was a time of transition, the effects of which would shape the future of American Catholicism for years to come.[1] The decade of the 1850s was especially significant insofar as it elicited a new tone of optimism in the community. In a very real sense the Catholic church was turning the corner and heading into the future in a surprisingly confident manner. An important consequence of this change was the emergence of the Catholic revival meeting. Prior to 1850 the revival was a relatively infrequent occurrence in Catholic America. But this would change in the next half century as revivalism quickly became the accepted technique in the evangelization of Catholics. To understand the emergence of revivalism during this period it is necessary to examine the changes that occurred in the Catholic community during the middle decades of the century. Understanding the growth and change of this transitional era will go a long way toward explaining the popularity of revivalism in Catholic America.

In a lecture given in 1854, Philip Schaff, the noted church historian, commented on the situation of American Catholicism. "Only within perhaps the last twenty years," he said, "has this church begun to make its influence felt in the public life of the United States."[2] Schaff's assessment was accurate. By mid-century the Catholic church had become the single largest denomination in the country, surpassing the Methodists by more than a quarter of a million people. From a population of 318,000 in 1830 the church had grown to over one and a half million members by 1850 (1,606,000). During the 1850s the number continued to rise reaching the level of 3,103,000 by the end of the decade. These thirty years, 1830–60, witnessed the largest proportionate population growth in the history of American Catholicism (876%).[3] No longer a minority religion, Catholicism had achieved a prominent presence in the nation.

The major reason for this rapid and unsurpassed growth was immigration. The natural population increase among Catholics was negligible during this period, whereas immigration accounted for 70 percent of the growth. Subsequent decades continued to chart the rise of the Catholic population, and by 1890 close to nine million Catholics lived in the United States (8,909,000).[4] Immigration remained a major source of the increase, but it never equalled the proportionately high levels of the antebellum period because of the steady rise in the natural increase in population.

The antebellum Catholic immigration was made up principally of Irish and Germans. By the 1880s the character of immigration began to change as more people emigrated to the United States from southern, eastern, and central Europe. For the church this meant an influx of new national groups—Italians, Slovaks, Lithuanians, and Polish, to name but a few. Like most immigrants, Catholics tended to settle in the city. How strong this tendency was in the nineteenth century was difficult to measure. In 1890 the Census Bureau compiled statistics on the various religious denominations. According to this data 48 percent of the 1890 Catholic population lived in cities of 25,000 and upward. More significantly the Catholic urban population represented 57 percent of the total urban church population in the nation. Even though 52 percent of its population lived in towns with a population of less than 25,000, the Catholic church was the largest urban religious community in America, outnumbering the urban population of all other churches combined.[5]

In choosing the city as their home, Catholic immigrants naturally gravitated toward the most rapidly urbanizing region in the country. In 1850 more than one-fifth of the Irish lived in New England and an equally large number lived in the Middle Atlantic region. The Germans traveled farther west; close to half of them settled in the North Central states.[6] The new immigrants of the late nineteenth century followed similar routes. Italians were principally attracted to New England and the Middle Atlantic states; the Polish and Slovaks settled in the North Central states, "where they tended to concentrate in areas devoted primarily to heavy industrial production."[7] Reflecting this pattern of settlement, the Catholic church was heavily centered in the northeast and the midwest regions east of the Mississippi and north of the Ohio river. In 1890, 70 percent of the Catholic population lived in this region, the urban and economic core of the nation.

It is not surprising that immigrant Catholics settled in the economic core of the country. This was the area undergoing the most rapid industrialization, and thus it offered the best opportunity for work. Immigrants were employed in factories and shops, working machines from sunrise to sunset. Their skills seldom qualified them for more than a blue-collar job, but their muscle and brawn were necessary ingredients for the growth of the nation's economic heartland. Because of its dominant immigrant constituency, Catholicism was primarily a church of the working class. This is a generalization continually used to describe the people who called themselves Catholic in the nineteenth century. Sufficient evidence is not available to substantiate the statement except in the most general terms. Yet, recent studies of individual urban communities do support this accepted impression. Stephan Thernstrom's study of Boston demonstrated that Catholics lagged behind Jews and Protestants in social mobility. A primary reason for this was that as a group

Catholics started out their careers heavily concentrated "on the lower rungs of the occupational ladder."[8] Better than 60 percent began work in skilled, semiskilled, and unskilled occupations—wearing a blue collar and working with their hands. A study of occupational distribution among Catholics in the early twentieth century confirmed this pattern with 62 percent of the group studied engaged in blue-collar jobs.[9] Research in parish communities also substantiated this pattern.[10] A small elite of businessmen and professionals existed and they provided the necessary lay leadership in the church, but the large bulk of Catholics belonged to working-class families.

The phenomenal growth of the Catholic population during the antebellum period and its subsequent expansion throughout the century carried with it certain characteristics that shaped the future of the church in the United States. In becoming a nineteenth-century immigrant institution, the trademarks of its charter members of the eighteenth and early nineteenth centuries were pushed into the background. The new immigrants driven to America by famine, unemployment, and poverty would determine the church's future development. Centered in the industrial heart of the nation and concentrated in the cities, Catholicism became the church of the working class, a distinction social-minded Protestants admired and Catholic leaders celebrated. To be Catholic in name, however, was a long way from being Catholic in practice; this was the problem that challenged the church throughout the nineteenth century.

The population boom from 1830 to 1860 was paralleled by a similar growth in the institutional church. During these three decades the number of clergy increased 863 percent (from 232 to 2235) and the number of churches from 230 to 2385, a 937 percent increase.[11] As was true of the population expansion, this was a period of exceptional growth as far as priests and buildings were concerned. Subsequent eras saw more numerical growth in clergy and churches but they could not match the 1830–60 period in terms of proportionate expansion. Thus, despite the unparalleled growth in population, the church was able to keep abreast of this expansion. In fact, the number of churches increased at a slightly more rapid rate than the population. In subsequent decades this pattern continued as priests and churches increased more rapidly than the population.

The growth of the institutional church was also reflected in the establishment of dioceses, the administrative and juridical rationalization of the church. As the frontier expanded west, geographical areas were mapped out establishing new dioceses so that the church could function more efficiently and effectively. In the more established areas of the Northeast the same rationale was followed as new administrative territories were carved out of older, more sprawling dioceses. By 1860 forty-three dioceses had been organized, one shy of four times the number in 1830.[12] Once again this period surpassed all subsequent decades in terms of the church's administrative expansion.

Another, more tangible index of the growth of the church in this period was its financial worth. In 1850 the Catholic church ranked fifth in the value of its property holdings among all religious denominations in the United States. Ten years later the value of its church property increased to 27 million dollars, about three times its 1850 level, and only the Methodists outranked the Catholics. If the census had included schools, convents, seminaries, and monasteries in its tabulations, Catholics would have certainly surpassed the holdings of the Methodist church.[13] In any event, the trend was clear. The church was becoming a financial power. People, priests, and pulpits had increased throughout the country, and in the process the church multiplied its financial resources. By 1890 its churches alone were valued at more than 118 million dollars.

The extraordinary growth of people and institutions obviously posed serious organizational problems for the American church. One such problem was how to forge some semblance of unity in a church made up of people from diverse national cultures, living in a land that was half-empty and underdeveloped, where people were constantly on the move. Rome initially was of little help. Vatican officials were astonishingly ignorant of America. Thus, when the question arose of establishing a new diocese in Virginia in 1819, the Roman cardinal in charge of such decisions proposed Hartford, Connecticut, as the episcopal center of the diocese.[14] As far as church law was concerned, the frontier mission of American Catholicism was *sui generis*. Roman officials resigned themselves to this fact and tolerated many things in America that would not have been allowed elsewhere. The United States was unique and "after all one could tolerate many things there since it happens, so to speak, in another world." Pope Pius IX underscored this attitude when one day, having been asked for an extraordinary favor, allegedly responded by saying that "unfortunately I cannot grant it to you; but ask some American bishop."[15]

The major remedy the hierarchy adopted to bind together a rapidly expanding organization was the church council. The council brought together all the bishops of either a particular region, or occasionally of the entire nation, for the purpose of creating a body of legislation that would regulate various aspects of church life. The diversity of peoples, the expanse of the country, and the burgeoning population demanded such a response. The church needed to be organized, and the council was the traditional means to achieve this goal. Thus, from 1829 to 1900 thirty-five major councils were held in the United States as a concrete response to this issue of ecclesiastical uniformity. This represented almost one-quarter of all the major councils held throughout the

Catholic world during this period. The extent of this conciliar activity in the United States was even more striking when compared with the church in Europe that had ten times as many dioceses but only forty-nine such councils from 1829 to 1900.[16] The extraordinary frequency of American councils, noted one historian, "represents without a doubt the paradigmatic conciliar example in the modern history of the Church."[17]

An obvious reason for the large number of councils was the missionary condition of the church. American Catholicism was an orphan child; it had no indigenous tradition to guide it. America was a new environment, an adopted homeland for Catholics, and everything had to begin from scratch. The vastness of the continent discouraged frequent communication, with the result that diversity rather than uniformity was the pattern of ecclesiastical administration. Since 1829 the hierarchy had tried to bring some order and harmony into church practices, but their efforts were not always successful. Individual bishops were not quick to give up the independence they enjoyed in their own dioceses and conform to the wishes of the episcopal majority. One area in which the variety of national traditions had created a state of chaos was liturgical practice. Germans had their own way of doing things and so did the French. To remedy this, the councils sought to impose one common style of liturgical practices as prescribed in the Roman Ritual.[18] This was only one of many issues that the councils attempted to resolve, but it illustrated the type of problem they confronted and the direction which they would follow. To create unity amid diversity the church fathers looked to Europe, especially Rome, for guidance. Unlike France or Germany they had no time-honored tradition to follow, and Roman practices, rather than any particular national tradition, furnished the model for many administrative and ecclesiastical decisions. The ultimate aim was to cement together a widely scattered, nationally diverse community. Martin J. Spalding, the arch-bishop of Baltimore and guiding light of the 1866 national council, emphasized this point in a letter to the Irish prelate, Paul Cullen. It was no easy task to meet "the exigencies of so many Provinces and Dioceses so differently organized and so remote from one another, with so many diverse nationalities," he wrote. "To harmonize all this and to pre-sent a Code of uniform discipline on which all could substan-tially agree" was his goal in the 1866 council and ultimately the aim of all American councils in the nineteenth century.[19]

In all of these church assemblies a good portion of legisla-tion focused on the piety of the people and how this could be further developed. Even though the councils were not primarily concerned with such issues, they inevitably were discussed, especially from the point of view of regularizing popular religious practices. This was an important dimen-sion in the development of nineteenth-century Catholicism since the church was undergoing a religious renaissance. "In its public worship and individual and group devotion," wrote Kenneth Scott Latourette, "the Roman Catholic Church experienced a mounting revival as the nineteenth century wrote toward its close."[20] In Europe the church was experiencing a devotional revolution and this "interior trans-formation of Catholicism" perhaps better than anything else represented "the true triumph of ultramontanism" in the countries north of the Alps.[21] This transformation can be thought of as ultramontane insofar as it bound the people more closely to the institutional church through the practice of officially approved and promoted devotions, with the result that the church enhanced its position as the one true and indispensable source of saving grace.[22]

From this religious revival emerged a type of piety that became normative in the late nineteenth century. It was of the Italian school, "more indulgent, occasionally more su-perficial but also more human and popular." Inspired by the romantic enthusiasm for the Middle Ages, there emerged a renewed emphasis on "Marian devotion, the cult of the saints, veneration of relics, processions, pilgrimages, and other public manifestations of the faith."[23] This was the most visible and most popular index of the "prodigious vitality," to use Kenneth Scott Latourette's phrase, that Roman Catholicism manifested in the second half of the nineteenth century.[24]

A very important component of this popular religious revival was the parish mission. During the nineteenth century the parish was the clergy's "field of action par excellence" and a favorite instrument of pastoral work was the parish mission.[25] This was especially true after 1850 as the church began to emerge from a period of religious malaise brought on by the enlightenment and the political upheavals of the late eighteenth and early nineteenth centuries. In Germany the 1848 Council of Wurzburg set the stage for a new epoch in the history of German Catholicism. The council encouraged the reform of parochial life and noted that the parish mission was "highly desirable in our time."[26] The Council of Cologne in 1860 reiterated the importance of the parish mission which was then enjoying widespread popularity in the area. During the 1860s the parish mission reached a high point of activity in the Cologne region only to be snuffed out in the 1870s by the *kulturkampf.*[27] In France the parish mission recaptured its former popularity during the 1850s and multiplied rapidly thereafter, reaching a peak in the 1890s when in some regions one hundred missions a year took place.[28] English Catholicism, as John Henry Newman described it, experienced "the coming of a Second Spring" at mid-century. The restoration of the hierarchy in 1850 and the appointment of Nicholas Wiseman as the new cardinal archbishop of Westminster ushered in a new age in the history of English Catholicism. During the 1850s church councils sought to resurrect the religious vitality of the church. An important aspect of this revival and one highly favored by Wiseman was the parish mission. It was viewed as a "new power" necessary in both the city and the country "to drive a wedge into the resisting block of aggregated and hardened sin."[29] As in France and Germany, the parish mission eventually became a trademark of the devotional revolution that transformed Catholic England.

The decade of the fifties was also a heady time for American Catholicism. The church was riding the crest of an unprecedented wave of growth. The number of people, priests, and pulpits was multiplying and the more astute individuals realized, along with Philip Schaff, that the church was beginning to make its mark in American society. It was a "time of foundation" for the church, wrote John Hughes, the fiercely confident archbishop of New York. Religion in the United States, according to Hughes, was taking on a "catholic form and tone."[30] A major impetus to this strain of Catholic boosterism was the conversion of native American Protestants to Roman Catholicism. The sensational conversion of the Englishman John Henry Newman attracted considerable attention in the United States; the conversion of the Episcopal bishop of North Carolina, Levi S. Ives, in 1852 was widely publicized; so too was the entrance of Orestes Brownson into the church of Rome. Other less notable individuals began to enter the church and Catholic apologists happily recorded these conversions, viewing them as harbingers of future success. They were concrete evidence "of the great movement towards Catholicity now providentially going on in this country."[31] Just about every parish revival recorded such conversions and the Catholic press publicized them as a sign of divine prejudice for Roman Catholicism. "The dispositions of the American people," wrote Orestes Brownson to Isaac Hecker, a fellow traveler on the road to Rome, "are much less unfavorable to the Church than is generally supposed . . .

their attention is turned to the study of Catholicity as it never has been before, and if approached now in a proper manner with earnestness and charity, in their own language and tone, I cannot but believe that a rich harvest of souls will be reaped."[32] During the 1850s Hecker, a newly ordained priest and member of the Redemptorists, and Brownson exchanged numerous letters touching on a variety of subjects. Interwoven throughout all this correspondence was the messianic theme that "America is the future hope of the Church." Writing to Brownson prior to one of his lectures, Hecker told the apologist that Brownson would stand before his audience "as an American and the champion of Catholicity." Even though it was just another Brownson lecture, Hecker raised it to an occasion of major importance, not because of the audience, but because of the significance of the speaker. "The reconciliation which has taken place in your own heart . . . is to take place also in the nation," Hecker said. "Never before had you such a task, the nation's destiny and the interests of God's Church are at stake."[33] According to Hecker, Catholics had a glorious future in America. "Our young men need to be told this, inspired with it and shown the means to attain it," the young priest exclaimed. "Let it be known that we have a future."[34]

Hecker and Brownson were not alone in expressing this theme of Catholic boosterism. Catholic journalists also took on a more aggressive tone in the 1850s, celebrating the glories of the church and how suitable a home Catholicism had found in the New World. One religious superior addressed a group of seminarians in 1856 and told them to consider themselves "as instruments in the hands of God which He will use to effect a wonderful change—a spiritual revolution in this country. . . ." "All America can be reformed," he said, "I expect this of you and I know God has predestined you for the accomplishing of this great work."[35]

The revival of Catholicism in Europe, the prodigious

growth of the church in the United States, and the sensational conversion of newsworthy Protestants contributed to this buoyant spirit of Catholic publicists. Sounding like their Protestant countrymen they spoke the language of manifest destiny, but it was the destiny of a Catholic America. Triumphal perhaps, but it made as much sense to them as the general belief abroad in America that the "Holy Spirit was endowing the nation with resources sufficient to convert and civilize the globe, to purge human society of all its evils, and to usher in Christ's reign on earth."[36] The only difference was that Christ would return looking like a Catholic, not a Protestant. Neither the impending crisis of slavery nor economic depression would dampen the enthusiasm of Catholic spokesmen. Americans were a "providential people, a people with a great destiny... a manifest destiny," wrote Brownson, and "it is only through Catholicity that the country can fulfill its mission in the world." "Catholicity," he proclaimed, "is the future hope of our country."[37]

The heady tone of such rhetoric illustrated how some Catholics were thinking in the 1850s. They did not speak the language of a "Second Spring" or "the resurrection of the Church," phrases that John Henry Newman used to describe the revival of English Catholicism. American Catholics were experiencing the first dawning of spring; they had no ancient tradition to revive, "no overpowering monuments of the past to check our fresh enthusiasm, or to dishearten us in our youthful attempts," as Hecker put it.[38] Much had to be done to build the church from scratch, or as it was more commonly expressed, to transplant the church of the Old World "in the new soil" where "it will strike deep its roots, it will spread out its branches on every side" and become "the adornment of the church" throughout the world.[39]

Such exuberance found its concrete expression in the expansion of church buildings, an increased commitment to parochial schools, and the recruitment of European religious orders. The Passionists set up their first establishment in the United States during this decade, the Benedictines came from Switzerland to establish a foothold in southern Indiana, and the Franciscans journeyed from Westphalia to Illinois in 1858. The number of Jesuits and Redemptorists increased, and their apostolate expanded. The 1852 national council inspired a flurry of conciliar activity; within the next decade fourteen major church assemblies were held, more than half the total number of councils in the second half of the nineteenth century.

The Catholic revival went hand in hand with this development. Progressive Americanists who wanted the spirit of Catholicism to be a dynamic force in reforming America viewed it as "the only means of propagating the Catholic religion on a great scale."[40] Isaac Hecker was so convinced of its value that he eventually founded a new religious community to promote Catholic revival meetings among English-speaking Catholics and non-Catholics. The more traditional wing of Catholicism who were suspicious of the Protestant American environment and were content to concentrate their energies on building up a strong island community viewed the revival as a way of strengthening the old-time religion in the New World. Such broad support strengthened the popular appeal of the parish mission.

Parish missions were never very numerous prior to the 1850s. But, during this decade they began to appear more frequently than ever before. Writing in 1858, Orestes Brownson observed that "the past few years have been marked by the unusual number and the great success of the Retreats or missions which have been given by the members of several Religious Congregations, in almost every ecclesiastical province and diocese; both in our overflowing city churches, and also in the country parishes both large and small." For Catholics "they were something altogether new and strange" and Protestants, he said, "have been astonished to find such an engine at work in the Catholic Church, and have usually styled it a new masterpiece of Roman policy."[41]

As Brownson noted, the missions were novel, "something altogether new and strange." This seemed true, only because relatively few Catholics in the United States had experienced them prior to mid-century. But with the arrival of additional religious orders from Europe and the numerical increase of groups already established the mission phenomenon spread like wildfire. What previously was an unusual event was now becoming a routine celebration in the cities and towns of Catholic America. Scores of parishes sought out the bands of revival preachers and asked them to come and give a mission. By 1852 one preacher noted that "we have missions ahead for a couple of years or more";[42] a decade later the same group of preachers was unable to meet the demands and had to turn down requests for their services.[43]

The Redemptorists and the Jesuits were two groups intensely involved in preaching missions. During the 1850s the Redemptorists preached 188 parish missions, more than five times the number in the previous decade.[45] In the Midwest about sixty-five missions took place prior to 1850; in the next ten years at least 280 were held with the Redemptorists and the Jesuits doing most of the work. One preacher, the itinerant Jesuit, Francis X. Weninger, accounted for over 170 of these midwestern revivals.[45] Other groups involved in preaching missions during this decade included the Vincentians, Franciscans, and Passionists.

A major impetus in the expansion of Catholic revivalism was the formation of an organized band of Redemptorist mission preachers. The guiding light behind this move was Bernard Hafkenscheid, a Redemptorist who had gained widespread renown in Holland and Belgium as a mission preacher. Appointed head of the American Redemptorists in 1848, Hafkenscheid set out to establish a more systematic approach to the mission apostolate. Previously missions took place in a haphazard manner depending principally on the availability of a preacher. Coming off a successful career in Europe, Hafkenscheid realized the value of the mission in reviving the religion of the masses and was determined to organize and expand this ministry in America. In 1851 he gathered together four American-born Redemptorists and coached them in the art of mission preaching. Two of the priests, Isaac Hecker and Clarence Walworth, had some experience in preaching revivals in England and they returned to the United States specifically to continue this work under the direction of Hafkenscheid.[46] The first mission given by the newly organized group took place in New York in April of 1851. Every evening for two weeks the little church of St. Joseph's in Greenwich Village was jammed with people curious about the "new spectacle" taking place. Catholic revival meetings were not very common in the metropolis and the novelty of the event reportedly attracted the attention of many people.[47] One of the preachers also noted in his chronicle that "the mission was conducted fully according to the method observed in Europe and no difficulty was found in introducing every usage at once."[48]

This link with the European tradition was also clearly evident in the publication of the first English language mission catechism. *The Mission Book*, as it was commonly known, was first published in the United States in 1853; it was a manual of instruction and prayer aimed at preserving the good effects of the revival and it had enjoyed wide circulation in Europe. The American edition, the preface noted, was "substantially the same book which, in other countries, particularly in Austria, Bohemia, Belgium, Holland, and France, has been already so greatly blessed."[49]

With the establishment of an itinerant group of preachers whose sole responsibility was conducting parish revivals and with the appearance of a mission catechism it was clear that

Catholic revivalism was undergoing a systematic organization. By 1861 the Redemptorists had formulated a set of
regulations to guide them, and govern them, in the preaching
of missions. The Passionists came up with similar guidelines
in 1866.[50] Another indication of the regularization of parish
missions was their official acceptance by the church hierarchy. The first official support occurred in 1858 at the second
provincial council of Cincinnati. At this gathering, which
represented the church in Ohio, Indiana, Michigan, and
Kentucky, the council fathers, noting the unusual success
which the missions had enjoyed in the region, urged that "all
means be used so that they could be provided in each diocese
in some regular manner."[51]

This was the key point in the development of Catholic
revivalism at mid-century. The Catholic revival meeting had
been tested and found successful. Now the task was to
organize and promote it so that as many people as possible
could experience a religious revival. Within a decade the
parish mission had become, as far as American Catholicism
was concerned, one of "the most powerful means for saving
souls that God has given to his Church."[52] Revivalism had
found a home in the American Catholic church and the
future looked promising.

In seeking an explanation for the increase in revivalistic
fervor during the 1850s several reasons must be considered.
The European churches were undergoing a similar revival
and many mission preachers came to the United States specifically to carry on the same type of ministry that was
proving so successful in Europe. The parish mission had
become "one of the features of the Modern Church" and in
transplanting Catholicism to the New World it was inevi-
table that the revival meeting would be part of the exchange.[53] A reason more indigenous to the United States
was the missionary status of the young church. The rapid
increase in the Catholic population and its dispersal across a

steadily expanding landscape demanded some type of extraordinary ministry. The itinerant style of the mission preacher, stoking the fires of religion at one place and then quickly moving on to another settlement, was ideally suited to the situation. It also compensated for the shortage of clergy in the more sparsely settled areas of the country. Despite the sensational conversions of notable Protestants, the Catholic clergy still feared the competition that Protestantism posed. By urging conversion to God and stressing the point that only one road, the Roman Catholic way, led to heaven, the revival meeting offered a counterattack to the Protestant threat. The popularity that revivalism enjoyed in Protestant churches was also conducive to a corresponding development in Roman Catholicism. Revivalism was a standard feature of American Protestantism at mid-century; as Timothy Smith noted, the revival was "the cutting edge of American Christianity... adopted and promoted in one form or another by major segments of all denominations."[54] What Catholics were up to was not much different. In fact, many observers began to recognize the similarities between the two, and it was not long before Catholic and Protestant revival meetings engaged in head to head competition. This type of competitive spirit in an environment that thrived on revival religion unquestionably had an influence on the ready adoption and promotion of the parish mission.

But a basic premise in all revival religion at this time was religious declension. It was an integral part of the revivalist rationale, needed not only to legitimate the holding of a revival but also to promote a sense of urgency and thus facilitate a religious conversion during the brief period of the revival. In the Catholic community the rhetoric of religious declension was commonplace. It was an ordinary feature of all mission reports during the 1850s, justifying not only the necessity of such preaching but also its critical importance. Admitting the formality of the religious jeremiad, however, does not exclude the possibility that religion was indeed in poor shape. As far as Catholics were concerned this definitely appeared to be the situation. Irish immigrants in the 1840s and 1850s were arriving in the United States religiously destitute.[55] Their countrymen who chose England as their adopted home manifested the same religious malaise. One witness after another, both clerical and lay, alluded to it in one way or another. Thomas D'Arcy McGee claimed that as far as New York was concerned "perhaps one half of the males do not even go to mass on Sundays."[56] A New York priest, writing in his private diary with no ax to grind in the public forum, came to basically the same conclusion. "Half of our Irish population here is Catholic," he wrote, "merely because Catholicity was the religion of the land of their birth."[57] Nor were German immigrants any better in this regard.

In one of his letters to Hecker, Orestes Brownson admitted "*inter nos*," as he put it, "that the mass of our Catholics are not Catholics."[58] Later he made the same charge publicly. "Numbers everywhere," he said, "have ceased to receive the Sacraments, to attend Church, to say their prayers even; are profoundly ignorant of their religion, and completely indifferent to it, and are bringing up their families without any religion, except a remembrance that they have been baptized and call themselves Catholics."[59] Even if the common religious jeremiad continually noted in mission accounts is excluded, other testimony pointing to the poor condition of antebellum Catholicism was still too widespread and too consistent to be ignored. Brownson's assessment was basically accurate. Religious practice was low, indifferentism was widespread and the "loss of faith" was real. Moreover, this pattern of religious malaise was the force that energized all the other influences which fostered the religious revival. Europe provided the model and Protestantism offered the competition, but the terrible condition of religion was the driving force that propelled the revival meeting into the foreground of the Catholic devotional revolution.

The turmoil of the Civil War did not halt the spread of Catholic revivalism. In the Midwest a total of 330 missions were held from 1860–65, more than the total of the previous decade.[60] In the Northeast the revival movement continued to expand. One impetus to this was the entrance of the Passionist order into the arena in 1856. Since their founding in Italy in 1720 their primary apostolate had been "the preaching of parish missions."[61] They carried this tradition to the New World and augmented the work being done by other religious orders. In eleven years, 1856–66, they conducted 160 revivals, mostly in the Northeast.[62]

Another event which was to have a significant impact not only on the parish mission movement, but also on the subsequent history of American Catholicism was the founding of the Congregation of St. Paul, more commonly known as the Paulists. In 1858, five Redemptorist priests, all American-born converts and led by the indominitable spirit and vision of Isaac Hecker, separated themselves from the Redemptorists and founded a new order of preachers whose principal purpose would be to conduct parish missions and hopefully "make Yankeedom the Rome of the modern world."[63] Described as "independent revival preachers" they promoted the Catholic revival among English-speaking Catholics.[64] In their first seven years the new community of priests traveled across the country preaching eighty-one revivals.[65] Death claimed the life of Francis A. Baker, the leader of the mission band, in 1865, and this forced the small group to abandon revival preaching for several years. In 1872 they resumed their work; by the 1890s they had established themselves in the forefront of the parish mission movement.[66]

Counting parish missions in the second half of the nineteenth century is like trying to number the stars in the sky with the naked eye. It is an impossible task and in the end not very useful either. But to gain some insight into the magnitude of Catholic revivalism such enumeration is illustrative. The Redemptorists preached a total of 3,955 missions from 1860 to 1890; the Paulists, numerically a much smaller community, conducted 1,111 parish missions.[67] The figures for the Jesuits are not as complete, but during those years for which figures are available the annual median number of Jesuit missions in the Eastern part of the country was 131.[68] Their premier preacher, Francis X. Weninger, traveled across the country from California to New York, Texas to Ohio preaching 519 missions.[69] Many other religious orders, as many as thirteen were conducting missions at any one time, were also engaged in the movement. How many missions they held is difficult to know for certain, but the pattern was clear. After 1850 the Catholic revival meeting swept across Catholic America like wildfire.

No region of the nation was left untouched. The Northeast and the Midwest, where the large majority of Catholics lived, were the most burned-over areas. But missions also took place in Georgia, Florida, Texas, and Louisiana as well as up and down the West coast and across the Great Plains states. Large cities were a favorite locale for the numerous bands of preachers, but small towns were also included in their itinerary. The city mission had all the marks of a large scale urban revival—newspaper publicity, handbills posted throughout the neighborhood, special choirs, notable citizens in attendance, and standing room only crowds. In smaller towns the missions took on the atmosphere of an annual fair. People journeyed from miles around to attend, often staying in town until the mission ended; all the Catholic townspeople appeared to be present and accounted for; work schedules in the mills and the mines were altered to allow workers to attend the morning sessions. Since small wooden churches could seldom accommodate the crowds, preaching and processions often took place out of doors. Like its counterpart the Protestant revival, the parish mission was not confined to large cities. The most widely publicized and most heavily attended revivals took place in large cities, but numerous others were held in the many towns and villages that made up nineteenth-century America. An examination of the Paulist revivals in New York State confirmed this pattern.

From 1858 to 1900 the Paulist missions in New York State were divided into 59 percent urban and 41 percent rural.[70] The prevalence of urban missions, however, did not mean that revivalism was primarily an urban phenomenon. Rather the urban-rural distribution of missions reflected the relatively high urban profile of New York State. Three out of every five missions took place in towns of 8,000 or more people during this period since New York, as the third most urban state in the nation, had increasingly more urban than rural communities. A further breakdown of the urban-rural distribution also reflected an absence of any uniquely urban dimension in Catholic revivalism (Table 1). In large cities over 500,000, and including only New York and Brooklyn, the percentage of missions was 37 percent and in towns of less than 5,000 the corresponding figure was 34 percent. As far as Catholics were concerned, they were consistently a very urban-oriented group. In 1890, 70 percent of them lived in cities of 25,000 or more, a population locale where only 48 percent of the missions took place.[71] Thus, despite the relatively high urban profile of New York State and the heavy urban concentration of Catholics, missions were not limited to nor necessarily concentrated in cities, but were also a frequent visitor to small rural towns.

Both the small town and the large city had the need for periodic revivals and it was not the size of the community but its needs that determined where revivals would take place. Religious backsliding was not limited to large urban

TABLE 1.

Distribution of Paulist Missions in New York, 1858–1900,
according to population of locale. *

Population of locale	Number of Missions	Percent of Total
500,000 and upward	111	37
100–500,000	6	2
25–100,000	28	9
10–25,000	25	8
5–10,000	29	10
Less than 5,000	102	34

*Information on the missions was calculated from the Mission Chronicles in the Archive of the Paulist Fathers; population figures were given in published U.S. Census reports.

parishes; it only appeared so prevalent in the city because backsliders were more densely concentrated there. Americans traditionally viewed the city as the devil's den whereas the small rural town was depicted as a garden of Eden. Yet, despite the romanticizing of the rural environment, the village parish was not immune to religious indifference. The geographical distribution of the Paulist missions pointed this out and reinforced the observation of preachers that in both city and town Catholics were in need of a religious awakening.

When a preacher boarded the railroad or the steamboat and set out on his revival itinerary, he seldom traveled alone. Each religious order, following the pattern adopted by the Redemptorists, eventually established a band of preachers whose sole responsibility was to conduct parish missions. The Dominicans organized their first mission band in the 1860s; thereafter they became intensely involved in the mission movement.[72] The Jesuits of the eastern province organized their first group in 1875. Three priests were assigned to the New England area and three to the Middle Atlantic and Southern states. The Jesuits in the Midwest also had a mission band centered in St. Louis. A Jesuit German-speaking mission band worked out of Buffalo and another was headquartered in Toledo. During the 1880s two Polish Jesuits came to the United States and took up the revival apostolate among Polish-speaking Catholics.[73] The Redemptorists had a mission band since 1851. In 1875, with the establishment of a western province centered in St. Louis, they divided their work geographically into two separate groups.[74] Another development in the organization of the Catholic revival was the appearance of how-to-do-it handbooks. The Redemptorist, Joseph Wissel, published one in 1875 and it remained in use well into the twentieth century.[75] Father Weninger compiled a similar handbook in German in 1885.[76] The Passionists had formulated an officially approved set of guidelines in 1866 and followed this with a more elaborate directory in 1884.[77]

A very important development in assuring the Catholic revival of continued support was the approbation and promotion given it by the church hierarchy. At the national council of 1866 the American hierarchy adopted a proposal promoting the parish mission. The guiding force of the council, Martin J. Spalding, had introduced similar legislation at the Cincinnati regional council in 1858, and now as archbishop of Baltimore and architect of the council he again promoted the parish mission.[78] It is clear from the discussions at the council, where little debate was given over to the question of parish missions, that the church fathers and their theologians were not introducing something novel or controversial.[79] The missions had been on the scene for some time, various European church councils (Cologne, Prague, and Westminster) consulted in preparation for the 1866 assembly had already approved similar legislation and the hierarchy was only promoting a "method of preaching the word of God" that had proven to be exceedingly effective both in Europe and the United States.[80] As an authoritative rationale for their action the bishops cited the 1745 encyclical of Pope Benedict XIV which was exclusively devoted to promoting parish missions.[81] After the 1866 council it became axiomatic for diocesan synods across the country to pass similar legislation endorsing what had become an event ranking "in solemnity with the highest festivals" of the church.[82] Along with attendance at mass and reception of the sacraments, attendance at parish missions had become a duty that immigrant Catholics were expected to fulfill.[83]

In the 1840s the itinerant preacher was a rare species and the Catholic revival meeting an uncommon event. By the end of the century organized groups of preachers crisscrossed the nation preaching a brand of religion that had become an integral ingredient of Catholic piety. The parish mission was a common occurrence which the hierarchy promoted, religious orders popularized and people supported. The revival meeting had become an accepted feature of parish life, a standard event scheduled to occur at regular intervals to boom up the religion of the people.

In relating the history of American Catholicism in the last half of the nineteenth century historians have focused on the major crises which occupied the time and energy of church leaders. The German question, the parochial school, Americanism, and the liberal-conservative debate on these and other issues appeared to be the main events in the history of the church in the closing decades of the nineteenth century. Yet, these issues constituted only one chapter of the story. A more popular and ultimately a more influential phenomenon was taking place—the emergence of revivalism as one of the most popular manifestations of Catholic piety. This was something that both liberals and conservatives agreed on, a piety they shared in common and a ministry they both supported. The liberal heroes, John Ireland, Isaac Hecker, and the Paulists, promoted the Catholic revival along with the vanguard of conservatism, the Jesuits and Redemptorists. Revivalism was not a divisive issue in the Catholic community. On the contrary, it enjoyed broad support and this enabled it to become a major current in the mainstream of the people's religion.

In tracing the development of Catholic revivalism, the 1850s stood out as the period when revivalism began to take off. Later decades reinforced the thrust of the 1850s and did not alter what eventually became a trademark of the Catholic devotional revolution. In the 1890s, however, certain changes took place in the Catholic revival movement. Like the 1850s this decade provided a benchmark in the history of Catholic revivalism. It did not mark the beginning of the end; this would come almost a half century later, but it did usher in a new phase in the movement. One of the most telling indications of the change was the way people reported the revival meeting. For decades clergymen wrote up extensive, glowing reports on missions. By 1900 these reports had disintegrated into perfunctory accounts, mere skeletons of their earlier counterparts. This was not due to a change in reporters; it was too frequent a pattern among various groups (Jesuits, Redemptorists, and Paulists) to be explained by mere individual idiosyncrasies. What was taking place was the simple fact of common, ordinary boredom. In becoming a routine feature of Catholic devotional life the revival had lost its original luster. Having been on the scene for decades it was no longer a novelty; priests and people took it for granted. Thus, the chronicles of the Paulist missions, faithfully written in a ledger book in a very descriptive and extensive style for more than thirty years were replaced by printed one page summary reports filled out with one or two perfunctory phrases. Redemptorist chronicles reflected the same pattern. The Jesuits, who reported their work in the *Woodstock Letters*, began to skip the pattern of annual reports; they appeared less regularly and certainly with less literary fervor. Newspaper accounts reflected a similar shift. In the 1870s missions were front-page news in the New York *Freeman's Journal;* by the middle of the 1880s they were reported less frequently and less prominently. Missions were no longer newsworthy even though they were occurring more frequently than ever before. The temperance crusade had pushed them off the front page.[84]

A more significant change at this time was the shift from Catholic revivals to non-Catholic missions. In its early stages the parish mission primarily aimed at the religious revival of Catholics; and the "conversion of Protestants," for Weninger and others, was "merely a secondary consideration."[85] Occasional talks, aimed specifically at Protestants, were given, but generally at the end of a mission tacked on as a sidelight to the main event. During the 1890s separate missions for non-Catholics began to take place inaugurating a new phase in Catholic evangelization. The person most responsible for this shift was the Paulist priest, Walter Elliott.

Civil War veteran, lawyer, and the youngest of nine children born to Irish immigrant parents, Walter Elliott entered the Paulist community in 1868.[86] After his ordination in 1872 he soon became one of the most popular mission preachers in the country. In September 1893, Elliott delivered a major address at the Columbian Catholic Congress in Chicago on "The Missionary Outlook in the United States." In his talk he called for an organized effort to convert America to Roman Catholicism, or as he put it, to make Catholics "missionaries to the American people."[87] Elliott himself inaugurated the work by holding missions for non-Catholics throughout the state of Michigan during the next nine months. This was a major shift for Elliott and the Paulists, since they would now begin to concentrate their efforts on the apostolate to non-Catholics. This had been the goal of Hecker ever since he founded the order in 1858, but it was never pursued in a vigorous and systematic manner until Elliott took up the cause in the 1890s.

Elliott promoted his crusade to "win America for Christ" by urging bishops to organize their own diocesan preaching bands. By 1900 twenty-five dioceses had established such groups. In 1896 Elliott and his Paulist colleague, Alexander Doyle, founded the periodical *The Missionary* as "the organ of the New Movement that has manifested itself so energetically in giving Missions to non-Catholics."[88] Another goal envisioned by Elliott and Doyle was the establishment of a center to train priests for the non-Catholic missionary apostolate. This plan was realized in 1904 with the opening of the Apostolic Mission House. Located on the campus of Catholic University in Washington, D.C., the mission house was a center "where the would be missionary could sit down at the feet of veteran missionaries and learn the whole art of giving missions; where, too, he would have the time and industry to prepare carefully a complete series of sermons and instructions on mission topics, and where he could learn the best ways of presenting Catholic truth and the art of persuading people to accept it."[89]

The non-Catholic mission generally took place after the Catholic revival meeting. Lasting for one week it featured evening lectures on the Catholic religion; included in the instructions were such topics as the church, the confessional, the mass, and why I am a Catholic. Both Catholics and non-Catholics attended, but the principal thrust was to gain new converts to the church. The Catholic revival promoted the lecture series by urging people to bring along a non-Catholic friend to the upcoming mission. Collections at the Catholic revival also provided the finances needed to promote the lecture series.[90]

By the turn of the century the non-Catholic mission was

emerging as a permanent feature of American Catholicism. Among the Paulists it was now their primary apostolate. For this group of preachers the Catholic revival was becoming less important, necessary to promote and finance the non-Catholic mission, but always secondary to this ministry. The increased activity of the Paulist apostolate to the non-Catholic was clearly illustrated by the dramatic rise in the number of converts around the turn of the century. Between 1898 and 1907 they recorded 3,208 converts, about one and one-half times the total number of converts claimed in the previous forty years since the founding of the order.[91] The number of non-Catholic missions had also increased substantially. As they became more self-supporting they even began to outnumber Catholic revival meetings. In 1909 *The Missionary* reported that in the previous decade 3,000 missions to non-Catholics had taken place under the auspices of the various mission bands associated with the Apostolic Mission House; the corresponding number of Catholic missions was 2,000.[92]

The new emphasis on the non-Catholic mission was not limited to the Paulists. Other religious orders, the Passionists in 1897 and the Vincentians in 1902, also joined the crusade to "win America for Christ." By 1904 eight religious orders were actively involved in the movement.[93] The increasing prominence of the non-Catholic mission did not, however, signal the end of the Catholic revival meeting. Parish missions continued to enjoy widespread popularity and remained a traditional event in the life of American Catholics. Growing up Catholic in the early twentieth century inevitably meant attending a parish mission. What was significant about the appearance of the non-Catholic mission was that it marked the beginning of specialization in the Catholic evangelization movement. Previously the Catholic revival sought to be all things to all people; it reached out to Catholics and non-Catholics, to men and women, to adults and children. By the turn of the century it was evident that a division of labor was emerging. The non-Catholic mission offered the best example of this, but there were others, chiefly the retreat movement.

In the early years of the century the term *retreat* was often used to identify the parish mission. But the resurgence of the mission in subsequent decades served to clarify the terminology, and the respective meanings of retreat and mission became quite distinct. In contrast to the parish mission, the retreat was a much more somber affair, aimed at a specific group of people and not opened to the public at large. The mission was aimed at the masses, but the retreat was more limited in scope, appealing to a particular class of people who could afford to take time off from their usual occupations for three days, a week, or even longer and spend the time sealed off from the world in prayer and recollection in a religious institution specifically designed for this purpose.[94] In the United States as in Europe, the *Spiritual Exercises of St. Ignatius* provided the best handbook for retreats. The Jesuits were also the best example of a religious group that shifted its energies from preaching Catholic revivals to conducting retreats. Conducting retreats had always been an integral part of the Jesuit ministry, and they continued this work in the United States during the nineteenth century. But only in the 1890s did the number of retreats for men and women religious begin to surpass the number of parish revivals.[95] Even more significant was the move toward retreats for lay people. Previously in vogue in Europe, there was little interest in them in the New World until the first decade of the twentieth century. Then the Jesuits actively began to promote retreats for laymen, inaugurating a work that would eventually become a trademark of their ministry in twentieth-century America.[96] At about the same time the Passionists also began an organized retreat movement for Catholic laymen. Such closed retreats had occasionally taken place prior to 1900, but only in a very informal manner.[97] After the turn of the century the layman's retreat became a nationwide movement promoted by several religious orders.

The layman's retreat along with the non-Catholic mission illustrated the trend toward specialization taking place in the Catholic evangelization movement. The parish mission remained a popular event in the local community, but it was no longer a novel and extraordinary phenomenon for the majority of Catholics. Among the more recent immigrants, Italians, Lithuanians, and Polish, the parish mission retained its original purpose of reclaiming spiritual backsliders and stoking the fires of religion among newly arrived immigrants. These communities were still beset with the problems of a mission church—too few clergy, religious indifference, and competition from Protestant missionaries. For these newcomers the Catholic revival continued to function as a religious round-up of neglected souls. Its goal was to bring back the lost sheep, convert the sinner, and build up the local church. For the bulk of Catholics, however, the revival meeting had become a routine feature of their devotional life. The urgent sense of reclaiming the religion of the people was gone, and the fear of Protestant competition was less acute. In fact, Catholics took to the offensive and sought to convert America to Rome. The world, the flesh, and the devil were still real dangers, and revival preachers lashed out at them with all the power they could muster from their oratorical arsenal. They aimed their missiles at church Catholics, and their sermons bristled with the heat of fire and brimstone; but their goal was not so much to reclaim the abandoned or the indifferent as it was to strengthen the religion of church-going Catholics.

Among mainline Catholics, second- and third-generation Irish, Germans, and Americans, the religious situation did not elicit the same concern it did fifty years earlier. Clergy and churches had kept pace with the population in the heartland of Catholic America, the northeast and north central regions. Schools and churches were popping up with determined regularity and from all appearances the institution was prospering. The indolent, indifferent Catholic was still around, however; in San Francisco the number was relatively very high. At the turn of the century only 44 percent of the estimated Catholic population of the city was accounted for.[98] In Cleveland a religious census noted astonishment "at the large number of renegade Catholics"; but compared with San Francisco the percentage of those "who had drifted away from the church" (24 percent) was relatively low.[99] On New York's West Side, St. Paul's parish had a regular Sunday church attendance that represented about 50 percent of the neighborhood Catholic population.[100] What evidence there was clearly indicated that the number of churchgoers had not increased dramatically among mainline Catholics; nor did the situation change much in the early decades of the twentieth century.[101] The Catholic revival, however, was increasingly less concerned about the other half. Mission reports hardly alluded to them. The focus was on the churchgoing Catholic. The mission's function as a means of mass evangelization had faded into the background in the established Catholic community as revivalism became a routine part of parish life. The lost sheep were still present, but revivalists focused their attention elsewhere. As one preacher put it, "leaving the 99 and hunting for the lost sheep outside is not quite applicable in our work, for the 99 are not good quiet sheep, but most restless rams and you must corral them even though a few stragglers may escape."[102]

In the 1850s the Catholic revival had been regarded as "something altogether new and strange." A half century later it was a standard event in the neighborhood parish. The passage of time had altered its goals and refined its constituency, but the ritual of revivalism remained basically intact. When people attended a revival at the turn of the century, they knew what to expect. Even though the element of newness had long since disappeared, people continued to crowd the churches during the time of a revival. They liked what they heard and enjoyed what they saw. Religious enthusiasm had received a welcomed reception from Catholics, and evangelicalism had become an accepted feature of Catholic piety.

The Catholic Revival Meeting | 3

Thus far this study has traced the development of Catholic revivalism throughout the nineteenth century. It is clear that by the 1890s the parish mission was a commonplace experience in the Catholic community. But in order to understand the revival phenomenon more completely it is necessary to examine the event itself and the men who made it work. The preachers and the themes they expounded in the pulpit, along with the rituals and ceremonies they performed, were the principal ingredients of the Catholic revival meeting. An analysis of these elements, the medium so to speak and not the message, will help to explain what the Catholic revival was like.

The scene is the West Side of New York in January 1895. The Ninth Avenue El is chugging its way downtown, jammed with the usual early morning crowd of commuters. As it passes by 59th Street, two huge structures rise up, dwarfing the rows of tenements that line the street. One is Roosevelt Hospital, the center of a continual flurry of activity and a familiar landmark. On the adjacent block is the other fortress-like building, St. Paul's Church, another landmark and also a daily reminder that the West Side is a Catholic stronghold. But on this particular day in January 1895 something unusual attracts the eye of the commuter. Stretching across the entire front of the church is a large white banner. Emblazoned on the sign in letters large enough not to be missed are the words, "A Great Mission."

Beneath the headline more particulars are given. The Paulist Fathers will conduct the exercises of the mission beginning at high mass on the following Sunday and continuing for the entire month of January.

The eye-catching banner was an unusual way to attract the public's attention, but parish missions were special events in the Catholic community, and no technique was left untried in promoting them.[1] What was taking place at St. Paul's and at scores of other parishes across the country was a Catholic revival meeting. A four-page leaflet distributed throughout the parish explained it in the following manner "for those of you who do not know what a mission is":

> A mission is a time when God calls with a more earnest voice than at other times all persons, but sinners especially, to work out their salvation with fear and trembling. It is an extraordinary time to make your friendship with God. It is a time when the greatest truths of religion—heaven, hell, the evil of mortal sin, the justice of God, his tender mercy—are preached to you. It is a time when priests from early morning till night wait in the confessionals for you, to absolve you from your sins, and restore you to God's favor. It is a time for you to remember that you have a soul to save, and to try and save it. It is a time when all things are made most easy and favorable for you to save that soul which will live on after your body is dead, and never die. It is a time when you are exhorted, by the cross and blood of Christ, if indeed you have a spark of gratitude or love towards God, to turn your face to him with contrition.[2]

A more graphic description given from the pulpit defined the mission as "something which gathers into one powerful showing all the warnings of Divine Justice: fully explaining the enormous folly and ingratitude of sin; it leads the sinner back to his very childhood and traces his downward track through youth and manhood towards his last death; which stands with him at his open grave; which calls in his ear the summons to the judgment seat of an offended God; which scorches his face with the fires of Hell and all in an atmosphere of fervor, aided by the entreaties of the sinner's friends, their prayers to God, their tears, the example of the repentance of other sinners."[3]

Four years had elapsed since the last mission at St. Paul's, and the revival would be a good occasion to round up many newcomers who during the interval had moved into the neighborhood. An economic depression had put many men and women out of work. The mission would help people to forget their distress for a while and remind them that God did not create them for this world, but for his kingdom in the world beyond. The salvation of their souls was to outrank all other concerns "for nothing can give truer comfort than to be in the state of grace."[4] This was a message applicable for both the best and worst of times.

During the week preceding the mission the parish neighborhood was alive with activity in preparation for the upcoming event. Fences and buildings were placarded with handbills—dodgers they called them—announcing the revival. It was also advertised in the daily newspapers with a schedule listing the time of services and the roster of preachers. The priests in the parish were busy making "a thorough visitation of the parish," urging people to attend the revival, because "in a city like New York it is very difficult to excite that general and popular enthusiasm comparatively easy in country parishes."[5] Prayers were offered each day during mass for the success of the mission. Local craftsmen were even involved; a preacher's platform had to be constructed as well as a cross, fifteen by seven feet, which would be mounted on the platform. The parish choir was busy with extra sessions preparing for the month-long revival. Down the street, Hutchinson's dry goods store had an ample supply of religious articles in stock in anticipation of the mission; the parish book exchange at 120 West 60th Street was also selling copies of *The Mission Book*, "a little manual of instructions and devotions" useful both during and after the revival.[6]

The elaborate preparations for St. Paul's mission were not unusual. Any parish in city or town underwent a similar routine if they were scheduled to have a revival. Revivalism had been "reduced into a kind of science,"[7] remarkably systematized with elaborate directions on how to promote, conduct, and prolong a revival of religion. Handbooks spelled out in detail the sermons that should be preached, the ceremonies that should be conducted and the atmosphere to be created. Father Weninger's instructions even included illustrations on how to build a mission cross correctly, what the candelabra should look like, how the church should be lighted, and how many flowers would be necessary. His instructions were so demanding and costly that some parishes refused to have a mission preached by Weninger. They simply could not afford it.[8]

The preparations for the revival at St. Paul's clearly indicated that parish missions were not the result of a spontaneous, popular religious awakening. They were manufactured events promoted by the clergy, and "specially calculated to excite the piety of the faithful and to prepare them for the sacraments of penance and communion."[9] This was not unusual in religious revivals. George Whitefield was a master promoter; Charles Finney knew how to get up a revival, and Dwight Moody's advance preparations were sometimes so elaborate that he needed a Wanamaker to finance them. Catholic revivals were also run according to a set plan. The unexpected could and did occur—a dramatic conversion, an extraordinary healing, even the sudden death of a hardened sinner—but generally people knew what to expect.

It was up to the pastor of the parish to decide when a

revival would take place. Usually they occurred at intervals of four to five years. This was the optimum lapse of time recommended by many church councils and suggested by the preachers themselves.[10] If they were more frequent, they became too routine; the more novel they were, the more enthusiasm they engendered since people had not been burned out by a continual succession of revival preaching. Missions were calculated "to startle, to terrify, and to rouse the consciences of the people,"[11] and this could best occur only periodically. According to the preachers, the degree of popular enthusiasm was in inverse proportion to the frequency of missions. If a community had been "missioned to rags," the revival invariably elicited little excitement. If "the mission was something new to the people, the interest and enthusiasm was greater."[12] As expected then, in the early years of the Catholic revival movement missions always aroused a great deal of excitement. But as people became more familar with them, the revivals were less a novelty and the possibility for "rousing great enthusiasm" diminished. It all depended on how commonplace the mission was in a particular locale. During the 1890s they were still "a kind of novelty" in California and "more attractive on that account."[13] It was not until 1879 that Catholics in Bridgewater, Massachusetts, experienced a mission. The preacher noted that it "had all the characteristics of a first mission—it was as lively as it could be."[14] Geneva, New York, had not had a revival for fourteen years; then in 1891 the Paulists preached a mission in the local parish, "an enthusiastic one" it was noted, "with the church always well filled." The following year they gave a mission in Mott Haven, New York. "It was like an old-time mission, rousing great enthusiasm not only among the Catholics but the non-Catholics as well."[15] There was no question that the best revival was one in which religious excitement prevailed. This could happen in any given year depending on the circumstances, but as missions became a standard feature of Catholic life, it was advisable to space them every four or five years so that they could be as effective as possible in exciting the piety of the people.

The promotional publicity associated with the mission and the calculated manner in which they were scheduled at first glance appears to undercut a basic rationale for Catholic revivalism—widespread religious declension and the urgent need to reclaim the fallen away. In a certain sense this was true. In the early stages of the revival movement the religious condition of Catholic immigrants was poor. The scarcity of priests and churches aggravated the problem, and the revival meeting was adopted as a ready remedy to an urgent problem. Over the course of time the revival was systematically organized and became an integral part of the church's devotional crusade. In established parishes it was a regular feature of their religious activity promoted to achieve the best possible results. At this level, revivalism was less an urgent response to unusual religious malaise and more a periodic spiritual overhauling. It supplemented the ordinary day-to-day parochial ministry by attempting to reach out to the lukewarm and the indifferent by soul-stirring, God-fearing preaching. The preachers had been called in to tune up the body religious, and after an interval of time had elapsed they would reappear ready to repeat their performance. Thus, what had begun as an urgent response to an unusual condition, a form of mass evangelization, became a special routine that took place at regular intervals.

But not all of Catholic America moved along at the same pace. Late into the nineteenth century and even into the twentieth century certain areas resembled the missionary conditions of an earlier age. In 1873 the manufacturing town of Fall River, Massachusetts, was in need of a "thorough mission." Scores of young people "were ignorant of the first rudiments of Christianity, several not knowing how to make the sign of the cross, nor indeed what the cross meant, did not know how many Gods there were, nor who Jesus Christ was."[16] Certain areas of the state of Michigan during the 1870s resembled the primitive religious conditions of other areas a half century earlier.[17] Further west, in the Dakota territory, the people were "in a wretched state spiritually."[18] The South was never a showplace of Catholicism and Catholics "generally were very negligent."[19] The new immigrants of the late nineteenth and early twentieth centuries suffered from the same lack of clergy and churches that earlier groups had experienced. The consequences were much the same, and for these groups the parish mission was often the first round-up of a community too long neglected by its spiritual overseers. In these instances the parish mission was a self-conscious effort to evangelize a spiritually impoverished community. The usual promotional trappings were employed, and the event was organized and regularized as usual. The sermons did not change, and no special ceremonies were added. But this was no routine revival. It was an extraordinary happening that took place under unusual conditions; according to the wisdom of the day, the general poverty of religion could be attacked in no other way.

Thus, on one level, the revival aimed at the overhaul of church Catholics. The spiritually destitute also showed up—they were always a special catch at any mission—but in established parishes they became less and less prominent. They were always around of course; in fact, preachers had coined a phrase for this special clientele, "mission Catholics," people who only came to church during a revival. At another level, however, the revival was primarily aimed at the spiritually destitute since they made up the bulk of Catholics in the area. Regular, church-going Catholics were not a common breed in those regions where the Catholic community was only recently organized and adequate numbers of clergy were lacking. This was the situation in St.

Paul's at the first revival held in 1859, shortly after the parish was organized. "The object of the mission was to give a start to the new congregation," and a highlight of the revival, according to the preachers, was the "great many young men who received communion for the first time during the mission."[20] Almost forty years and seven missions later the great revival of 1895 took place. "The number of negligent was very small," noted the mission chronicler, and the highlight of the mission was the "booming up" of the parish societies, "and best of all a Holy Name Society was started among the men with a membership of 850."[21] In St. Paul's, as in many other established parishes, revivalism had ceased to be a technique of mass evangelization, but it remained an integral part of the religious experience of Catholics.

Once the pastor had decided that the time was ripe for a revival, he set out to choose a group of preachers. He had a wide variety to select from, and it did not make much difference what group he chose. They all were specialists trained in the art of revival preaching, and only minor differences distinguished one group from another. The Jesuits encouraged devotion to the Sacred Heart; the Redemptorists put a special emphasis on Mary; the Passionists singled out Christ's passion for particular attention; and the Dominicans fostered the rosary. These were about the only points of difference among the groups. This became especially evident when several religious orders collaborated in canvassing a city or a diocese. Each group dressed differently, fostered its own favorite devotions or saints, and followed a particular rule of life. But when they stepped into the pulpit, their goal was the same—"to excite the piety of the faithful and to prepare them for the sacraments of penance and communion."[22]

In the early years preachers often traveled alone. Later as the movement became regularized and more priests were available they generally traveled and worked as a group. At least thirteen different religious orders conducted parish missions between 1875 and 1885.[23] Each order had its own band of preachers numbering as few as two or as many as six or seven depending on the size of the parish to be evangelized and the length of the mission. The roster of preachers continually changed depending on the needs of the order in other apostolates and the demand for missions. Between 1832 and 1865 at least fifty-two Redemptorists traveled the midwestern mission circuit.[24] Within a twelve-month period in 1890–91, twenty-two Jesuits journeyed up and down the Atlantic seaboard preaching missions. The core group was made up of seven priests, but other Jesuits periodically stepped in to help out.[25] Theoretically, any Jesuit or Redemptorist was able to preach a mission, but the nature of the work demanded special oratorical talents, and the full-time revivalists were men who best possessed these skills.

As in any profession, certain men stood out above the crowd. Among Protestants names like Finney, Moody, Jones, and Torrey were front-page headliners, giants in a profession that had hundreds of practitioners. Catholic revivalism also had its star performers. They never made it into the textbooks of American history, but in the Catholic community they were as popular and as important as a Sam Jones or a Dwight Moody. A look at some of these revivalists is necessary to better understand the profession and the type of men it attracted. To accomplish this I selected eight preachers whose achievements set them apart from the scores of other revivalists.

In studying this group of three Paulists, three Jesuits, and two Redemptorists certain characteristics were more common than others.[26] Two of the group were converts to Catholicism, the Paulists Clarence Walworth (1820–1900) and Alfred Young (1831–1900); six were immigrants to the United States, the Redemptorists Joseph Wissel (1830–1912) and Francis Seelos (1819–1867), the Jesuits Francis X.

65

Weninger (1805–1888), Bernard Maguire (1818–1885), Arnold Damen (1815–1890), and Young. Walworth and another Paulist, Walter Elliott (1842–1928), were the only American-born priests. The immigrant character of the group mirrored the nineteenth-century Catholic population. As the number of American-born Catholics increased the number of native clergy also grew. This shift was very noticeable among the Redemptorists. At mid-century they were overwhelmingly a community of foreign-born clergy; by the end of the century three of every four Redemptorists were native Americans.[27]

Weninger was the only preacher who came to the United States as an ordained priest. The others emigrated with their families or traveled to America as young men, eager to work as missionaries in the New World. The immigration of Seelos and Wissel was particularly illustrative of the attraction that the New World had on a young man's imagination. Born in Bavaria, Francis Seelos studied at St. Stephen's Gymnasium in Augsburg and later entered the Maximilian University in Munich, an institution whose faculty included such scholars as Schelling, Döllinger, Möhler, and Görres. As a young man, Seelos was familiar with the United States, having frequently pored over maps of the New World with his younger brother. In 1842, while still a student at the university, he decided to become a priest, not in Germany, but in America as a missionary of the Redemptorist order. Seelos had read about the work of the Redemptorists in the United States in the German press and had seen newspaper advertisements written by the superior of the American Redemptorists urging young German men to come to the "rescue" of their countrymen who "were in danger . . . of losing their souls" in the New World. Inspired by the thought of becoming a missionary, Seelos cut short his university education, left family and friends and emigrated to America to prepare for the priesthood.[28] How much influ-

ence the newspaper articles had on him is difficult to determine, but it was clear that the New World held a special
attraction for Seelos and not even his close family ties could
weaken his determination or delay his speedy departure once
he had made up his mind.

Joseph Wissel also came from Bavaria, the birthplace of
many German Catholic immigrants. In 1848, at the age of
eighteen, he decided to study for the priesthood, much to the
dislike of his parents. Without their approval he was refused
admittance to the seminary. Shortly afterwards he read an
immigrant letter from the son of a neighboring family; as was
true for many immigrants, the letter from America provided
the necessary spark. For Wissel the deciding influence was
the letter's reference to the dearth of priests in the United
States. "This letter set me thinking," he said. "The thought
of going to America entered my mind and never left it
again."29 This time his parents approved and within a
fortnight Joseph and his brother left home and set out for the
New World. The two brothers arrived in New York City
penniless. His brother quickly found a job, while Joseph, in
fluent German and occasional Latin, spent ten days pleading
with various priests to help him gain entrance into the seminary. His efforts were unsuccessful until he finally contacted
John Hughes, the bishop of New York. Within a week he
was enrolled in the New York seminary at Fordham. Later
he left to join the Redemptorists who at that time were
working principally with German-speaking Catholics.

For both Seelos and Wissel, America possessed a special
attraction; it was a missionary territory desperately in need
of German-speaking priests, and this fired their youthful
imagination and inspired them to travel to a distant foreign
land where they could work as missionaries.

Seelos, in particular, possessed an attribute that was
common to the group—a solid nineteenth-century college
education. Young was a graduate of Princeton; Walworth

gained Phi Beta Kappa distinction at Union College; Elliott attended Notre Dame; Weninger earned a doctor of divinity degree in Vienna. Maguire and Damen, like Wissel, pursued their higher education in Catholic seminaries. All of them were better than average students and their subsequent careers testified to their intellectual talents. Before he died Weninger had written at least seventy-four books and pamphlets, including three books on the art of preaching missions; Elliott wrote the popular and controversial, *Life of Father Hecker*, translated the sermons of John Tauler, compiled a mission manual and contributed numerous articles to the Paulist periodical, *The Catholic World*. Wissel wrote a three-volume mission handbook for the Redemptorists which remained in use well into the twentieth century. Young was an occasional poet, an exceptional musician and composer, as well as the author of an apologia for Roman Catholicism. Maguire and Seelos were the only ones who were not accomplished authors, but they had their own special talents. Maguire was president of Georgetown College; Seelos was the holy man of the group, one whose cause for beatification by the church began shortly after his death in 1867.

All but Weninger and Elliott had spent a substantial amount of time in the ordinary parish ministry acquiring the necessary pastoral experience judged essential in revival preaching. As was true of most mission preachers, the majority of the group began their full-time work during their thirties,[30] after some years of pastoral experience had demonstrated their oratorical skills and when they were still young enough to endure the rigorous schedule of an itinerant missionary who was on the road for at least six or seven months a year.

Another common trait that linked this group of preachers was their basic emphasis on preaching to the hearts of their audiences, a style that was "of the greatest importance in the mission."[31] Their aim was to move sinners to repentance and conversion, and they aimed their sermons at the heart, seeking to elicit an emotion-filled response that was ratified by a confession of sins. Intellectual arguments, the doctrinal dimension of their sermons, were often interspersed in their preaching, but only insofar as they reinforced the stirring appeal to the heart of the sinner. Some made this appeal with more flair and drama than others.

Clarence Walworth was certainly one of the most forceful preachers to step into a pulpit. As a student at Union College he had undergone a conversion at a Protestant revival in which he said, "a real, substantial, and lasting impression was made upon me which changed the whole current of my life."[32] Later as a young Catholic priest in England, he wrote to his father to describe his mission work; he told him that "he was giving a spiritual retreat, that is, as you would say in America, a revival."[33] Later, as head of the Redemptorist mission band in the United States and then as a member of the Paulists, he excited his audiences with his drama-filled preaching. He himself had experienced the religion of revivalism, and as a mission preacher he knew what he was about. He was a revivalist, that is how he described his work to his Protestant father and that was the style of preaching he adopted. A young teen-age girl said that his sermons were "impossible to describe. . . . His gestures, his delivery, gave it [the last judgment scene] the appearance of reality, that is, made it pass in imagination before us." First he would speak in a quiet, gentle manner, then he "screamed out so that the walls of the Cathedral reechoed it back again; it reverberated and resounded. It was magnificent and terrible and the people cried, groaned, beat their breasts . . . and when he spoke of the wicked they all cried out Oh Oh Oh Oh My God, My God and then crosses all over their faces."[34] Appropriately he was described "as the one with the clarion voice."[35] His flair for the dramatic included a particularly striking trait. During his sermons he not only pointed to the mission cross, "but he even clung to it, till it swayed back and forth with the weight of his body, whilst the people conscience-stricken and pale with emotion watched and listened in almost breathless silence."[36]

Joseph Wissel was the foremost Redemptorist revivalist, a recognized authority on how to conduct missions. During his career he preached close to one thousand missions in both German and English.[37] Catholic folklore remembers the Redemptorists as singularly forceful preachers, prototypes of the hellfire and brimstone school of preaching. A contemporary said of them that they used

> stern, strong words. They are men who do not believe in treating evil with politeness.... Rough truth rather than smooth phrases is their motto.... They preach with power, hence sinners throng about their pulpits and crowd their confessionals.[38]

The regulations which the Redemptorists issued in 1861 to standardize the parish mission alluded to this penchant for "tumultuous and clamorous" preaching and urged the priests to tone down their preaching style lest they be subject to ridicule.[39] Wissel was particularly known for his "vehement" style, and Seelos urged him to treat the people "softly," not like the battering ram that he usually was.[40] Described as "frank, plain, and forceful in his delivery," he also advised others to be "forcible" in their language with "the delivery impressive and vigorous";[41] certain sermons, he said, demanded "a tone of severity (but not passion) and the attitude of an inexorable judge." Though he counseled against an eagerness "to make people shed tears," Wissel was known for his ability to elicit such a response from his audience.[42] On one occasion he delivered a sermon on the death of Christ in such a manner that "one woman began to cry aloud; twenty others joined in as a chorus; and the whole congregation showed similar symptoms when the preacher said: 'Don't cry now but cry at your confession: then bewail your sins.'"[43]

Another effective preacher was Walter Elliott. He was the foremost authority on missions in the Paulist community, spending better than twenty years crisscrossing the country preaching Catholic revivals. For Elliott the mission sermon was calculated to arouse "the emotions of fear, reverence, awe, hatred of sin, and the love of God." It must "convict them of sin and infuse the fear of the Lord into their hearts by the terrors of judgment."[44] Six feet three inches tall, his presence in the pulpit was truly impressive and his preaching was "intensely dramatic."[45] One priest noted that he "trembled" during Elliott's sermon on hell and added, "what must have been the effect on the people."[46] His sermons bristled with picturesque, fear-inspiring images, but he always saved his best for the temperance sermon. He was ruthless in his denunciation of drunkenness, and his enmity toward saloon keepers was such that he even refused them absolution in the confessional unless they abandoned their trade. The temperance cause was a special crusade with all revivalists, but none could match the Paulists for their persistent denunciation of the demon rum. The Paulist, Alfred Young, was described by Elliott as "a powerful and dramatic preacher, but not at all theatrical."[47] He wrote out his sermons in their entirety and read them. Unlike Elliott's or Walworth's they lacked fervid imagery and emotion-packed drama; they were bland, all except the sermon on temperance. Then, predictably, Young rose to the occasion and preached a terrifying attack on the evils of drink and its perpetrators, the saloon keepers.

Among the Jesuits the premier revivalist was Francis X. Weninger. He had volunteered to work in the United States as a missionary specifically to preach parish missions, and for nearly forty years that is about all he did. There is little doubt about the effectiveness of his preaching; numerous accounts of his missions attest to his "straightforward," direct style, and he could massage the hearts of an audience as effectively as anyone.[48] Weninger's principal genius was his calculated, systematic approach to the parish mission. He arranged every aspect of the revival to suit his goal of gaining the conversion of sinners. He was the tactician, the master planner, of Catholic revivalism whom German, French, and Irish pastors called upon to revive the religion of the people.

Arnold Damen was recruited for the American missions by the famous Jesuit missionary, Pierre-Jean De Smet. While visiting the school in Belgium where Damen was studying, De Smet spoke to the students in such a compelling manner of the needs and opportunities in the United States that Damen decided to dedicate his life to the American foreign mission. As the pastor of a growing parish in Chicago he took time out every year to hit the mission circuit. For a time he was the only Jesuit preaching English missions in the Midwest; then in 1861 the Jesuit, Cornelius Smarius, teamed up with Damen.[49] Weighing close to three hundred pounds and possessing a booming voice, Damen was judged to be "a most successful preacher to the masses of people."[50] He himself admitted that he preached "with great vehemence," and he "strongly favored the dramatic method of presenting a subject."[51] One woman recalled the impression he made on her as a young child:

> After a thrilling sermon on the Passion he held aloft in the pulpit a huge crucifix and addressed the Saviour as follows: "My God, it was my sins of wantonness and rebellion, leading me to occasions of sin that caused those fearful wounds in your sacred Feet; my refusal to walk to Sunday Mass drove the nails deeper and deeper; my cursing, swearing, my uncharitable and blasphemous speech that caused the awful parching of your sacred lips. . . ." As he went on, the sobs and cries that broke forth from the congregation of

men and women were terrifying to me. The words "wanton-
ness and rebellion" never left my memory.[52]

From this brief sketch it is clear that these preachers
adopted an evangelical style of oratory. They went straight
to the heart of their audiences, seeking to stir the emotions
and to move people to conversion. Expectedly, some had
more flair for the dramatic than others. They were individuals and each had his own particular style in the pulpit. Seelos
was admittedly more mild than Wissel; Young's sermons
were more refined and less dramatic than Walworth's; the
Jesuit Maguire, who worked the eastern mission circuit, did
not have the dramatic style of Damen, but like all Catholic
revivalists "his fervid eloquence carried conviction to the
heart of the unbeliever and strengthened the faith of the
wavering."[53]

With all the preparatory and promotional activities completed, the mission could then begin. It commenced on
Sunday and would last for one, two, or even four weeks.
Weninger's revivals seldom continued for more than eight
days, but other missions preached by a group of at least three
missionaries, could go on for two weeks, occasionally even
four. The length of the mission varied, depending on the size
of the community. It never was less than a week, and only
occasionally did it go beyond fifteen days. A practice which
was followed by many mission bands was to hold a two-week
mission, dividing it up between men and women. One reason for this was that the churches were not large enough to
accommodate the large crowds, and such an arrangement
would also spread out the number of people going to confession over a longer period of time. Another reason was that
the women, who made the mission first, were of "great help
to the missionaries to induce the men to attend the men's
mission."[54] The great mission at St. Paul's went on for a
month. Each week was aimed at a specific clientele, married

women, then single women; afterwards married men and then single men. This arrangement "contributed immensely to the convenience of the people and to the thoroughness of the work."[55] It was not the customary arrangement and only took place in large city parishes, but it was said to have "met with extraordinary success."[56]

The daily schedule was very similar regardless of what religious order was involved.[57] Each day began with a mass, usually at 5 A.M., followed by a thirty-minute instruction. "Punctuality must be strictly observed," it was noted, "so as to give time to those attending the instructions to go home, take their breakfast, and be on time for their work, that begins usually at seven o'clock."[58] Later in the morning a second mass and instruction repeated the earlier exercises. The next service took place in the evening. A brief instructional talk was followed by the recitation of the rosary; then came the highlight of the day, the mission sermon, which lasted for about one hour. The day closed with benediction of the blessed sacrament which together with the rosary was a traditional devotion in the Catholic community.

The morning instructions or doctrinal sermons focused on the sacraments of penance and the eucharist as well as the commandments of God. Their aim was to teach, not to exhort, and to complement the major sermons that were given in the evening. Since confession, or the sacrament of penance, was the heart of the mission, the instructions emphasized this a great deal. In a two-week mission, the first week of instructions would be given over to explaining the sacrament of penance, hitting on such themes as the necessity of confession, how to make an examination of conscience, the true spirit of contrition, and the need for a firm purpose of amendment. The following week would focus on the necessity of attendance at mass and receiving communion as well as on one or two of the commandments.[59] The instructions comprised the catechetical aspect of the mission and were thought to be especially necessary in the United States where

> on the one hand Catholic education still labors under great defection, and on the other Catholics are continually associating with an unbelieving population. Many are deficient even in the rudiments of faith, or at least have not a sufficient knowledge of their meaning.[60]

In the evening, before the rosary, another but briefer instruction was given. This centered on either the great truths of Christianity outlined in the Apostles' Creed or on the meaning and appreciation of certain "objects of piety and devotion" such as the rosary, wearing of medals, the scapular, crucifixes, and sacred pictures.[61]

A practice strongly favored by Weninger and also used by other preachers was a series of instructions on the different states of life, that is, married and single men and women. Generally given in the afternoon, or in the evening for men, they centered on the principal duties of each state of life. The main thrust in each instruction was on marriage, correctly preparing for it or faithfully living up to its responsibilities.[62]

A mission for children occasionally took place during the adult mission. It was aimed at school children between the ages of ten and fourteen. The sessions were held in the early morning and afternoon; ordinarily the superintendents of public schools "showed some generosity in allowing the Catholic children to leave school sooner for such purposes."[63]

The highlight of the revival was the evening sermon. As one Jesuit put it, they were "the big guns in our engagement, with boom and reverberation overwhelming by irresistible force."[64] According to Walter Elliott "the mission sermon ought to be a masterpiece, arousing the emotions of fear, reverence, awe, hatred of sin and the love of God."[65] The evening was a time for "invective; intreaty [sic]; reproach;

pleading; impassioned remonstrance; warning and threatening: all resulting in horror of sin, terror of the Divine wrath; and towards the end of the mission compassion for Jesus Crucified, and tender sentiments of hope and love."[66] The style as well as the content of the evening sermons sharply differed from the morning instructions. The latter were plain, simple catechetical lessons delivered in a didactic manner; the sermons were basically moral "harangues," as one revivalist described them.[67]

When the preacher mounted the platform to give the great sermon of the day, he was following a centuries-old tradition. The themes he addressed himself to had been tried, tested, and confirmed by the great masters of Catholic revivalism in the seventeenth and eighteenth centuries. A schema of sermon topics had developed over the centuries and throughout the nineteenth century it remained fundamentally the same.[68] The traditional themes were occasionally supplemented by topics which responded to the particular needs of the age (Catholic schools, temperance), by apologetical sermons (the church), or by certain devotional topics (the Sacred Heart, sodalities, the Holy Name). After studying mission sermons for over a century, one scholar concluded that "the main stream, the general direction and the peculiar form of mission sermons remained the same until very recently, right up to the second world war."[69] The framework for this schema was to be found in Ignatius Loyola's *Spiritual Exercises* where the themes of the first week furnished the fundamental motifs of the Catholic revival: salvation, sin, death, judgment, hell, and the ways of conversion. Alphonsus de Liguori, Vincent de Paul, Paul of the Cross, and Paul Segneri preached sermons that, "apart from a few negligible variations," were "more or less identical."[70] The same can be said of Walter Elliott, Joseph Wissel, Clarence Walworth, and Francis X. Weninger. They all followed a similar plan, preaching the great truths of salvation which aimed at a religious revival by bringing people face to face with the evil of sin and the harshness of God's judgment.

At the first mission held in St. Paul's in 1859 the opening sermon took place at the Sunday morning High Mass, the customary time for beginning a parish mission; that evening the sermon topic was salvation. In the next seven days the revivalists preached on mortal sin, death, penance, judgment, mercy of God, occasions of sin, and the closing sermon on perseverance and the renewal of baptismal vows.[71] A recommended schema for a one-week Jesuit mission began with a sermon on the end of man, followed by sermons on sin, hell, death, judgment, mercy, and the closing ceremony; on the last Sunday, the eighth day of the mission "a sermon on the Sacred Heart will be appropriate and encouraging."[72] The core of a Redemptorist revival included the following themes: salvation, mortal sin, general judgment, hell, Blessed Virgin Mary, precepts of the church, and means of perseverance. These themes were never to be omitted, but could be added to according to the length of the revival.[73] Depending on the needs of the parish, a point that every preacher was to familiarize himself with, certain sermons were added, such as intemperance, attendance at mass, duties of parents, Catholic schools; or they became the concrete specification of a more generic topic, such as intemperance for occasions of sin and attendance at mass for precepts of the church. The basic thrust of the mission, however, was clear. The first stage of the revival aimed at conversion which was then followed by the theme of perseverance. A more theological breakdown of the sermon topics further illustrates the design of a Catholic revival. It aimed at conversion by (a) making man return to himself to recognize his sinfulness (sermons on salvation and sin); (b) arousing in his soul a fear of God's justice (sermons on death, judgment, hell); (c) awakening hope in his heart (sermon on mercy); and (d) finally trying to rekindle the love of God and the Christian life (sermons on perseverance, precepts of the church).[74]

The design of revival sermons underscored the point that revivalism had been "reduced into a kind of science." From the opening-day ceremony to the final sermon everything was arranged to achieve the best possible results. For a week or more the drama of salvation was acted out on the preacher's platform. To emphasize certain scenes, the words of the preacher were reinforced by the ritual of ceremony. One of the more dramatic was the ritual that accompanied the sermon on death. Among the Redemptorists the custom was to use a catafalque, placed "so that it can be seen from every part of the church"; candles were placed around it and lighted just before the sermon, then "some mournful piece is sung. . . . It is well to begin the sermon abruptly with the solemn question, Who is dead? Then continue by answering: The sinner is dead! Dead to God! dead in his soul! He shall die another death this night at the foot of this catafalque: die to sin, lest he die in sin sooner than he expects. Then, addressing himself to all, the preacher asks them where, they think, their souls would be if their bodies were lying there ready for burial. But how soon may not one or the other be there, etc. This ceremony never fails to make a very deep impression."[75]

The Passionists occasionally used the figure of the dead Christ to dramatize the sermon on his passion and death. The paraphernalia used to decorate the mannequin were so unique and tradition-bound that priests repeatedly wrote to Italy requesting the desired costume.[76]

The sinner's bell was another ritual used in many missions. It tolled each evening at the close of the services "to carry to the ears of the wayward sinner the report that the congregation is just now praying for him on their knees before the Blessed Sacrament."[77]

Francis X. Weninger was unquestionably the most dramatic performer of his day. His handbook on missions minutely described in over two hundred pages how his revivals were conducted, and it was evident that for Weninger ritual as well as rhetoric was an indispensable ingredient for a successful parish mission. Elaborate processions were scheduled throughout the mission; bands and choirs marched in these processions and performed at all the services. Every detail of the mission, including the placing of flowers and candles, was designed for the best possible effect. Weninger was such a stickler for detail that he even carried his own incense, since American priests were using all types of unorthodox mixtures.[78]

But the *pièce de résistance* of a Weninger mission, and of many other missions as well, was the erection of the mission cross. Almost every page of Weninger's autobiography alluded to this ceremony. At first the cross was erected outside the church, preferably on a knoll or hillside to enhance its prominence. Thirty to fifty feet in height, inscribed with the names of Jesus, Mary, the word *Mission* and the date, along with the inscription, "He who perseveres to the end will be saved," the cross stood as a continual reminder of the mission. Experience eventually determined that it was better to place the cross inside the church; outside in the open air it was subject to deterioration, during the bad weather the ceremony could not take place and the cross also was exposed to desecration by "scoffers of religion."[79] Inside the church the cross was naturally smaller in size, only ten feet in height, but the ceremony of the mission cross, inside or outside the church, was always an inspiring ritual. Isaac Hecker described an outdoor ceremony which took place in Loretto, Pennsylvania, and it conveys as well as any account the pomp and splendor of this popular ritual.

I must describe to you in a few words the closing ceremony, the plantation of the cross. We all assembled in the church on Sunday afternoon at 3:30 to recite the Rosary. The procession then was formed outside the Church. First came the processional cross with the boys, then the men carrying a large cross 40 feet long entwined with garlands of flowers borne by 60 of them; on each side of the cross was a file of soldiers with a band of music; then came 20 or 30 Franciscan brothers of the third order with their cowls; then the clergy; after them the missioners in their habit, followed by the Sisters of Mercy, and these by the girls and women. The number of the procession was about 4,000. We marched through the village to the site of the cross with music, and there we blessed and erected the cross in a most conspicuous place. The farewell sermon was preached at the foot of the cross and the papal Benediction given. It was a novel scene for America, a famous one for our holy religion, and one which never will be forgotten by those who witnessed it. The cross overlooks the whole village, and when you look that way you will always see some one or more saying their five paters and aves to gain the indulgence of 10,000 years which is attached to the missionary cross.[80]

None of the rituals were unique to the United States; like the mission itself they were European imports. But some ceremonies popular in Europe never made it to the United States, or if they did they were not long on the scene. The major reason for this was that too much emphasis on the theatrical "in this country . . . would only excite the ridicule of the people."[81] This particularly applied to the ceremonies of the Italian-style mission developed by Alphonsus de Liguori, Paul of the Cross, and others. In contrast to the mission north of the Alps, the Italian mission put a great deal of emphasis on extravagant ceremonies that appealed primarily to the senses. The process of adaptation that some of these ceremonies underwent was best illustrated in the Passionist order. Founded in Italy by Paul of the Cross in

1720, the order had its roots in the baroque period when gaudy, even grotesque, practices began to creep into the mission program. To emphasize the passion of Christ, the keystone of their spirituality, Passionist preachers employed such ceremonies "as the repeated processions with the mission crucifix, the taking of the discipline at the foot of the cross, and the impressive ceremony of the burial of Christ."[82] None of these rituals made it to the United States; few of them ever got outside of Italy. They were too Italian, too culturally conditioned, and younger Passionists looked unfavorably upon them as too theatrical for an Anglo-Saxon audience. One unique Passionist ritual did make it to America. Father Anthony Calandri was the only one who employed it, "and with impressive results," noted the American historian of the order. After the sermon on death, Calandri placed a rope around his neck and a crown of thorns on his head, and then while he knelt at the foot of the crucifix facing the congregation, he begged pardon for his sins. Then the people were to beg pardon of each other.[83]

The Redemptorists had a special ceremony to drive home the evil of a sacrilegious communion. The 1861 directives spelled out the ritual which was carried over from the days of Alphonsus de Liguori. First, the eucharistic host was exposed in a monstrance placed on the altar; then the preacher, kneeling before the altar, gave a stirring sermon on the eucharist, gradually introducing the theme of sacrilege. The monstrance was then covered with a veil; at this point the preacher could publicly bemoan his own sins or end his sermon with an act of reparation. Having aroused the people to a "sense of most profound humility and most intense contrition," he then ordered that the veil be removed from the monstrance, once again exposing the eucharistic host for all to see. He concluded the ceremony by asking the people to make a solemn act of atonement for the evils done by sacrilegious communions.[84] Such a bland description hardly conveys the emotion that accompanied such a ritual during the course of a mission. Priests objected to it because it could do more harm than good. It was thought to be too dangerous, exciting the people too much, even frightening them and keeping them away from the sacraments. Eventually the Redemptorists abandoned the practice and incorporated the theme of a sacrilegious communion in another sermon in a more subdued manner.[85]

The abandonment of certain old-style rituals, however, did not mean that the American Catholic revival lacked emotion-packed ceremonies. The entire mission was a dramatic process, and there were enough ceremonies available, even for an Anglo-Saxon world, to intensify the drama of salvation. Some were planned; others like the reconciliation of sinners before a packed church, the public validation of marriages, and the reception of converts into the church were more spontaneous and arose from the circumstances of particular revivals. If things were not going well, the preachers even took to the streets in elaborate processions to arouse the lethargy of the community and boom up attendance at the mission.

To enliven the ceremonies and the sermon, music and song were incorporated into the revival. They were a natural, necessary ingredient and "ordinarily a very attractive one."[86] Each evening the services began with the traditional hymn, *Veni Creator*, and closed with the customary hymns at benediction. In addition, other vernacular hymns specifically composed for revivals were sung to accentuate various themes emanating from the preacher's platform. The songs of Father Faber, the noted English spiritual writer and preacher, were very popular; the Paulist Alfred Young also composed mission hymns. Other parish song books generally included a section of mission hymns.[87] The church choir usually did the major work, but in the late 1880s the Paulists introduced the practice of congregational singing, "a feature entirely novel and experimental" at that time.[88] They continually fostered this practice, and it did catch on with other religious orders. The Jesuits adopted it in the 1890s, but at the close of the century congregational "singing at missions was not common."[89] Twenty years later Walter Elliott was still trying to promote it. The choir was the key to revival song, and only occasionally, at the closing ceremony especially, did the people raise their voice in song. Like the ritual of ceremony, revival music was used to create the appropriate atmosphere and to reinforce the sense of conversion and repentance urged upon the people; to loose "the chains that have bound me," as one hymn put it, so that "by the mercy of God the poor slave is set free."[90]

To break the "chains of sin" was the goal of the revival; for Catholics this was achieved through the sacrament of penance, or confession as it was more commonly referred to. Half of the instructions focused on it, and the first group of sermons sought to move people toward the "sawdust trail" that led to the confessional. Priests began hearing confessions only on the third or fourth day of the mission, after the people had been sufficiently warmed up so that they could seek the sacramental ratification of their conversion. Since it was a private affair between priest and sinner, extra priests had to be recruited to help out with the large crowds that lined up day and night at the confessional. The revival was theoretically limited to people who belonged to the parish; to enforce this admission tickets were often distributed to the parishioners. This restriction was also observed in the confessional where only those people who made the mission were allowed admittance. Such a regulation was not always easy to observe, but preachers were urged to "be strict in enforcing this regulation."[91] The sacramental complement to confession was communion. To highlight this as much as possible, Weninger urged that different groups of people, specifically married and single men and women, receive the sacrament in a body at a specified mass. For Weninger it was a natural complement to his emphasis on singling out the various states of life for special treatment. Other preachers were less specific, but in a two-week revival divided up among men and women, a similar effect was achieved since one week the mission was limited to women and then the next week to men.

The last night of the mission was the capstone of all previous ritual, song, and preaching. In some instances it was the occasion for the erection of the mission cross in the church; at other times it featured the renewal of baptismal vows; occasionally both ceremonies occurred together. Perseverance in the Christian life was the theme for this service; the mission cross ritual underlined this as did the renewal of baptismal vows. The church was always packed with a standing room only crowd. Elaborate arrangements of flowers and candles decorated the altar; during the renewal of their vows the people, with lighted candles in hand, stood up to renounce the devil and proclaim their faith in Jesus and the church. Oftentimes the mission scorecard was read which included the numbers who had received communion and those who had been converted to Catholicism. The preachers were making their final appearance, their grand farewell. Newspaper reports always singled out this event as the climax of the revival. The Newburyport, Massachusetts, *Daily Herald* gave the following description of the closing of a Paulist mission where the renewal of baptismal vows took place. As well as any account it conveyed the sense of religious enthusiasm that pervaded the revival's grand finale.

> We are not unacquainted with revival meetings, and we have before seen people at camp meetings and other excited gatherings, stand up and vow; but we never before saw such a scene. The multitude looked as though they would have sunk into the earth or been burned together at the stake, before one

of them would in the slightest manner have denied the faith. We saw before us both the material of which martyrs are made and the fiery zeal that would make them.

During some parts of the service, especially at the farewell, the people were greatly moved. The speaker held them as by a sort of electrical influence, and the whole audience quivered like the leaves of a tree in the breeze. Now they sunk; and now the rising tide found vent in sobs and moans.[92]

One event which often took place at the closing of a mission, and on other evenings as well, engendered a good deal of controversy. It was a typically American theme—the collection of money. In reading over the conciliar legislation of several countries the similarity of concern and the importance attached to the mission was universally apparent. Only in the United States, however, does the question of money arise. The discussion of missions at the 1866 Baltimore council was relatively brief, but the one issue that aroused the concern of the theologians was this issue of "filthy lucre." The preliminary acts of the council referred to the practice, urged preachers and pastors to avoid scandal in this regard, and stated that before such collections or the sale of religious articles took place the preacher had to obtain the consent of the pastor and the bishop. The theologians thought that such practices were unwise and out of order and wanted to abolish them entirely. Their advice was overruled, and mission collections and the sale of religious articles were allowed to continue with the caution that any action which might arouse suspicion of any semblance of "filthy lucre" and thus cause severe harm to the mission be zealously avoided.[93] Subsequent events indicated that such scandal could not be avoided, given the zeal with which some preachers and pastors acted.

The reason for the collection was ostensibly to cover the expenses of the revivalists. But the records indicate that their stipend was generally a small portion of the total collection—two, three, or even four hundred dollars—the rest went to the pastor.[94] Mission collections also took place to raise money for a new church, a new school, or any other parochial expense. For some pastors the only reason for having a mission was to raise money for their parish. Yet, such crass motivation was more the exception than the rule.[95] Despite the possibility of causing scandal, the collection continued to be a regular feature of Catholic revivals. Preachers approved of the practice and on occasion even took up the collection themselves to dramatize the need for a new church, a new school, or a new altar. Later on, the collection was used to support the non-Catholic mission.

The selling of books and religious articles was also commonplace at missions. Such materials were an integral part of Catholic piety. Weninger carried his own supply of books which he had written, and his zeal in selling them eventually led his superiors to forbid such sales at the mission. Damen followed a similar practice and ran into the same trouble.[96] Naturally the volume of sales varied. At a Redemptorist mission in Philadelphia 1,825 books and religious articles were sold, netting a total of $3,000; at a Cleveland mission the sales brought in $600.[97] The proceeds went either to the parish, to the preachers, or to a local merchant who had the franchise for the mission. People freely purchased these items, and it did provide an outlet for the mass distribution of Catholic literature and devotional materials. It was primarily through mission sales that Cardinal James Gibbons's *Faith of Our Fathers* got into the hands of thousands of Catholics and non-Catholics and became one of "the most widely read books on religion in the English language."[98]

Another controversial aspect of Catholic revivalism was less tangible. It was the debate over the propriety of religious enthusiasm at Catholic revivals. The two major essays on

Catholic revivals in the nineteenth century both addressed themselves to this issue.[99] One, written by Father Frederick Faber in England, was conditioned by the English environment and was an apologia for religious enthusiasm over against Anglican critics. The second, by Orestes Brownson, which also appeared in the 1850s, was another apologia for "religious excitement" in Catholic missions against those "superficial observers" who claimed that Catholic and Protestant revivals closely resembled each other.[100] Both authors articulated an attitude which was common to many Catholic publicists. They were opposed to religious enthusiasm as an end in itself, or better, to the "base" type of enthusiasm that they associated with Methodism; for Brownson this was most evident in the western camp meeting. As he put it, "in Protestant revivals, excitement is carried to excess, and made the end aimed at. In Catholic retreats and missions, it is wisely managed and made simply a means."[101] He acknowledged that in some Protestant revivals it was not carried to excess, but ultimately it was not useful since, in his opinion, such a revival did not offer salvation. Catholic revivals, however, were "a vehicle of the supernatural graces and gifts of God."[102] Faber's argument was basically the same: grace sanctified religious enthusiasm and made something which was not decorous legitimate.[103]

Within the Catholic community there definitely appeared to be some people who criticized the revival because it was "an imitation of the old Methodist revivals."[104] This was not a widespread concern, but it surfaced periodically in oblique comments in parish mission accounts. One such report of a Redemptorist mission observed that

> Catholics never forget themselves in the house of God as to disturb its solemn stillness by any audible expressions of feeling. They never fall into what is called "religious excite-

ment," even when their hearts are most deeply moved. . . . Their excitement is all within, quiet, subdued, working to salvation, never noisy or demonstrative.[105]

Another account noted that the Paulists discarded "the rant that characterizes so many religious leaders and teachers who strive by stage effects and sensational recitals to charm or frighten proselytes into their ranks."[106] It was clear that such references were apologias on behalf of Catholic revivals against any type of religious excitement which Catholics associated with Protestant revivalism. Indeed, parish missions did not evidence the physical frenzy associated with the early western camp meetings, but it was also apparent that religious enthusiasm, despite any disclaimers to the contrary, was an integral part of Catholic revivalism.

It was principally a question of style. Some individual preachers, like Weninger and Damen, were accused of appealing too much "to the heart" and thus effecting only temporary results.[107] Wissel too was cautioned about the vehemence of his style, and the Redemptorist regulations urged their priests to tone down their preaching. Other preachers prided themselves on "the total absence of any striving after excitement or sensational effect."[108] The enthusiastic style was believed to effect only temporary results, and for some it was not decorous and proper. But this issue of religious enthusiasm was clearly a marginal concern that surfaced only occasionally. It was never a major debate and did not cause the type of divisive conflict which took place over Finney's new measures. Church councils never alluded to it; a reading of newspaper accounts and mission reports indicated that it was not a major concern. Nor can it be associated with the style of any one religious order over against another. All groups had their fiery, dramatic performers, and those were the men most celebrated by the community and singled out in historical memory.

The issue of religious enthusiasm was a question of pre-ferred style, and the majority of preachers, certainly the giants in the profession, were soul-stirring, exciting preachers. This was what the revival was about. It was designed to excite, to shock, the religious sensibilities of people. Too much theatrics did not go over well with Ameri-can Catholics, and revivalists had to abandon some of the rituals common in European countries. But some theatrics were necessary since revivalism thrived on dramatic, evan-gelical preaching. By adopting an evangelical style parish mission preachers fostered a type of religious experience which tradition has generally assumed to be uncharacteristic of modern Roman Catholicism. But revival religion not only found a home in the Catholic community, it also became the most popular religious experience of Catholic Americans in the second half of the nineteenth century. Its popularity, however, was not entirely based on the drama of its ritual or the appeal of the preacher. Surely these were critical ele-ments in the success of the revival, but equally important was the message of the preacher. People came night after night, not only to see him in action, but also to hear what he had to say. And in the final analysis what he said was to have a more lasting effect on the culture of Catholicism. Thus, not only the medium, but also the message of revivalism has to be examined for a fuller appreciation of the evangelical strain in American Catholicism.

Evangelical Catholicism | 4

The Catholic revival was an evangelical summons to conversion. To say this, however, introduces a term, *evangelical*, that has a variety of meanings. It can be so rigidly defined theologically as to become a test of orthodoxy, or it can be described more generically as a perspective from which religion is viewed primarily as "an experience of personal conversion" that issues forth "in a pursuit of personal piety."[1] Understood in this sense the term *evangelical* represents a mood or style of religion which is not peculiar to any one denomination and thus best describes the central thrust of the revival tradition in American history. Catholic revivalism fostered such a religious experience, and for this reason it deserves to be included in the history of American evangelicalism. The basis for this judgment rests on an analysis of the sermons preached at the parish mission, as well as the explicit purpose of the revival rituals. This judgment is not so astounding as it first appears, given the long tradition of evangelicalism in the history of Christianity.

Ever since the days of the apostles the spirit of evangelicalism has been present in the Christian community. The prophetic tradition of Isaiah, Jeremiah, and other Old Testament prophets pushes its roots even further back into the past. The prophets' plea to Israel to repent and turn to Yahweh has provided a model for the preachers of Christianity ever since. With the reform movement of the twelfth century and the itinerant preaching of Bernard of Clairvaux came a renewed regard for preaching. Francis of Assisi and Dominic of Spain were but two of the many preachers who traveled the roads of thirteenth-century Europe preaching repentance and conversion. The Reformation reiterated the importance of the spoken word and the experience of conversion. Pietism and later Methodism kept the tradition alive as Protestantism began to grow cold and formal. Catholics also recaptured the spirit of evangelical Christianity during the reform period of the sixteenth and seventeenth centuries, an era that not surprisingly gave birth to the parish mission.[2] In modern times evangelicalism has been almost exclusively identified with Protestantism, but evangelical religion is not so readily categorized. It is a style of religion with which Catholics as well as Protestants have felt comfortable. The margin of difference has been the emphasis that different denominations have placed on the spirit of evangelicalism. For some Protestant churches it is the mainstream of their religion; for other more ritually oriented denominations it is a strong current which only periodically has achieved a prominent presence in the mainstream of popular religious experience.[3] This is what happened in American Catholicism during the second half of the nineteenth century.

Two principal points distinguish evangelicalism—its conversionist thrust and its urging to pursue personal piety. The pursuit of piety, or more accurately the effects of a successful summons to conversion, will be examined more thoroughly in later chapters. For now the focus will be on the concept of conversion and how this was expressed in the Catholic revival meeting.

Since evangelicalism is aggressively conversionist, it puts a great deal of emphasis on personal religious experience. It confronts the individual with the central truths of Christianity—sin, repentance, and salvation through the redeeming love of God manifested in the savior, Jesus Christ. "The evangelistic message," noted an historian of evangelism, "is a persistent, pleading invitation to seize the preferred hour for repentance from sin and for surrender to

Christ."[4] Coupled with this invitation to conversion is a sense of immediacy which envelops the preacher's call with an aura of urgency and emphasizes the importance of a decision for Christ. In addition to the emphasis on a personal religious experience and its necessary immediacy, another quality of evangelicalism must be acknowledged. This is the stress given to the affections, or to religion as a heartfelt experience. Such an emphasis has been a major characteristic of the revival tradition. It does not exclude the intellectual component from evangelical preaching, rather it accents the importance of the heartfelt experience of religion over against a more intellectual, more rational experience. Evangelicalism clearly fostered an experiential religion, and this experience was most often described by the symbolism of the heart, not the head. Such a distinction is legitimate and useful insofar as it serves to underline the experiential quality of evangelical preaching. These three elements, then, conversion, its immediacy, and a heartfelt experience, were the major ingredients of evangelical religion, and they were visibly present in the sermons and rituals of Catholic revivalism.

The parish mission was something extraordinary, a "special time of grace" when the central saving truths of Christianity were pressed upon the people like "an irresistible steam engine of grace, which can grind a heart of quartz to dust."[5] There was nothing else like it in the repertoire of Catholic evangelization. The ordinary pastoral ministry was much more ritually oriented with the primary emphasis being on the liturgy of the mass and the institutional administration of grace. This ritualistic style of religion was the image that most nineteenth-century Americans had of Roman Catholicism. To some it was decisively appealing and eventually persuaded them to enter the Roman Catholic fold. To others it represented the "chilling formalism" of an ignorant mind for whom "one sprinkle of holy water was worth a volume" of the comforting words of religion.[6]

It is indeed true that in such a ritually oriented religion the preacher's word is of secondary importance. In the nineteenth century the Sunday sermon was a special event, mainly because it occurred only at the principal liturgy of the day; other masses dispensed with the sermon or only offered a few minutes of instruction. The Sunday sermons were quite different from those preached at a revival. They were principally instructional in tone and style, relying very much on the dry, formal theology of the catechism. The tradition of the church, expounded by the popes, the councils, and the ancient fathers, together with the opinion of theologians and proof texts from scripture formed the basis of the argument pursued. In the United States very often it took on a defensive, apologetic tone as well. Obviously every sermon emphasized the necessity of personal salvation, but doctrine, not conversion, was the primary thrust. This was particularly evident in the importance given to the catechism of the Council of Trent. This Roman catechism was the *vademecum* of the Catholic preacher throughout the nineteenth century. It was a handbook of Catholic dogma and included everything the preacher needed to compose his sermons, but its formal, theological presentation made for correspondingly dry, dull preaching. By the end of the century one priest, commenting on the state of Catholic preaching, noted that the preacher and the sermon had become "veritable cures for insomnia."[7]

Sleep-filled pews were not a problem at the revival. The preacher's message loudly resounded off church walls, and his stern words and vivid descriptions were calculated to keep the audience attentive, if not on edge. On one occasion a Redemptorist preacher, Henri Giesen, was so loudly vivid in his description of the fires of hell that his booming voice roused the firemen tending a nearby station; they quickly charged off to church to put out the fire that Giesen's oratory had fabricated.[8] This style of preaching was designed to persuade the sinner to turn from a life of sin to a life of grace. The whole tenor of the mission—its ritual, its music, as well as its dramatic oratory—was geared to the goal of the conversion of sinners. In the words of Alfred Young, the mission was "a call to conversion."[9] Throughout his autobiography, Father Weninger continually referred to the mission as a time of conversion, an event "intended to produce repentance and to convert the contrite sinner."[10] Every sermon touched on this, and one in particular, the delay of conversion, explicitly hammered home the message in a tone of "stern severity and menace."[11]

Consistent with the evangelical thrust of the mission the preachers enveloped their plea for conversion with a sense of urgency. "There is no time like the time of the mission," Walworth said, to attend to the "great affair" of salvation. "Pray now for it is a time of mercy, the time of the mission; pray now, tonight, for tomorrow it may be too late to pray."[12] Another preacher reminded his audience that God's mercy was not timeless; while acknowledging that God is merciful and "promises to pardon you today, God did not promise you pardon for tomorrow," he argued, "and he who today is your merciful God, might be tomorrow your infinitely just judge, and he might then send you into Hell."[13]

This was the key to the urgency of conversion, to instill in people fear of eternal damnation. The angel of death was capricious in its work and could strike at any time, suddenly and without warning. One revivalist directed his message to the young people in his audience in the following manner:

> Oh the short graves in the graveyard! Are there then so few of them? Have they no voices to the youthful sinners? Yes, they cry out. Come, and look at us. Come and number us. Come

95

and see how we far outnumber the long graves of the old!
Delay not to be converted. Put not off the time of seeking the
Lord.[14]

God, he went on to say, "is calling you in a loud, earnest
voice. Repent, repent. Delay not to be converted to me, and
put it not off from day to day, for my wrath will come upon
you on a sudden and in the time of vengeance I will destroy
you."[15] If the rhetoric of persuasion was not sufficient, the
preacher could present statistics which indicated that "sixty
percent of the vast number who die in a day are ushered into
eternity by a sudden death."[16]

Even more persuasive, in the mind of the preacher, were
the examples of sinners who died, suddenly and uncon-
verted, having refused the grace of the mission. Weninger
told his audience about a man in LaCrosse, Wisconsin,
whom he met on the street during the time of a revival. The
pastor of the parish pointed the individual out to Weninger,
informing him that he had not been to confession for a long
time, "perhaps not for ten or twenty years." The pastor
urged the sinner to come to the mission and to go to confession. "No, not today, the man replied. O yes come today.
No, he said scornfully, not today, tomorrow." He was not
sincere, Weninger noted, as he concluded the tale in a predictable manner: "That very same evening he was a corpse;
he suffered a stroke and we could not bury him in conse-
crated ground."[17] Every preacher had such stories to relate
of people who died suddenly—struck by lightning, hit by a
train, or the victim of a heart attack; a sudden and unexpected death was the best example to persuade a sinner to
repent immediately since "it is not known whether you will
still be living tomorrow morning."[18]

Such efforts to arouse the sinner did achieve their desired
effects, at least occasionally. In a rural parish in Virginia, one
sinner, having heard the sermon on death, was "impelled by

terror" to change his mind and convert to a life of grace. In Johnstown, Pennsylvania, an individual heard the sermon's warning and was so upset, he could not sleep that night. "Fearful," the preacher noted, "he went to confession the next morning."[19] Similar episodes recorded by observers indicated that the preachers' desire to elicit a sudden conversion was not in vain.

With the whole thrust of the mission being the conversion of sinners, the preacher's first task was to shock people out of their complacency by instilling in them a fear of death and the eternal punishment of hell. The preacher took his audience to the deathbed of a sinner and described in vivid detail the consequences of such a destiny. As pulpit artists, revivalists continually painted picturesque scenes of sin, death, judgment, and hell, in order to impress upon the people the horror of sin and its punishments. Walter Elliott did it as well as anyone. His deathbed victim had been suddenly cut down by the "sword of Damocles" in the prime of life. The sinner's family filled the room, a priest was called but to no avail since the sinner remained unrepentant; at the end "the Angel of Record scores another mortal sin against his name—a sacrilegious confession." Then the room becomes haunted with evil spirits and each one beckons him: "Come adulterer, come thief, and a bloated face with a drooling mouth and bloodshot eyes appears and cries out, come, come thou drunkard; come thou hypocrite, cries another evil spirit." Elliott went on to paint the scene of demons dancing around the sinner's deathbed, shouting, joking, laughing, weeping, mourning, gnashing teeth. The sermon ended with the preacher speaking in the second person and addressing the audience as sinners, telling them to beware of a sudden death and a sinful life "for 10,000 priests and sacraments cannot save a man who damns himself."[20]

The sermon on hell was part of every preacher's repertoire. Its purpose was not to present an apologia on behalf of the existence of hell, although one of Walworth's three sermons on hell did defend the doctrine against Henry Ward Beecher's denial of the eternity of hell. But as Walworth himself admitted in this sermon, he had little time to spend on such controversy. "I have too many other things to say," he noted.[21] What interested him most was not a doctrinal exposition of hell, but a sermon which would produce conversions, and there was no better instrument of persuasion than a rousing and vivid portrayal of the devil's den.

Night after night people listened "to a stern and unfaltering course of denunciation; every sentence armed with that awful threat of eternal fire."[22] Indeed, the fires of hell continually burned throughout the mission, but the strategy of the revival necessitated a special sermon to arouse the fear of the Lord in the people; as Elliott said, "the fear of the Lord is the fear of Hell."

> And so tonight it is that same dire necessity which makes it my miserable business to concentrate in a single sermon all the threatenings of an angry God, to bring forward what has so far been the dark background of every picture for your sole consideration by a more particular description of the torments of the lost. And brethren, if we knew of no hell to preach of, if we had only the sentiment of honor, of gratitude to appeal to, we should never give any missions: they would all be failures. Ah! but when the sinner hears of a fire which is never going to be quenched, of a gnawing worm which shall never die, it strikes terror to his soul, you will see his face turn pale, you will see the tears start unbidden to his eyes.[23]

This exhortation sought to arouse the emotions of the listener. Hell's "grim shadow of horrible doom" served to instill fear in the people; then the preacher, pointing to his one major prop, the mission cross, sentimentally extolled the sufferings of the crucified savior. He knew, as the hymn said, that all it took was "one look to my Savior, and all the dark night like a dream scarce remembered, was gone from my heart."[24] The sermon on hell was "to strike the heart of the sinner with the fear of the Lord" by a "description of the pains of hell."[25] Then the crucified savior preached his own silent sermon, speaking a language of the heart which reinforced the preacher's urgent call to conversion. This peroration, as the preachers called it, summarized the core of evangelical religion—an immediate heartfelt conversion.

To effect this "change of heart" the preacher had to speak primarily to the heart not to the head. As Walworth put it, "a word which speaks only to the ear and not to the heart is a word without life."[26] He had to "touch the hearts" of the people, and if he failed the mission was not a success.[27]

Each evening the preacher carried a "bucket of blood" into the pulpit. The cross that stood beside him needed to come alive with the awful sufferings of the crucified Jesus. The thorns, the nails, the wound in the side were recreated through the revivalist's picturesque rhetoric. Bloody, painful suffering was the price of salvation, and the preacher painted the scene like a Baroque master. All that God asked was a heartfelt conversion "for the heart is His one only fee."[28] Like the themes of conversion and its urgent necessity, the appeal to the heart of the sinner was woven throughout all mission sermons. But it was in the second stage of the revival, after the fear of the Lord had been aroused by the grim pictures of sin, death, judgment, and hell, that the preacher really appealed to the feelings of the audience. The key was the sermon on mercy. Here in all their detail the sufferings of Jesus were portrayed. Most often Jesus himself spoke to the people from the cross:

> All my bleeding wounds cry for mercy, and if you will but come, it shall not be denied. If I did not intend to have mercy, you would not see me in this piteous state. Go not away until you kneel before my cross and ask for mercy.[29]

To reject such a plea was a one-way ticket to hell as once again fear of the Lord pushed aside love of God as the central motivating force. Sorrowful tears were always viewed as a sign of conversion and the preacher frequently asked for them "for God cannot resist the weeping sinner."[30] Indeed, the mission was a "blest time of contrite tears,"[31] and journalists always noted the weeping and crying that took place at revival meetings.

The hymns sung at the mission reinforced this appeal to the heart. Designed to awaken the emotions, their lyrics dripped with the blood "ever streaming from Jesus' holy Side."[32] "All hail, then, all hail," they sang, "to the dear Precious Blood/ that hath worked these sweet wonders of mercy."[33] Like the sermons, the hymns focused on the crucifixion of Jesus to arouse the emotions and produce conversion. But the strain of sentimental religion went beyond the cross to include another equally moving image—the family.

The men and women who made up the crowds at the revivals were immigrants or sons and daughters of immigrants. They had either experienced at first hand the journey of separation from the Old World or had heard tales of the voyage "into that sunset far/ across the western waters."[34] Capitalizing on the immigrant's nostalgia for the homeland left behind, the preacher often used the metaphor of separation to touch the hearts of the people. His listeners had experienced the sorrow of separation from family and loved ones, and sin would have the same effect. Sons and daughters would die in the prime of life, and the grief of parents would be increased since children dying in sin would be separated forever from mother and father. Weninger, in particular, frequently incorporated the immigrant experience into his sermons. One especially touching scene made up a major portion of his sermon on the last judgment. Sons and daughters begged their parents' blessing as they left the homeland for America. Receiving the blessing and the prayer that they live well, "they departed in sorrow." Such sorrow, Weninger reminded his audience, will be repeated at the last judgment where sin will separate husband and wife, sister and brother, parents and children.[35] Another immigrant saga further dramatized his point. A family had left Germany for America, but a storm blew up and the ship they were on was wrecked; another ship came to the rescue and they were saved. "O what a jubilation. Then almost immediately the parents anxiously ask—children are you all here? One— two— three— six? Where is the seventh child? Where is your brother? Your sister? A child has drowned. What a grief. The family stands there and weeps." Then Weninger told the people that there will come a time "when the children will be counted again, at the last judgment. Where will the children be, on the right or the left? Where will the father and the mother be, on the right or left hand of God the just judge?"[36]

Walter Elliott preached mainly to English-speaking Irish communities, and his scene of the last judgment was equally nostalgic. The damned soul bid his last "farewell". "They are to be separated from all that is good or happy and separated forever. They must bid farewell! Oh the pangs of that separation." Then he continued by recalling a scene that all understood:

> Do you remember leaving home? Ah till that day you never knew how much you loved your country and your home. How dear the old place seemed, though but a humble cottage and how sad a parting from good old Father and Mother and beloved Brothers and Sisters and relatives and neighbors. And when the ship sailed out of the harbor and the green hills of the dear old land gradually faded from sight, was not yours a heavy heart? Yet you had hope. Many a time you promised these friends to write, to send them gifts, and you fondly

> dreamed of returning some day and seeing them again
> before they died, and you knew full well that they would love
> you only the more for the oceans and continents that divided
> your hearts from theirs.[37]

But the condemned sinner, unlike the immigrant, had no hope; he must bid farewell forever "to Jesus, Mary, the Saints, father and mother." Then, Elliott asked the key question: "Sinner, which side will you be on that day of judgment?"[38]

Another aspect of this sentimental appeal to the love of one's family was rooted in the classic biblical theme of scandal, more precisely the case of children cast into sin by a neglectful mother or father. "There can be no more heart-sickening or harrowing scene . . . [than] to see a son brought up and compelled to witness against his own father or mother in a court. But on the last day how many miserable parents will find themselves accused by their own guilty children. When God shall demand of the wicked child, 'Tell me, why did you not keep my commandments? Why did you not frequent my divine worship? Why were you so impure, so fond of cursing and blasphemy, why so vindictive, unforgiving, and dishonest?'" The son then summons his parents before the Judge and accuses them of leading him into all these sins through their neglectful, sinful conduct. "Home—a mockery of the name. It was a den," the accusing child said. "To escape its horrid roof I fled to drown my memory of it in drink and evil company. But I learned the first lessons from them. Come up wicked, unnatural father and mother. What have you got to say to Almighty God about me."[39]

This theme of scandal on the part of parents permeated mission sermons; the harshest condemnation was always reserved for the drunkard father who, preferring a "glass of poison . . . that glass filled with the blood of your starving wife and children,"[40] brought poverty, sickness and general ruin upon home and family. The grogseller, that "doorkeeper of hell," also came in for severe denunciation because he lived on "blood money—money that belongs to wife and children."[41] His trade wreaked havoc and destruction for countless families who were ready and waiting to condemn him at the last judgment. "The grogseller would soon change his business if he knew what awaits him" in hell, warned Elliott, a fierce opponent of demon rum. "There is the poor drunkard, there his wretched widow, driven by poverty to drink and worse and so to Hell, there the drunken orphans, turned out on the street to beg and steal. Brethren there are thousands of souls this night in hell whose only joy forever shall be to torment the grogseller; who this moment are sending up a frantic prayer to God that the grogseller may die tonight suddenly in his bed."[42]

The emphasis on the family and the utter destruction that sin wrought on hearth and home together with the image of the cross and the bleeding savior provided the preacher with numerous opportunities to touch the affections of his audience. Such appeals reflected the romantic mood of evangelical religion prevalent in the latter half of the nineteenth century. Catholic preachers were especially adept at incorporating romantic, sentimental imagery into their sermons. As many observers noted, revival sermons were "full of unction" and "touched the hearts of all."[43] Few images were as conducive to "heart-stirring appeals" as the bleeding savior and the sin-wrecked family.[44] The imagery of the family, however, was always referred to in an oblique manner. The revivalist did not explicitly preach any sermons extolling the virtues of home, hearth, or motherhood; but in his stern denunciation of sin, these symbols entered through the back door. The ruin of the family and the desecration of motherhood as well as fatherhood were the wages of sin; to neglect the duties of parenthood, a standard mission theme, was to raise children to become "tenants of hell" by making the home into a devil's den. The implications were clear: the sacredness of parenthood and the environment of a Christian home were cherished ideals, and they could only be preserved by living a life free of sin.

Catholic revivalists, however, were not given to excessively saccharine sermons; they were more inclined to threaten and to intimidate people by the "fear of the Lord which is the fear of Hell," and their sentimental appeals to the cross and the family must be viewed in this context. Such symbols blended the sweetness of sentiment with the terrors of hell, but in the end it was always fear that remained the dominant mood in revival preaching. Sentimentalism had its place, but only as a means of intensifying the horrors of sin and the fear of hell.

Even though Catholic revivalists were fostering the spirit of evangelical religion, they were doing it in a way that was characteristically Roman Catholic. The people to whom they addressed their call to conversion were already professed believers. As Weninger said, "my call is primarily to Catholics."[45] Thus, there was little need to enter into apologetical discourses on various religious dogmas. Faith was presupposed since the revival "does not for the first time establish the Christian religion in the hearts of people, but merely repairs whatever has become defective."[46] It was an appeal to a second conversion; not the first conversion of people preparing for baptism and entrance into the church, but the conversion of baptized believers who had fallen into mortal sin which, according to Catholic theology, had snuffed out the life of grace. The mission sought to restore this state of grace by revitalizing the dormant virtues of faith, hope, and love planted in the soul in baptism. The grand finale of the revival explicitly had this as its aim—to renew the vows of baptism already vicariously made in childhood

through an adult godparent and thereby restore the individual to the "holy innocence of baptism."[47]

In stressing the personal conversion of "sinners," the
phrase generally used to address the audience at a revival, the
preachers were striving for a change of heart that for
Catholics necessarily had to be sealed by the reception of the
sacraments of confession and communion. This was the first
step in their pursuit of holiness. The evangelical tenor of
their preaching emphasized "the conversion of the heart,"
but the Catholic version of evangelicalism added a sacramental component to such conversion. "Open your heart to the
voice of summoning grace," the preacher pleaded, "answer
the call—say yes—convert—confess."[48] Here in a very brief
passage Weninger summarized the ingredients of Catholic
evangelicalism. God's grace summoned the sinner through
the preacher's mighty word; it penetrated the heart, the
affections of the sinner, urging him to convert, to make a
decision for Christ and to "say yes" now; then the last stage of
the process was to confess the sins of the past. Walworth
made a similar appeal to a penitent sinner despairing of hope:

> Suddenly in the midst of his gloom, a sweet vision of hope
> arises. He sees the dear emblem of salvation—the holy Cross,
> etc. and on that cross a crucified Christ, whose face even in
> the stillness of death has a smile left to cheer the penitent
> sinner. He sees the open side from which water and blood
> come streaming down as from a fountain of mercy. It is the
> symbol of baptism. Baptism! but he has already forfeited that
> grace. He has lost the innocence of his baptism already. Alas!
> alas! what shall he do now? Even the wounded heart of Jesus
> seems to reject him, etc. Again he looks up. Still the Christ is
> on the cross, and still he smiles. A new hope springs up in his
> breast, for see the arms of the savior are extended, and his
> wounded hands tell of another refuge, a second baptism of

> penance. The hands of Christ preach penance, the open wounds preach penance. These extended arms are the symbols of penance. Baptism is no longer enough.[49]

To the evangelical appeal to the crucified savior Walworth added the Catholic emphasis on the sacraments, but baptism was not enough since sin had "forfeited that grace." Conversion without confession was not sufficient, but equally important, as Alfred Young noted, was the point that "confession without conversion is not penance. Communion without conversion is not penance—not being truly converted, the communion does no good."[50] Both elements had to be present, conversion and the sacraments; one without the other was incomplete.

Mission hymns also stressed the importance of the sacraments. In fact, they most often centered on the salvation won by Jesus and received through the sacraments. For the sorrowful sinner confession " 'twas the labor of minutes, and years of disease/ Fell fast from my soul as the words from my tongue."[51] Communion was the "food, the pilgrim needeth . . . the manna from above" that was symbolized in the "fount of love redeeming/ O River ever streaming/ From Jesus' holy Side."[52]

The conversion sought was not a lifeless, ritualized act but a radical decision for Jesus rooted in true repentance. This was illustrated in the emphasis given to the importance of a general confession. The sinner must tell all, "shamelessly go to the bottom," and confess all his sins lest in omitting something he would make a bad confession, and worse a sacrilegious communion.[53] Normally confession of sins only included those misdeeds since the last confession, but for many at the mission this was often five, ten, twenty or more years past; thus confession became equivalent to a general review of life. Even more important was the fear that somewhere along the way the sinner had made a bad confession, having chosen to omit some grievous sin. Such a confession nullified everything that followed until a general confession, which included as far-reaching a review as possible of one's spiritual life, was undertaken. Not everyone had to make a general confession, and the decision as to whether or not it was necessary should be left "to the Father when he [the penitent] comes to confession."[54] Since such a confession can be "injurious to the penitent" who has a scrupulous conscience, the priest should be particularly cautious about encouraging this general review. "After he has satisfied himself about the necessity of such a confession," Father Wissel noted, "let him conduct the examination with great care."[55] Such caution illustrated the pastoral concern for the delicate conscience, but in encouraging this general review of life, it was clear that the preacher was striving for a total conversion. He wanted the slate of sin wiped clean so that the converted sinner could begin anew the Christian life wrapped in the "innocence of holy baptism."

The sacrament of confession, according to the preacher, strengthened conversion, making it long-lasting. "Compare the conversion of a sinner at a [Protestant] revival and of one at confession," Elliott said. "In a revival there is sudden repentance; in excitement, perhaps frenzy. With Catholics it is in patient searching of the heart done with calm deliberation. In one case a man judges his own heart and approves his own motives; in the other a learned and discreet officer of the Church tests and approves his dispositions in addition to his own judgment, administering warnings drawn from the past and exacting guarantees for the future. Protestant conversion is done in a hurry, in excitement, without any act of humility, done in the vanity of self-judgment, done without reparation for the past and without provision for the future. No wonder such a change of heart is notoriously uncertain."[56] For Elliott the sacramental ritual obviously added something extra to conversion, and it is significant that the comparison chosen was a conversion at a Protestant revival since in Elliott's mind conversion at a parish mission was similar although superior because of its sacramental fulfillment.

The emphasis on the sacraments was also evident in the way that the preachers and the press recorded the success of the revivals. The measure of success was the number of confessions and communions since these figures supposedly indicated how many people had been converted at the revival. Obviously, not every confession and communion represented the radical second conversion sought for since not everyone was in such a spiritual condition, but the one sure indicator of conversion in the mind of the preacher was the number of confessions heard at a mission. At the close of a mission they announced these figures as an indication of the mission's success and of God's bountiful blessing on the revival.

The sacramental evangelicalism promoted by Catholic revivals placed a great deal of stress upon the role of the human person in the conversion process. This was an obvious legacy of the post-Tridentine theology which emphasized "the need and value of man's own efforts to save himself—to such a point that [it] often forgot to mention the prevenient saving action of God which complements them and comes first."[57] The sacraments were the fulfillment of a personal conversion decision, but the process leading up to this strongly accentuated the human instrumentality of conversion. The more forcible the sermon, the better chance the preacher had to "overwhelm the mind, penetrate the heart, pervade the whole substance of man and absorb all his faculties."[58] The entire mission schema was designed to produce conversion, to persuade people to repent. This emphasis on the importance of effective preaching overshadowed the role of God's grace, though it hardly denied it. It was a question of emphasis, an Arminian approach to the process of conversion that highlighted the importance of the human person.

"God's promise of forgiveness," said Elliott, "is like the Bank's promise to pay: any time this side of the moment of death will do to present it. You may repent when you please; God will forgive you anytime."[59]

"Save your soul . . . it is your affair"; this is how Walworth put it.[60] Of course "we are saved by God's grace" and "true sorrow for sin is born of God's grace," noted the preacher,[61] but this side of the conversion process was far overshadowed by the emphasis on the human activity necessary for salvation. Such theology placed the individual in the foreground of revival preaching. The preacher's "only business is to help you save your souls," and he told the people in no uncertain terms that if they wanted to be saved, all they had to do was ask; the only fee demanded was their heart.[62]

The paramount concern for the individual in the conversion process was complemented by a rigorous moralism. The obsession with salvation fostered a religion concerned primarily with obligations and duties. What must I do to escape hell, or, more accurately, what practices must I avoid (rarely was a sermon on heaven included)? The answer came back loud and clear—stop your drinking and your carousing. Drunkenness and impurity were the two cardinal sins to be avoided; they were also thought to be the vices most prevalent in the United States.[63]

One evening was given over to a sermon on the occasions of sin, and predictably the two major vices touched on were drunkenness and impurity. Drunkenness was the worst of all since it takes away the individual's rational faculties; thus, "it is the only sin which deprives God of his power to forgive."[64] It was "the seven-headed monster of the Apocalypse, a vice that encircles the globe and stops short of nothing" in subduing its victims.[65] Seldom did a mission go by without a sermon on drunkenness or intemperance and throughout the course of the revival the evils of drink were continually alluded to. Invariably it headed the catalogue of sins to be

109

avoided, its evil effects on the individual and the family being always highlighted in very vivid and sentimental detail. The most prominent "tenant of hell" was the drunkard father and its "doorkeepers" were the liquor dealers who lived off the "blood money" exchanged for a "glass of poison."

Sex has always been a touchier topic than drink for Catholics to deal with. Characteristically, Wissel advised that the sermon on impurity "be preached with utmost precaution." "Whatever the people do not know in reference to this vice," he said, "they need not and should not learn from the missionary."[66] Frequently the theme of impurity was treated together with intemperance; in this arrangement it was sufficient for the preacher to "dwell a little while on the subject of impurity, express, in two or three sentences, his abhorrence of it, and then dismiss it in disgust, as being too abominable to be treated before a Christian audience, and to be left to the awful revelations of Judgment Day."[67]

In avoiding those places which gave rise to sins of impurity, one institution in particular came in for severe denunciation—the dance hall. The code of morality fostered by the revival strongly condemned dancing; at the last judgment the sinner's body would be recognizable not only by "drunken lips," but also by "dancing feet."[68] For the young girl who "lost [her] soul at the night dance," there was waiting for her "in Hell a burning floor for her giddy feet."[69] Dancing was an "inveterate evil," so prevalent in one town, St. Genevieve, Missouri, that the popular idea of heaven seemed to be that of "an endless ballroom where there was nothing but everlasting dancing and fiddling."[70] The preachers were so opposed to the practice that they sometimes asked for acts of public penance from the young people who were engaged in such frolicking.[71] On one occasion a Redemptorist, preaching a mission in New Trier, Illinois, was so persuasive in his denunciation of a local dance hall that "all turned against that ballroom-keeper, his two sons were sent out of their situations, and on the day after the mission not only his, but all the other ball-tents were broken to pieces."[72]

In addition to dancing, the revival's code of morality condemned other forms of entertainment. "Bad reading" meant the frivolous novels and magazines that abounded in the marketplace as well as "heretical" works of Protestants. To combat this the mission had available a recommended home library of books for purchase. Gambling, most often in the setting of the saloon, was another forbidden recreation; excursions and picnics, shows and the theatre also came in for condemnation. Parents were also advised to be watchful about their children's companions, especially when it meant "company of people of different sexes" lest such relationships lead their children astray.[73]

The stern moral code encouraged by the revival promoted an individualistic moralism that blended in with the evangelical thrust of Catholic revivalism. Morality, not dogma; right doing, not correct believing was the thrust of the revival message. Fear was the chief means of inspiring correct behavior; by expressing the central truths of Christianity in terrifying imagery the preachers impressed upon people what must be done, or more often, what must be avoided in order to gain salvation.

The evangelical spirit of Catholic revivalism with its emphasis on morals and its strategy of fear did not mean that the intellectual component of religion was completely excluded from the mission. Each morning instructional talks were given, and they were considered an important part of the mission. For Walworth this was the distinguishing feature that set the Catholic mission apart from the Protestant revival "which appeals only to feeling and gives no instruction."[74] But even the instructions were shaped by the mission's focus on conversion; they aimed at preparing people for a proper sacramental conversion and little else; they were a catechesis on conversion and were useful only insofar as they instructed people on how to make a good confession and communion. As one preacher put it, the instructions were "rapid firing guns." The evening sermons were the "big guns" of the mission; they set the dominant tone.[75] Expressed in "plain, strong, simple language, and nothing which smacks either of learning or controversy," they represented the epitome of evangelical preaching.[76] As Elliott said, "The Catholic mission should be dominantly moral with a doctrinal influence."[77] "Convict them of sin, Infuse the fear of the Lord into their hearts by the terrors of judgment," was the advice offered by another preacher.[78] Catholic revivalists sought a change of heart, not a change of opinion, and this was the key to evangelism. They wanted to arouse "the emotions of fear, reverence, awe, hatred of sin, and the love of God."[79] Significantly, love of God came in last since it was fear of the Lord, not love of God, that was the chosen way to persuade sinners to convert. To intimidate and terrify the sinner, thus arousing an immediate conversion of the heart, was the goal of every preacher who stepped into the pulpit.[80]

Catholic revivalism blended the gospel of evangelicalism with the ritual of the sacraments; the end result was a sacramental evangelicalism. This gave Catholic piety a new tone by placing the heart above the head, feeling above reason. Personal religious experience became an important ingredient in the pursuit of holiness. The sacraments ratified this experience and nurtured the converted as they struggled to attain "the perfection of the saints." Through the revival meeting, evangelicalism had become a trademark of Catholic piety. No one understood this better or experienced it more fully than the people who listened to the preacher's "harangue."

Revival Catholics | 5

An important question to be answered in a study of revivalism is who was listening to the preacher's word? Most often historians of revivalism have focused on the message of the preacher and answer the question of who was listening by referring to impressionistic evidence left behind in eyewitness accounts. The reason for this is obvious: preachers left behind written versions of their sermons or had them recorded by others for public consumption, but few lay people recorded their observations for posterity. Thus, the eyewitness accounts of the person in the pew are meager, while the volume of sermons is extensive. As a result, little is known about who was listening to the sermons beyond the general impressions contained in the relatively few contemporary accounts made by journalists, educated and articulate churchgoers, and the preachers themselves. These are certainly legitimate and valid, but they often are so general as to be of little use, more suggestive than anything else; a mere hint as to who was really present at the revival. Nor do such accounts always answer the questions that historians of a later age ask. Thus, it is necessary to go to other sources to answer the critical question of who was listening to the preacher's word.

In the case of Catholic revivalism this is especially true since few Catholics wrote diaries; nor is it the expected behavior of immigrant workingmen and women. What diaries do exist were often written by clergymen and not surprisingly they are concerned with ecclesiastical affairs, and only occasionally, if at all, do they speak about the people at a revival. Immigrant letters abound, but they too seldom allude to the participants at a revival. If they mention the revival at all, more often than not they focus on the priest, the main attraction at any parish mission. Because of this lack of literary evidence, then, it is necessary to consult parish records, census materials and a host of other sources which together with the extant literary evidence can offer an answer to the question of who were the people in the pew listening to the preacher's word.

The impressionistic evidence gleaned from traditional literary sources indicates that Catholic revivals took place in large city churches and in "country parishes both large and small."[1] All types of people were attracted to this unique offering of saving grace. In Oxford, Indiana, the dirt roads that led to the local church were busy with the coming and going of wagons driven by farmers who traveled fifteen to twenty miles, several times a day, to hear the preacher's word.[2] Webster, Massachusetts, was a factory town specializing in cloth and cotton goods, and the popular demand for revival religion persuaded "the superintendents of the three different factories" to change "their hours of work in order to suit the exercises of the mission."[3] In Bellefonte, Pennsylvania, men laboring in the steel mills took time off from work so that they could participate in the revival. In a nearby mining town workers were on "strike for wages" and "they had only the thought of the mission to occupy their minds during the whole week."[4] The large city revivals attracted people from all walks of life: "the rough laborer . . . the aristocratic gentleman . . . clerks . . . mechanics of every trade . . . politicians . . . the professions too were represented—lawyer, physician, surgeon . . . the professional bootblack and professional pickpocket."[5]

Revivals not only cut across class lines, but also broke the racial barrier, at least for a time. In Savannah, Georgia, soldiers and sailors "who had sailed to every port of the world except into a confessional" joined "our fellow citizens of the African persuasion" at a Redemptorist revival.[6] In Louisiana, black and white Catholics crowded together in the small rural churches evangelized by the Redemptorists.[7] The Jesuits were frequent visitors to Maryland and occasionally their travels included an interracial revival. But the Maryland revivals, even in the 1880s, reflected the old-time tradition of black and white together, equal but separate, with blacks occupying seats in the galleries.[8] Moreover the nature of the Negro apostolate was changing. Following the pattern of national parishes for different immigrant groups, separate black parishes began to emerge as the chosen solution for the evangelization of black America. As this trend developed, the revival ceased to be an interracial gathering and became more typically the religious awakening of a particular parish community. Revivalists followed the trend and included the black parish in their itinerary. But whether it was interracial or not, the revival was viewed as a particularly effective way of evangelizing the black population. The 1866 Baltimore Council explicitly pointed this out by noting that the revivalist's method of preaching the word of God would be particularly effective among Negroes since, "ignorant of divine things and measuring everything by the senses, they need a more vigorous stimulus so that they can arouse themselves to perceive celestial truths."[9] The 1884 Baltimore Council again alluded to the usefulness of revivals among the Negroes since "experience" had demonstrated that they were necessary for "their salvation and Christian education."[10]

The black Catholic revival, infrequent as it was due to the small number of black Catholics, illustrates how inclusive the parish mission was. No race, nationality or class escaped its influence. Weninger's revivals illustrate how far-reaching the appeal of revivalism could be. This itinerant preacher traveled to small rural communities and large metropolitan parishes; he preached revivals to plantation slaves and California gold miners. German, French, Irish, and American-born Catholics came under his spell, and not infrequently he even had to preach in three different languages because of the ethnic mixture of his audience. The versatility of Weninger was unique, but the varieties of people he evangelized illustrate the widespread attraction of the revival movement.[11]

These general impressions have only partially answered the question posed at the beginning of this chapter—who was listening to the preacher's word? Other more important answers need to be given. Were these people middle-class churchgoers or did they represent a broader segment of the population? Were they the lukewarm or the devout? Were they all Catholic and, if not, from what denominations did they come? Was the revival a female phenomenon, or were men attracted as well and in what proportions? An answer to these questions will not only reveal more specifically who was in the pew listening to the sermons, but equally important, it will determine just how broad the appeal of evangelical religion really was.

To answer these questions and to fill in the ambiance of the revival, a microstudy of a single parish community was undertaken. Such a study, like the evidence gleaned from impressionistic accounts, has its limitations, since it can never fully represent the breadth of the total Catholic community. Yet, it does fill in the broadly stroked pictures left behind by individual eyewitnesses and offers a level of understanding which the history of revivalism has traditionally not achieved.

St. Paul's parish, located on the west side of New York's Manhattan Island, was the community chosen for this local study. An urban parish, it represented the favorite locale of Catholic immigrants in the nineteenth century. A northeastern community, it was located in the core of Catholic America in a city whose Catholic population was the largest in the nation. The city was the locale that all revivalists were eager to subdue. Dwight Moody put it as clearly as anyone when he said, "water runs downhill and the highest hills are the great cities. If we can stir them, we shall stir the whole nation."[12] "The great need of the mission," wrote one Catholic preacher, "lay in the cities and large towns where dense masses of Catholics were gathered and where churches, clergy, and religious organizations of all kinds were inadequate to the spiritual wants of the people."[13] Invariably revivalists reserved their most severe epithets for metropolises like New York, "another Sodom"; Chicago, that "place nearest hell"; or San Francisco, the "Babylon of the Pacific."[14] It did not really matter what city was being castigated, the charges were predictably identical: "the occasions of sin are so numerous and of such a character as to make it, practically speaking, too much for flesh and blood to resist."[15] This concern for the viability of religion in the city was reflected in the Paulist missions that took place in the state of New York during the last half of the century. The one locale which outdistanced all others as the most burned-over area was New York City. Among the midwestern Redemptorists a similar pattern was evident, with Chicago leading the list.[16] Revivals took place in small towns with a great degree of frequency, but the urban revival was more significant insofar as it reached a greater number of Catholics. If the preachers could revive the religion of city dwellers, then they were going a long way toward awakening the religion of the vast majority of Catholics who lived in the urban, economic core of the nation.

St. Paul's parish was organized in 1858, and from its very beginning the Paulist Fathers were in charge of it. Initially the parish boundaries extended from 52nd Street to 109th Street, bordered on the east by Seventh Avenue and Central Park and on the west by the Hudson River. Between 1858 and 1900 the boundaries contracted as new parishes were organized in the area. During the 1870s the northern limit was 75th Street and the southern boundary was 54th Street.

In 1887 a further shrinkage took place with 64th and 54th streets becoming the northern and southern boundaries; these streets remained the geographical limits of the parish into the twentieth century (Figure 1). Despite this geographical contraction the parish population steadily increased as the area attracted more and more inhabitants.

In 1859 the church was located in the center of a district that was "as yet sparsely populated," and 59th Street was the last street opened for traffic on the West Side.[17] To the north was the rocky terrain of the Manhattan countryside and what was soon to become Central Park. By 1890 59th Street was no longer the line of settlement on the West Side and the area north of it was becoming more densely populated each year. The population within the parish boundaries in the early years is difficult to determine accurately. An 1864 survey reported that at least 16,105 people lived in the area between 50th Street and 86th Street. Though this is admittedly a low estimate, it does reflect the relatively sparse settlement in the neighborhood.[18] More accurate figures are available for later years. In 1890 an estimated 28,860 lived within the parish boundaries, and by 1900 the number had increased to 39,120.[19] Though these estimates are low, they indicate the growth taking place in the neighborhood and in the parish as well, despite its continually shrinking boundaries. The census reports confirm the pattern of rapid growth. The parish was located in the 22nd Ward which extended from 52nd to 109th Street and in 1860 it housed 61,725 people; thirty years later its population was 153,877.[20]

The parish population, or the number of Catholics living in the area, is even more difficult to determine accurately. In 1875 one observer stated that the parish numbered eight thousand Catholics.[21] In 1893 the estimate was eleven to twelve thousand parishioners.[22] These were figures of church-going Catholics and not of the total Catholic population in the parish. To arrive at this latter figure the number of

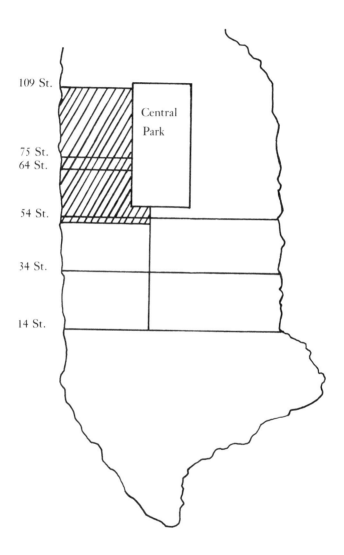

Figure 1.   St. Paul's Parish—New York City

baptisms in the parish for a given year was used in conjunction with birthrate figures. The use of birthrate figures to determine the population of a nineteenth-century urban immigrant community is not the most reliable index; thus, the results are more suggestive than definitive, but they do illustrate the relative growth of the parish in this period. In comparing these estimates, given in Table 2, with the population figures for the neighborhood in 1864, 1890, and 1900, and realizing that the area was predominantly Irish, the Catholic population estimates do not seem exaggerated. In 1900, for example, the parish contained 14,083 tenement house dwellers with a second-generation Irishman as the head of family (36 percent of the neighborhood population); add to this the foreign-born Irish, about 30 percent of the population, and the native-born Catholics of American-born parents and the figure of 25,606 Catholics out of a neighborhood population of 39,120 does appear plausible.[23] In fact, many nineteenth-century urban parishes numbered 20,000 people and more. In any event St. Paul's parish was a rapidly growing community whose population peaked in the 1890s, a decade which one observer described as the "high point of the parish."[24]

From 1859 to 1900 ten missions took place in St. Paul's. The first mission was in 1859 when the parish was being organized. Fourteen years later the second mission took place.[25] In subsequent years, missions occurred in the parish at a rate of three each decade. A study of the ten parish missions showed that they mainly attracted adults, both men and women, single as well as married. At first, the revival audience was a mélange of males and females. Gradually the revival was divided up, with males and females being separated. Eventually married and single people were also set apart with each group having its own mission. The reasons for this are not hard to discover. The size of the church could not accommodate more than a standing room crowd of

TABLE 2.
*Estimated Catholic population of St. Paul's parish.**

Date	Baptisms	Est. N.Y.C. Birthrate per 1000	Catholic Population
1860	213	41.8	5,096
1875	519	41.8	12,416
1885	635	31	20,484
1895	845	31.1	27,170
1900	740	28.9	25,606†

*Baptisms were recorded in the parish registers; birthrate figures were given in Ira Rosenwaike, *Population History of New York City* (Syracuse, 1972, pp. 61–62).

$$P = \frac{\text{baptisms} \times 100}{\text{birthrate}}$$

†A study in 1901 concluded that 28,000 Catholics lived in the 17th Assembly District, located between 49th Street and 60th Street (*Federation* 2 [June 1902], 168).

thirty-five hundred to four thousand, and the expansion of the parish population surpassed this limit. The division also permitted the preacher to focus on a particular class of parishioners and shape his message to their needs.

The attendance figures for the ten missions suggest that from 53–59 percent of the audience were females, their average representation being 57 percent (Appendix). Although they outnumbered men at each mission, their presence was not so overwhelming as to characterize the Catholic mission as a female phenomenon. If mission confirmations are considered, then the pattern is reversed with more men receiving this sacrament than women. Two out of the three adults who were confirmed during a mission were male. A second category of mission confirmations, that of working boys and girls above the age of seventeen, reflect a similar pattern, with 59 percent of those confirmed being male.[26]

The pastor of St. Paul's called the parish neighborhood "Shantyopolis," and few New Yorkers would have quarreled with this description. The area north of 57th Street contained an estimated 552 one-room wooden shanties in 1864 with an Irish and German population. But the large majority of people did not live in makeshift shanties; their homes were two-room tenement apartments. Many of them were day laborers employed in the construction of streets along the Upper West Side. A number of the city's railroad car barns were located in the area, along with the necessary horse stables, and many men were employed in one or another aspect of the city's transportation industry. A "large class of mechanics, as tailors and shoemakers, and many of those engaged in retail business on the avenues" lived in the tenement houses. A small percentage of the neighborhood lived in "the better class of houses" and were "engaged in business downtown as merchants, clerks, real estate agents, brokers, bankers, etc."[27] The Catholics in the area were described as "a people, almost entirely, who do manual labor."[28]

Like most city parishes, St. Paul's contained a diversity of nationalities, but the Irish were in the majority. During the 1860s and 1870s the foreign-born Irish represented between 60 and 65 percent of the families that had children baptized in the church. The next largest contingent were the American-born, but a large number of these were clearly of Irish heritage; throughout the period the Irish flavor of both the parish and the neighborhood remained predominant.[29]

The people who attended the missions in St. Paul's came from the surrounding neighborhood. For most of the parish revivals very little information about the audience is available except for the fact that they lived in the parish. At the 1879 revival the mission chronicler noted that the parish was in a lamentable state. One reason he gave for this was "the hard times which threw so many out of work and into idleness . . . causing the men and grown boys to spend their time loafing about the street corners and in bar rooms coming into contact with the worst company." People also lacked "decent clothes to go to church in." Hundreds of this group of poor and unemployed did attend the mission and he noted that "many of them had scarcely heard mass once since the last mission" held almost two years before.[30] In 1885 at a neighborhood slaughterhouse and on the freight docks along the Hudson River, "the hours of work were fixed so as to allow the men to make the mission," and the distinct impression given was that these men did attend the revival.[31] Three years later, "it was remarked by some engaged in the missions that during the past few years a better class of Catholics has come into the parish. There was less of the material part of man with its low coarse vices at this mission than at the previous ones given in the parish."[32] This particular assessment of the mission audience corresponded with the growth and change of the neighborhood during the 1880s.

In 1880 the built-up area of the neighborhood did not extend beyond 59th Street. But in the next decade the population movement of the city shifted from the east side to the west side of Manhattan and the neighborhood acquired a new look.[33] One observer noted in 1891 that "no part of New York City has developed more rapidly within the past ten years than the section west of Central Park and above Fifty Ninth Street."[34] The West Side was the scene of widespread housing construction and by 1893 the 22nd Ward numbered 4,146 tenement houses, an increase of 3,150 new tenements since 1864.[35] Construction was changing the neighborhood and the shanty population was "fast being crowded out."[36] The priest described the change by stating that "a better class of Catholics had come into the parish"; the policeman observed that in certain sections of the neighborhood "the unruly and worthless inhabitants were being stamped out."[37] However one described it, the neighborhood was changing, and Shantyopolis was no longer a correct description.

Prior to the late 1880s then, the revivals at St. Paul's attracted people who exhibited "low coarse vices," men "out of work and into idleness," dock workers, and men employed in slaughterhouses. Who else attended the mission is unknown, but from the data available, the revivals of the 1870s and 1880s clearly attracted a lower-class clientele.

Both the neighborhood and parish population increased dramatically in the 1890s. An estimated eleven thousand more people crowded into the area during this decade, and the Catholic population peaked at a level of approximately twenty-seven thousand in 1895.[38] During this decade the parish held missions in 1891, 1895, and 1898 and the crowds at those gatherings numbered 11,650, 10,520 and 12,850 respectively (Appendix). The people who attended these missions lived in the neighborhood and were mainly Irish men and women. But the type of Irish Catholic in the area had changed over the years and by the 1890s the number of second-generation Irish had increased significantly. In 1875 65 percent of the fathers of newborn children had been born in Ireland. Ten years later the number had declined to 43 percent, and the remainder were largely American-born Irishmen.[39]

In 1890 the families in the neighborhood with Irish-born mothers represented 37 percent of the district's population.[40] For subsequent years, census data for the neighborhood foreign-born was not recorded but the trend in the city was quite clear. The foreign-born Irish were declining and the number of second-generation Irish was on the increase. By 1900 the second-generation Irish heads of families had reached a level of 36 percent in the parish neighborhood and the foreign-born represented about 30 percent.[41] These figures suggest that the Irish-born heads of families in the district and the parish were declining and American-born Irish were on the increase. The parish remained decidedly Irish, but the shift was to the American-born rather than the foreign-born. The map of the parish (Figure 2) indicates the areas where the second-generation Irish represented at least one-third of the block population. A twentieth-century resident described the neighborhood by stating that the "respectable Irish lived above 59th Street while the laboring class lived below this street."[42] Nor does this seem to be an inaccurate recollection, since the further removed one was from the area south of 54th Street, known as Hell's Kitchen, the more respectable was the address. Moreover, the closer one was to Central Park, the better his chances were of finding a first-class residence. In contrast, an address closer to the river indicated a more adverse environment. Significantly, the least desirable areas of the district numbered the largest percentage of second-generation immigrants. An American birth did not necessarily propel one to upper-class status with a respectable address.

The transition in the neighborhood from foreign-born to American-born Irish did not necessarily mean that the working-class character of the parish changed. On the contrary, an occupational analysis of the fathers of newborn children in 1880 compared to a similar analysis in 1895 strikingly indicates that the parish was still largely composed of manual workers (Table 3).

In his work on poverty and progress in Boston, *The Other Bostonians*, Stephan Thernstrom noted that despite the fluidity of Boston's social system, "there was a ledge at the lower white-collar level above which workers rarely rose and below which men from the upper classes rarely fell."[43] The 1880 and 1895 profiles of St. Paul's parish show that the large majority of West Side Catholics, 77 percent, lived and worked on the lower side of this ledge; close to half of both

125

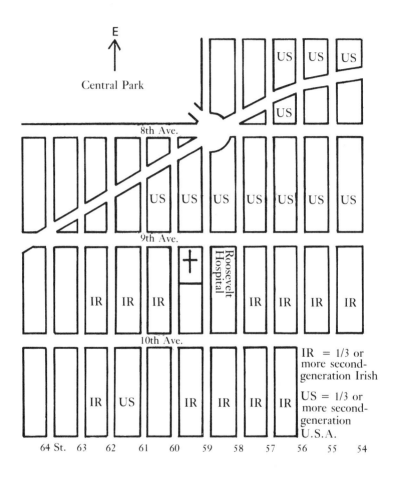

Figure 2.   St. Paul's Parish in 1900

TABLE 3.
Occupational distribution (percent) of St. Paul's parish in 1880 and 1895.**

Occupational Rankings†	1880 Parish N = 268	1895 Parish N = 539
High White-Collar	2	3
Low White-Collar	21	20
Skilled	30	30
Semiskilled	20	21
Unskilled	27	26

*Profile of parish was taken from list of fathers of children baptized in 1880 and 1895; for 1880, 268 of 483, 55%, of them were located in the City Directory; for 1895, 539 of 845, 64%, were so located.

†Occupational rankings are those used by Stephan Thernstrom in his study, *The Other Bostonians* (Cambridge, Mass.: Harvard, 1973). In Appendix B he explains this socioeconomic ranking of occupations.

groups, 47 percent, were engaged in low manual trades (semiskilled and unskilled). In 1895 the largest occupational group was the unskilled laborers, who represented 19 percent ($N=102$) of the heads of families. Next were men employed in the transportation industry— drivers, motormen, etc.—they represented 12 percent ($N=67$) of the Catholic population. These figures have a built-in bias since the study included only those men who were married heads of families and excluded single workingmen. If the occupations of these men could have been included, the percentage of low manual workers, and thus the working-class nature of the parish, most likely would have been greater.

The supposition is that people who attended the missions

came from the parish, and all available evidence supports this assumption. The missions were primarily parish-centered, and outsiders were not encouraged to attend. In some instances, tickets were distributed to prevent them from attending. People from outside the parish undoubtedly went to the mission, but the large majority of the audience lived in the parish neighborhood. In St. Paul's this meant that the participants at the revival were mainly manual workers.

Additional information for the missions in the 1890s confirms this general conclusion. During the course of each of these three revivals a mission confirmation took place, and the names of those people receiving the sacrament were recorded.

The mission confirmation was a special event and was clearly aimed at adults who had delayed receiving this sacrament. The normal age for confirmation was from ten to twelve, and Catholics were expected to receive this sacrament as an integral part of their sacramental initiation into the church. The mission provided an opportunity to round up the delinquents. Those who received the sacrament were obviously present at the mission and were persuaded by the preachers to take this step to complete their spiritual initiation. To discover who they were, the males were identified in the City Directory and ranked according to their occupations (Table 4). The females could not be so identified, and all that is known about them is that they were not the wives of the male contingent.

Indeed, the men confirmed represented a very small percentage of males who attended the missions. In 1891 they were only 2.19 percent of the male adult audience, only 2.4 percent in 1895 and 1.6 percent in 1898. Despite this small percentage, the group was significant since it represented those men whom the mission reached in a special way. Nor is it surprising that their number was so small, since the group represented only those adults who had delayed receiv-

TABLE 4.

*Occupational distribution (percent) of adult confirmations
at missions in St. Paul's parish.*

Occupational Rankings	Total N = 169*	1891 Mission N = 70	1895 Mission N = 53	1898 Mission N = 46
High White-Collar	2	2	4	0
Low White-Collar	27	21	21	41
Skilled	33	30	34	35
Semiskilled	19	24	19	13
Unskilled	19	23	22	11

*The names located in City Directory represented 60 percent of the total list, 169 of 283; in 1891, 70 of 100 were located; in 1895, 53 of 101; and in 1898, 46 of 82.

ing the sacrament of confirmation, a ritual generally received during childhood.

Taken as a group the confirmations mirror the social composition of the parish in 1895. Thernstrom's ledge is again suggestive with 71 percent of the men confirmed living and working on the lower side of the barrier and 38 percent of them engaged in low manual occupations. The principal differences between the parish profile and the confirmation groups are that the latter included 7 percent more men employed in low white-collar jobs and 7 percent fewer unskilled workers.

The percentages given in Tables 3 and 4, however, are more suggestive than definitive. The principal reason for this is the large percentage of individuals listed in the parish registers and omitted in the city directories.

Neither the City Directory nor the parish registers provided enough information to trace people with common names who had changed their place of residence between their listing in the parish register and the annual directory canvass in June. Although the common name problem accounts for some omissions, the major reason is the general tendency of the City Directory to exclude transient individuals.[44]

The City Directory tended to include only those individuals who had lived in the city for a prolonged period of time, whereas the parish registers recorded individuals at one particular moment in their lives. Since people of low economic status were more transient than upper-class individuals, the directories had a built-in bias to omit a disproportionate number of lower-class workers.[45] As a result, the percentages of both lower-class conversions and lower-class members of the parish are underestimated. They are minimum figures and the real percentages of lower-class workers in the parish and at the revival would undoubtedly be higher.

Although the bias of the City Directory against lower-class transients made it impossible to determine the precise percentage of white-collar and blue-collar workers in St. Paul's parish, it is still significant that the results of the study evidence a consistent pattern of blue-collar dominance. The bias of the directories does not impair this general conclusion, but it does weaken the exactness of the findings. The margin of error, however, favors the pattern of blue-collar predominance. In this regard the quantitative data not only supports the literary evidence on behalf of the working-class composition of the parish and the revival, but it also suggests that it was more extensive than one might imagine.

Throughout the period of parish revivals the neighborhood retained its working-class character. Despite a natural turnover in population the district remained one in which skilled trades and low manual occupations dominated.[46] The one change that was most noticeable was the decline of the foreign-born Irish and a corresponding rise of American-born Irish men and women. It appears that this was the "better class of Catholics" that was moving into the neighborhood. Like their predecessors they mainly worked with their hands, but their American background suggested to some observers that they were a "better class" than the foreign-born workers who dominated the district in the 1860s and 1870s. They were not the rough and rowdy shanty Irish who helped to sow death and destruction in the 1863 Draft Riots and battled the Orangemen in 1870 and 1871. The native-born newcomers lived in tenement houses and draped their windows with lace curtains. To the native-born priests who noticed the changes, what apparently made the newcomers "better" was their American background. In other words, they were a "better class of Catholics" because their native birth made them more similar to the priests; goodness in this case was in the eye of the beholder.

The lower-class audience at the revivals is not surprising given the predominance of the Irish in the parish and the working-class nature of the neighborhood. Yet the appeal of revival religion to blue-collar Catholics does modify the impression given by historians who, in studying Protestant revivalism in the late nineteenth century, have concluded that revivalism was primarily a middle-class phenomenon. Among Protestants this was indeed the case; among Catholics, however, both the impressionistic and quantitative evidence indicates that the appeal of revivalism was much broader.

Another indicator of the lower-class composition of revival Catholics comes from the pulpit. In their sermons the preachers often alluded to the poverty of the people, consoling them with the vision of heaven where "the poor shall rest. In heaven they shall look back upon the time of need . . . and see that what they lacked in perishable things God was

131

heaping up for them in riches that never waste."[47] In the United States, "the high places of wealth, power and fashion are occupied by heretics," noted one Redemptorist preacher, but not possessing such positions should not make Catholics any less proud of their religion.[48] Walter Elliott exalted "the man who makes something" as a more noble person "than he who sells something." This reference to having a trade as "something next to God" was also reflected in the occasional references to the occupations of the audience.[49] The Redemptorist, Joseph Kautz, addressed his audience in the following manner:

> If I should ask you—one and all what your occupation is, I would receive a variety of answers: I'm a merchant—a mechanic—laboring man—railroader—machinist—fireman—head of a family—farming—living under guardianship—mother of a family—housework—take care of children—living out—make my living by washing—sewing. . . .[50]

Kautz realized that he was speaking to people who were concentrated in lower-class occupations, the occupations which predominated in his rhetorical list of jobs. Such internal evidence from sermons, though infrequent, parallels the impression gleaned from the study of St. Paul's parish. Catholics were concentrated in the lower levels of the social-economic hierarchy and not surprisingly those who attended the revivals reflected this class composition.

A typical participant at a Protestant revival in the latter decades of the century was not only a member of the middle class, but generally one who regularly attended church and practiced his or her religion. In the Catholic community revivalism again evidenced a broader, more mixed constituency. Quite clearly many members of the audience were regular church-going types and the mission aimed "to excite the piety of the faithful," mainly those whose religious fervor was "cold and formal."[51] Yet, the revival also appealed to more marginal Catholics. Born and raised in the Catholic tradition, they had neglected the sacraments for an extended period of time. They were not church Catholics, but nominal Catholics; they occupied a prominent position in the minds of the preachers and the Mission Chronicles mentioned them in a mixed tone of distress and satisfaction.

How numerous this group was is difficult to state. Referred to as "hundreds," "a great many" or "very small," their presence was always noted. An analysis of St. Paul's parish population indicates that the number of adults attending the missions in the 1890s exceeded the number of regular church-going adults. During this decade the consistent contemporary estimate of the parish membership hovered around twelve thousand, or about 40–50 percent of the number of Catholics actually living in the area.[52] The adult parish population (20 years or older) was thus about 7,440.[53] Adult attendance at the missions, however, exceeded this figure. In 1891, 11,000 adults attended, in 1895 their number was 9,700, and 12,150 were present in 1898 (Appendix). It is impossible to determine the ratio of adult church members to nonmembers, but the general impression is sufficiently convincing—the revivals attracted men and women who were not regular members of the parish. They resided in the neighborhood, were Catholics by birth, but lived on the periphery of parish life. During a mission, however, they emerged from their anonymity and sought the consolation and rewards of revival religion.

The mission confirmations further indicate that about 2 percent of the adult audience felt the need for this additional sign of saving grace. The information on adult confessions, however, is the most persuasive evidence. They soared into the thousands, and though these were not exclusively confessions of marginal Catholics, the impression given by the priests was that such confessions were quite commonplace.

In fact, one frequent type of "conversion" was the periodic acceptance of saving grace by one who had last received the sacraments at a prior mission. Although they were not regular church-going types, they were regular mission repeaters. The priest could count on them showing up at each mission and then disappearing from view until the next revival. The ordinary ministry "cannot cope with them" it was said and "it is only during a mission that they are discovered, if even then."[54] Preachers coined various names for them—hickory Catholics, mission Catholics, or rounders—"a mission bird whom the fowlers of Christ manage to insnare with the nets of the Exercises once every three or four years and restore for awhile to the graces of the Church."[55] Commenting on this type of religious behavior, one Paulist lamented that

> it is not yet two years since the last mission in our church and yet this one reveals a lamentable state of things. Hundreds made this mission who had been last to the Sacraments only at the last Mission, many of whom had since then scarcely heard Mass once.[56]

Another type of participant at the revival was obviously peculiar to Catholic revivals. This was the seeking Protestant who attended the mission and ended up being converted to Roman Catholicism. They were a cherished prize at any mission, and both the Mission Chronicles and the parish registers noted them with distinctive pride. The Paulists were especially desirous of this type of participant since one of the principal reasons for their organization was "the conversion of American people." As their most distinguished spokesman, Isaac Hecker, put it, "we must make Yankeedom the Rome of the modern world."[57] Like Hecker, the founding group of Paulists were all converts to Roman Catholicism, and for a number of years the community remained predominantly a group of American-born, Protestant-bred, Catholic priests.[58] Such a background furnished them with a better understanding of Protestant Americans than most Catholic preaching orders, and in time the work of the Paulists became closely identified with the non-Catholic apostolate.

From the very beginning the conversion of Protestants at a mission was always noted and the more prominent the convert, the more lengthy the coverage. From 1858 to 1900 the total number of converts at Paulist missions across the country was 2,935.[59] This type of conversion was also common at missions given by other religious orders; Paulists merely worked harder at it.

At the ten missions given in St. Paul's the converts numbered sixty-one. This was not a very significant achievement considering the large mission crowds, but it does underline the predominantly Catholic dimension of parish revivals during this period. These converts mainly came from two denominations, 30 percent being Episcopal and 19 percent Lutheran. Twenty-three percent claimed no prior religious affiliation.[60] This pattern is also evidenced in a random sampling of all converts in the parish from 1860 to 1900. This group includes converts at missions as well as outside the mission. The largest representation came from the Episcopal church, 34 percent, and this figure was significantly different from the Lutherans, 13 percent, and all other denominations. Squeezed between Episcopalians and Lutherans were converts who had no prior religious affiliation; they represented 24 percent of the sample.[61]

It is not surprising that the Episcopal church contributed the largest number of converts. In their emphasis on doctrine and ritual the Episcopalians were very similar to Roman Catholics. Moreover, the second half of the nineteenth century was a time when English and American members of the Episcopal church were finding Roman Catholicism particularly attractive. Lutherans also tended to be more ritualistic than other denominations and this might also explain their movement to Roman Catholicism at a level higher than other, more pietist, denominations. The problem with such an explanation is that despite the marked ritualist perspective of Roman Catholicism, and thus its affinity to Episcopalianism and Lutheranism, Catholics did evidence characteristics at their revivals allegedly reserved only for more pietist sects. Historians who have used this religious classification have noted that the primary emphasis in the pietist perspective "is on right behavior."[62] But this was precisely the thrust of Catholic revivalism. That a ritualist sect should evidence pietist characteristics indicates the limits of such a classification. Indeed, Catholics were more ritualistic than Methodists or Baptists, but they also evidenced a strain of pietistic fervor as did Lutherans and Episcopalians. Whether it was Catholic ritualism or Catholic evangelicalism that attracted converts, or possibly something entirely different, is impossible to determine. What is certain is that more converts to Roman Catholicism came from the Episcopal and Lutheran denominations than from all the other Protestant churches. Why those converts whose denomination was labeled "nothing" became Roman Catholic remains more of a mystery. The fact was, however, that many members of "nothingism" did become Roman Catholics.

Age is a more precise category than motive, and the data in this area are more satisfying and illuminating. The age of converts during the course of a year was given in the baptismal records, and a study of three groups in 1875, 1885, and 1895 was made to arrive at some general conclusions about the age of converts to Roman Catholicism. The most obvious pattern is that the great majority—81 percent of the total— were generally under thirty years of age. This pattern is true both for the group in its entirety and for each of the three years. Another pattern evidenced is that the majority of converts, 54 percent of the entire group, were in the twenty to twenty-nine age bracket, 27 percent were under the age of twenty, most often in their late teens. As was true with the mission converts the majority of this group of converts were males.

From these data no composite picture of a typical convert can be precisely drawn, but the chances were that in eight out of ten cases he was under thirty, more than likely in his twenties; in one out of three instances he would have been a member of the Episcopal church, and the odds were about even that the convert would be a man.

Catholic revivals clearly attracted a broad spectrum of people—lower-class as well as upper-class, church members and non-church-members, men as well as women, Protestants and Catholics. Like a parish fair it seemed to offer something for everyone—renewed commitment for the zealot, momentary consolation for the negligent, and a new religious adventure for the seeker. It represented the church's best effort in the evangelization of "the masses and the poor," of the large working-class population that made up the bulk of American Catholics. Yet, any community, regardless of its location or its social status, was a potential candidate for the revival. Rich and poor, professionals and laborers, farmers and steelworkers were all touched by the enthusiasm of revival religion. The variety of ways in which their lives were changed illustrates the extraordinary impact that revivalism had on the people and the church.

Conversion and Reform | 6

Through its rituals, music, and preaching the Catholic revival meeting established an atmosphere conducive to conversion. It induced a mood of personal guilt through the ever-present image of an ungrateful sinner confronted by a stern God. But moods, "like fogs . . . just settle and lift."[1] While they are present, they have a pervasive and powerful effect, but they evaporate quickly. By themselves they change nothing; they have no directional thrust. Yet, directly related to the mood induced by the revival was a motivational component that sought to direct the sinner to conversion and the pursuit of piety. This was the goal of all evangelical preaching. Every revivalist wanted to effect a change of heart and elicit a personal, experiential decision for Christ. For Catholic evangelicals such a conversion included the reception of the sacraments. This was the principal type of conversion at the Catholic revival and the all important first step in the pursuit of holiness. But other types of conversions also indicated the powerful effect that revival preaching could have on people. At parish missions Protestants were converted to Catholicism, young people were persuaded to pursue a religious vocation, and many men and women were converted to the cause of temperance. On a personal level these various types of conversion were the major achievements of Catholic revivalism. In order to appreciate the impact of revivalism on the person in the pew, it is necessary to understand the nature and extent of mission conversions.

The single most persuasive indicator of sacramental conversion was the number of confessions. After the proper mood and atmosphere had been formed during the first few days of preaching, confessions began to be heard. From then on people lined up at the confessionals, heeding the call of the preacher to confess their sins before it was too late. Extra priests had to be recruited to take care of the large number of penitents, and when it was all over the number of confessions, having been tabulated by the confessors, was announced at the closing ceremony of the revival. In Manhattan's St. Paul's parish the number of confessions reached into the thousands, hitting a peak of 12,850 in 1898.[2] Other city parishes recorded equally high numbers of confessions. A mission preached by Father Damen and other Jesuit revivalists in 1863 at St. Francis Xavier church in New York claimed the extraordinary figure of 20,000 confessions. A Redemptorist mission in St. Patrick's church in San Francisco in 1886 numbered 8,213 confessions; in Chicago during a Redemptorist mission in 1895 the priests heard 7,939 confessions.[3] Undoubtedly many of these sacramental conversions were the confessions of practicing Catholics, pious folk who desired a spiritual uplift, and as time passed this type of penitent became more frequent. But originally the revival was not aimed at this group of Catholics; its primary purpose was to gather in the negligent, the spiritually destitute, and the evidence indicates that this more radical type of conversion was commonplace. One of Father Damen's coworkers, Cornelius Smarius, estimated that one out of five people present at the missions were "self-styled Catholics who haven't been to confession for ten, twenty, thirty, or forty years."[4] Other missionaries, avoiding the hazard of enumeration, left the clear impression that many long-time sinners lined up for confession. The presence of "hickory Catholics," whose last trip to church was during a previous mission, also testified to the frequency of the second conversion called for by the preacher.

Revivals did indeed motivate people to change their lives, to convert from the habit of sin to a life of grace, but the persistent criticism leveled against revival conversions in general has been that they were more distinguished by their transiency than by their permanence. Conversion at a Catholic revival was no less ephemeral. The religious enthusiasm generated by the revival quickly died down, and there was little evidence of a continued upsurge in piety once the preachers left. Parish registers of baptism and marriage were strikingly devoid of any unusual upsurge in religion. The number of baptisms did not change, indicating that very few parents converted at a revival felt the responsibility of having their children baptized at advanced ages after years of neglecting this parental duty. Nor did couples married in a civil ceremony come forth in any significant number to have the priest bless and legitimate their marriage with a church service. The registers recorded each year with a striking similarity, giving no hint whatsoever that a revival had taken place. The preachers knew this and bemoaned the short-lived impact of the revival.[5] The Redemptorists had even adopted the practice of having renewals of the mission; the reason given for this clearly indicated that the preachers had little hope for the permanency of revival conversions. "It is to be remarked," wrote Joseph Wissel, "that the many and extraordinary conversions produced by the mission are very rarely so permanent as not to be followed by a relapse." The renewal should not be delayed too long, he noted since "experience proves that the majority of those converted at a mission remain steadfast for about four or five months, then they begin to neglect the means of perseverance and consequently fall into sin again. It is precisely then that the renewal should come to their timely assistance. . . ."[6] Less than half a year was Wissel's candid assessment of the permanency of revival conversions, and there is little evidence to repudiate his experienced judgment.

The transiency of revival conversions, however, should not detract from the value of such a religious experience in the lives of countless individuals. Revival religion did enrich and even change the lives of many people by revitalizing their religious sensitivity; it offered something extraordinary to the person in the pew. It was a soul-stirring event that presented the pious folk with an opportunity to advance further along the path of holiness. For the spiritually impoverished it was an opportunity to become a saint for a day, if nothing more, and thousands of men and women desired at least this touch of holiness offered at the revival. To live continuously in the presence of God is an ideal sought by many a holy person; most mortals, however, do not achieve such mystical heights, nor can they even fathom what it means. To experience the saving grace of God periodically, perhaps only occasionally, is more akin to the human condition. This was the limited aim of revivalism—to awaken in the sinner an awesome experience of the holy that would lead to a change of heart. How long it lasted was an entirely different issue. Religious enthusiasm, conjured up by a revival, was of its very nature an ephemeral experience. From a religious perspective to have undergone this experience was good in itself, to prolong it was only better. To criticize revivalism by emphasizing its transient impact is to miss the point. Revivalism fostered only one variety of the religious experience and an ephemeral one at that, but, like a moon eclipse, it was a unique event whose significance was not diminished by its transiency.

Not all conversions which took place at a revival were as temporary as the sacramental conversions. Although they were not as numerous, two other personal decisions were very common and by their nature were much more permanent. One was the conversion of Protestants to Roman Catholicism; the other was the decision to enter the religious life.

The Catholic revival meeting did not actively seek out converts from Protestantism. This was a bonus the preachers hoped for, but they did not direct the revival to this goal.

Their primary concern was the religious conversion of Catholics, and if in the process they gained some new recruits from Protestantism, so much the better. Occasionally talks or lectures on controversial topics might be given during the revival, and Protestants were invited to attend. A crusade for converts did develop in the 1890s as an offshoot of the Catholic revival movement, but for the greater part of the nineteenth century Catholic revivalism focused on the conversion of Catholics, not the recruitment of Protestants. Despite the secondary concern for Protestant converts, Catholic missions did gain a considerable number of new recruits for the church. The Redemptorists listed a total of 4,322 converts from 1840 to 1890; from 1858 to 1900 the Paulist missions gained 2,935 converts from Protestantism.[7] Gilbert J. Garraghan, the Jesuit historian, "reckoned that Father Damen and his associates had made twelve thousand conversions to the Faith" in a period of twenty-two years (1857–1879).[8] This is an extraordinarily high estimate considering the more modest and more reliable figures of the Redemptorists and the Paulists. Other religious orders engaged in the revival movement also recorded substantial numbers of converts.[9]

This desire to enumerate the number of converts along with the number of confessions, evident in every mission report, was an implicit testimony to the importance attached to winning Protestant converts. Although it was not their central concern, the preachers attached great importance to these conversions and publicized them accordingly. Along with the number of confessions the revival scoreboard always included the number of converts. Frequently, elaborate public ceremonies took place during a revival to receive these "lost sheep" into the fold. Rich in catechetical value, these ceremonies drove home the message that Roman Catholicism was the one true church. They were ritualized apologias that strengthened the faith of Catholics by the moving example of a personal decision to renounce Protestantism and enter the "one true church."[10] Such ceremonies were also desirable since they demonstrated the bountiful blessings of God poured forth during the revival. All the more reason not to reject this extraordinary opportunity to convert and be saved.

Missions were also a breeding ground for vocations to the religious life. Some preachers, such as Weninger, made an explicit appeal for vocations to the priesthood. True to his flair for the dramatic Weninger would gather the altar boys around the mission cross during the solemn blessing and erection of the cross and ask them to pray that God "will give many a vocation to the boys of this parish. Boys, for —— years, since I have been giving missions in America," he said, "I have extended my hand to many a young boy at the foot of the cross who is now a priest and has invited me to preach a mission in his congregation."[11] Religious orders viewed the mission as a potential source of vocations and even sent priests to areas where missions were being held since this was "thought to be a proper time" to try "to obtain vocations."[12] One of the most notable recruits was James Gibbons, the cardinal archbishop of Baltimore who as a young man of nineteen heard a mission sermon on the priesthood given by Clarence Walworth in New Orleans. "It was Walworth's sermon," wrote John Tracy Ellis, "that settled James Gibbons' doubts and solidified his decision to devote his talents and effort to this high calling."[13]

The goal of the revival was individual conversion, and it was apparent that it achieved its aim in a variety of ways. The numerous sacramental conversions, the large number of conversions from Protestantism, and the occasional vocational decisions illustrate how effective the revival was in producing the proper mood conducive to a radical change of heart and how powerful a motivational force it was in gaining such conversions.

Another example of the revival's success in establishing an aura of the holy and thereby providing people with a unique religious experience was the enthusiastic response given to the ceremony of blessing the sick. Not all religious orders practiced this custom, but two groups did occasionally incorporate it into the revival, and the results were extraordinary.[14] In 1857 the Passionists conducted a mission in Brooklyn and during the revival an event took place that "stirred the entire metropolitan area and brought people, Catholic and Protestant, by the thousands to the doors" of the church. The preacher gave the following account of what happened:

> The people had conceived such high opinion of the missioners that they expected them to work miracles to cure every kind of bodily disease;—more than 3,000 suffering persons came or were brought to the missioners for cure. This pious importunity encreased [sic] the labours of the missioners— the sick were blessed with the relic of our Blessed Founder. Their faith in several instances was rewarded with graces of a miraculous character. Some cures were effected by our missioners thrugh [sic] the relic of Blessed Paul. More were mentioned to them by priests and by secular witnessess [sic].[15]

During other missions, similar extraordinary cures were reported. In Lockport, New York, a young paralytic woman was brought to the mission; the Passionist preacher applied the relic of Paul of the Cross, and the woman walked out of the church under her own power before numerous witnesses.[16] Protestant journalists scoffed at such reported cures, but Catholic apologists defended them, cautiously yet adamantly. They might not "stand the test of the Sacred Congregation in Rome," wrote the editor of *Freeman's Journal*, but they certainly were extraordinary and "in the popular sense . . . miraculous."[17] Jesuit revivalists also blessed the sick from time to time, and the distinct impression given at both the Jesuit and Passionist missions was that such a ritual was in response to popular demand.[18] People brought in the sick and the lame, lined them up in front of the church, and waited in hope for a cure through the application of some sacred relic.

Father Weninger always included the blessing of the sick on the last day of the mission. He did not wait on popular demand, but solicited the presence of the sick and the lame at his revivals. Weninger told the people that for some, sickness, such as blindness, may be a saving grace just as for others good health can be a blessing from God. He cautioned them not to expect any immediate results but to pray as follows: "Blessed Peter Claver, help me, if it so be the Holy Will of God, if it be better for my salvation, that I be cured; if not, O then obtain for me the patience to bear my sufferings meritoriously."[19] Then after a reading from scripture and a prayer, Weninger applied a relic of Peter Claver to the sick brought to the church for this special event. The extraordinary point about Weninger's ritual was that numerous cures were reported to have taken place. "For nearly forty years," Weninger wrote, "cures followed cures without interruption."[20] He was cautious about claiming any supernatural power at work, but eventually he was led to believe that such was the case. He sent reports of some of these cures to Rome in support of the canonization of Peter Claver, and at least two of them did stand the test of Rome's scrutiny, were accepted as miraculous, and "used accordingly for the saint's canonization."[21]

The reported cures at Catholic revivals, regardless of the question of their miraculous authenticity, illustrated the popular assessment of the mission. People did believe that this was a special moment when God was present in their midst in an extraordinary manner. His power was visible in the public conversion of hardened sinners, in the reception of Protestants into the Catholic church, and to expect the healing power of God to touch the sick and the lame was not an illogical leap of faith for many people given the unusual events of these holy days. The entire revival stressed the point that this was a special moment in their lives, and it established a mood that lent support to this claim. The people "expected [the preachers] to work miracles" and brought sick friends and relatives to church in anticipation of such cures. Once incidents of healing did take place the expectations of the people escalated. Subsequent revivals would attract large crowds of sick and lame because people believed that the power of the divine was working in mysterious and surprising ways. It was not only able to cure the soul, but it could even heal the body.

The atmosphere of the revival, conducive to the popular demand for the "miraculous" and to the widespread acceptance of conversion, fostered another type of experience replete with both religious and secular overtones—the temperance pledge. Temperance had always been a concern of revivalists throughout the nineteenth century. It was a major theme in their program for the reconstruction of the social order, and during the closing decades of the century they put most of their efforts at social reform into the temperance movement.

The Catholic concern for temperance first peaked with the visit of the Irish crusader, Father Theobald Mathew, in 1849. Thousands of Catholics took the pledge from Father Mathew and the number of total abstinence societies increased substantially. During the second half of the century the crusade continued as the tide of reform and the movement toward prohibition gathered strength.[22] Catholics continued to be swept up in the movement, and the total abstinence pledge became a major instrument of the temperance movement. The pledge could be given at almost any time or place, but the Catholic revival soon became a popular setting for the decision to abstain from all intoxicating drinks.

The preoccupation with temperance was common to all religious orders engaged in the revival movement, and it was a crusade that permeated every region of Catholic America. It did not originate with the emergence of revivalism, but the mission reinforced the crusade for temperance and enveloped the pledge in an aura of a life or death decision. The drunken sinner was a nightly visitor to the revival meeting. He appeared in just about every sermon as a classic example of the sinner, and his vice was always singled out as one of the most destructive plagues to have befallen mankind.[23] By the 1870s these cameo appearances of the drunken sinner were eventually incorporated into a specific sermon, labeled drunkenness or intemperance. His nightly appearances continued since the preacher never hesitated to call upon him as a powerful and persuasive deterrent to sin, but the prevalence of the vice and the increased tempo of the temperance crusade demanded that one entire evening be given over to a detailed examination and denunciation of demon rum and its victims.

Frequently joined with the sermon on drunkenness was the total abstinence pledge. Not every religious order promoted the pledge; this was especially true among those who worked in German communities. Their attitude was more cautious, recommending the pledge only as a last resort for the habitually intemperate drinker since "the missionaries should not exact more than the law of God obliges us to."[24] Weninger's attitude toward intemperance and the pledge was indicative of how revivalists handled the problem in German communities. "Water, wine which is made from vine produced grapes and also beer and cider" God had given for nourishment and may be imbibed in, but temperately; "brandy, whiskey and all types of liquor or distilled drinks" which an individual takes as medicine are permitted but "only out of necessity and only as little as possible."[25] Weninger strongly urged temperance upon his audience pointing out the spiritual, physical, and social evils attached to the intemperate use of alcoholic beverages; but he never administered the pledge nor did he appear to favor total abstinence societies. Temperance or moderation was sufficient in itself, and it was not necessary, though it was laudable, to renounce totally "the usage of nourishing drinks."[26]

The Paulists were ardent supporters of the temperance crusade and zealously promoted the total abstinence pledge. In the 1860s they occasionally had a special sermon on drunkenness; during the following decade the sermon, its name now changed to temperance, became a standard feature of the revival and pledges began to be solicited. Up until 1888 they recorded only 700 pledges at their missions. The low number of recorded pledges was not entirely indicative of its importance at the mission; the Paulists were just not keeping good records. But as the temperance crusade began to revive in the Catholic community after a brief lull in the 1870s the Paulists emerged as leading promoters of the reform movement. As if to demonstrate their ardent support for the crusade as well as their recognition of the increased importance of the issue in the community, they began to count the number of pledges administered at each mission. Together with the number of confessions and converts the number of pledges was announced at the end of the revival as another indicator of God's wonderful work. From 1888 to 1897 they listed 15,000 pledges; in the following decade the number dropped to 12,200. As late as 1913 they were still counting the number of pledges, but the number had dropped off considerably from the peak years of the 1890s.[27]

At a Paulist mission people were urged to take the pledge for a period of three years. The preacher realized that it was not a "law of God," but it was "a virtue very pleasing to God" and "the fittest penance" a person could do.[28] The pledge was made "for the love of Jesus Christ and with the grace of God." The promise was first explained to the people and

149

pledge cards were distributed. "The people had twenty-four hours to deliberate before hearing the sermon on temperance"; after the sermon another explanation was given and "then all who had decided to sign the cards took the pledge in the usual way. The Fathers then collected the cards and if others desired them gave new ones out also."[29] In St. Paul's the percentage of pledges to adult participants ranged from 37 percent in 1888 to 27 percent in 1891, 16 percent in 1895 and 23 percent in 1898. Only adults took the pledge and in 1898, the only year when the figures were enumerated by groups, the distribution was 850 single men, 450 married men, 800 single women, and 650 married women taking the pledge.[30] As these figures suggest, temperance was a concern for both men and women. Intemperance was not sexually discriminatory and in some factory towns the practice of "snuff scouring," rubbing scotch snuff about the interior of the mouth to produce a partial intoxication, was said to have prevailed among female factory workers "to a great extent."[31]

The increased importance given to the pledge was rooted in the rise of the temperance movement in the nineteenth century. Studies of temperance in the United States have generally explained the temperance crusade as one aspect of the widespread reform movement that swept across the country. Brian Harrison's study of the temperance question in England indicates that such a generic analysis is inadequate; the reform thrust only partially explained the rise of the temperance movement.[32] Until similar groundwork in the history of American temperance is done, any explanation of temperance and revivalism will necessarily be limited. The mission chronicles, however, do provide some insights into the phenomenon.

The revivalists continually bemoaned the presence of intemperance in America and the evil it had wrought among Catholics. The Irish were always singled out as special victims of this vice. In Ireland, "intemperance," wrote one priest, "formed a part of the national character," and leaving the Emerald Isle did not change the Irish in this regard.[33] St. Paul's parish in Manhattan was an Irish enclave where drunkness was said to "run wild among the men—young and old," intemperance being a habit of "too many."[34] In the mind of the preacher the principal enemy was the saloon and antisaloon tirades became an accepted part of the temperance sermon. It was the devil's den and saloon keepers were the demon's "visible ministers on earth."[35] The pastor of St. Paul's put it very emphatically:

> I have such a hatred of the saloon that if it were in my power tomorrow to take the liquor traffic out of this country and sink it into the Atlantic, I would do it. The saloon evil is at the bottom of most of our misery. It is the source of 99 percent of the intemperance that exists in this country.[36]

He did not have to look very far to find the object of his wrath. In 1885 the neighborhood supported 487 liquor and beer saloons; only two other areas of the city had a higher number. The number had declined to 387 in 1894, but the district still ranked third in the city in the number of saloons it supported.[37] In subsequent years the number of licensed neighborhood saloons decreased; one reason for the decline was the passage of high license legislation and a Sunday closing law in 1896. Another reason was the source of the statistics, the Police Department. Their collusion with the liquor trade was so well known that it resulted in an investigation of the department.[38] Thus, their data indicating the decline of saloons and consequently the effectiveness of policing the system would necessarily be suspect. Yet, other sources do indicate that the number of saloons in the neighborhood did actually decline.[39] The decline cannot be directly linked to the temperance spirit fostered by the revival or to the parish priests' battle against the saloon; other societal changes must be considered to account for the decline of saloons. Nor did the decrease mean that people were any more temperate. In fact, in the early years of the twentieth century, a time when the antisaloon crusade was riding high, the per capita consumption of alcohol was higher than at any time since 1850.[40] If the intensity of the preacher is any indicator, the saloon was as much of a villain in 1900 as it was in the 1880s.

The clergy recognized the social function of the saloon as a place where men go "to play a few games of cards or have a friendly chat,"[41] but the temptation to drink was too irresistible, even for one who had taken the pledge; thus, the saloon was to be avoided at all costs. To combat the attraction of the saloon, parishes established clubhouses for young men "as a substitute for the saloon."[42] How successful a deterrent this practice was is not known, but a recent study of Irish drinking habits suggests that "the temperance ethic of nondrinking came off a poor second to the bachelor group ethic of hard drinking which had almost full community support."[43] The authors of this study concluded that hard drinking was a prerequisite for membership in the Irish bachelor group, and this observation was reflected in the mission chronicles. Drunkenness was most often referred to in relation to young bachelors: in 1898 the largest group taking the pledge in St. Paul's parish were single young men. Whether these were conversions of the temperate or the intemperate is not known, but the correlation between hard drinking among bachelors, young men taking the pledge, and substitute saloons for young males suggests that the bachelor was a special concern of the temperance preacher.

The church hierarchy also supported the crusade against the saloon. Bishops urged the clergy "to do all in their power to break up low grog shops and order them to refuse Christian burial to those who die of its effects, as well as to those who sell liquor to drunkards."[44] Some even decreed that saloon keepers could not hold office in Catholic societies and those "who persist in selling liquor on Sundays, or otherwise conduct their business in an unlawful manner" were to be excluded from the sacraments.[45] The Third Plenary Council of Baltimore (1884) urged pastors "to induce all of their flocks that may be engaged in the sale of liquor to abandon as soon as they can the dangerous traffic, and to embrace a more becoming way of making a living."[46] Catholic revivalists supported this episcopal crusade, denouncing saloon keepers at every opportunity. Their attacks on intemperance and the saloon did result in the occasional closing of saloons, but they also stirred up controversy with their sledgehammer attack against an ethic and an institution that were too popular and too ingrained in the community to be overcome by "the flying visit" of the revivalist. Saloon keepers were often prominent members of the local Catholic community; in Boston they were "so strong . . . as to completely hush the mouths of the priests," and the archbishop even censured a priest because "he dared to preach against the saloon."[47] Saloon proprietors resented the "injustice" heaped upon them by the revivalists; "the utter denial or banishment from the confessional without receiving absolution is a grave step," wrote an Irish saloon keeper to Father Elliott. Before "real reform can become lasting," he said, the clergy and the people must support it.[48]

But it was obvious that both the laity and the clergy did not unanimously support the crusade, despite the hierarchy's repeated condemnation of the saloon and the revivalist's denunciation of the "door keepers of hell." To the working-class Catholic the saloon was more than just a place to buy a drink. It "was a natural social center" and a center of "the workingman's leisure-time activity."[49] Even that fierce temperance crusader, Archbishop John Ireland, admitted that the saloon was "the sole clubroom" open to Catholics.[50] The preacher might denounce it as the primary cause of society's misery, but the workingman viewed it differently. As one observer commented, "very few temperance reformers have, or ever had, any conception of what the saloon meant to the workingman."[51] It was his political clubhouse, his employment office, and his bank as well as a refreshing waterhole after a long day's work. Temperance preachers could not do away with such a popular institution, however vigorously they tried. Moreover, they were going against the tide of changing social mores, the liquor industry was expanding with the passage of each decade, and people were drinking more, not less, than ever before as the century drew to a close. Coupled with other political forces, revivalism did help to bring about prohibition, but even this was a momentary victory.

As an agent of temperance reform the revival also fostered the growth of temperance societies, and in this area it achieved its most permanent gains. Local temperance societies were an important cog in the movement, and priests were encouraged "to have a society or more than one, in [their] parish to assist [them] in [their] work."[52] The revival promoted such societies by either inaugurating them in a parish or encouraging people to join already existing societies. Mission reports frequently noted the number of people who joined the local society, and significantly it was much lower than the number of pledges. In St. Paul's the men's society was organized in 1873, and its largest enrollment was 450, most of the time about 150. Few of those who joined "have taken the pledge from absolute necessity," according to Walter Elliott.[53]

Membership in the temperance societies clearly appealed to those who most identified with the values of an aspiring middle class. Temperance was not only a religious virtue, but a social attribute that could be "profitable" for its practitioners. The "great work" of the temperance society was to cultivate "sobriety and good citizenship, . . . to uplift man to a higher morality, and to battle incessantly against all those agencies that tend to destroy the home, to debase citizenship and to degrade manhood."[54] An analysis of the membership of St. Paul's parish society in 1898 illustrated the upper- and middle-class dimension of the group. About half of the group, 51 percent, were engaged in white-collar occupations and 7 percent of these were professional men. The skilled trades accounted for 37 percent of the membership and no unskilled laborers belonged to the society.[55] This distribution was more weighted toward the upper rungs of the social ladder than either the parish profile of 1895 or the mission confirmations of the 1890s. In this regard it reflected the upper-class character of other temperance societies in England and the United States.[56]

Temperance has been viewed as a symbol of middle-class membership and "the movement par excellence of the self-made man."[57] St. Paul's society was not an exception to this pattern. Thrift and industry were allegedly outstanding virtues of the members, and "many families owe not a little of their worldly prosperity to the principles which the Guild lived to enunciate."[58] The middle-class individual and the aspiring workingman were the most likely persons to join the movement. It was with this group of men, more than likely temperate to begin with, that the preacher made his most permanent gains, and even these were modest.

St. Paul's women's temperance society was much larger than the men's, having an enrollment in 1898 of 968 compared to 132 for the men. At that time, only four years old, it was said to be "the main support of the Temperance sentiment in the parish."[59] Both societies supported the cause of temperance and the battle against the saloon. Their most noticeable achievements were organizing the parish settlement house and founding a reading club. Their meetings were generally oriented toward providing music and entertainment interspersed with a talk on temperance. In a sense, the society was a substitute for the saloon, and their meetings were a "respectable" form of recreation for reform-minded men or women. The over-representation of females mirrored the hearty support that feminists were giving to the temperance movement and their "strong desire to curb the self-assertive, boisterous masculinity of the saloon, to support and protect the family, and to return the husband—immigrant workingmen in particular—to the home."[60]

The religious aura of the revival surrounded the taking of the pledge; it was a way to solidify conversion and a practical step toward prolonging and preserving this change of heart. But blended together with such religious motivation were other equally prominent motifs. The physical benefits of temperance were clearly stressed. "Disease of the body and imbecility of the mind are notorious results of drunkenness," and it was a "scientific fact" that "the brains of children born of drunken parents" compared unfavorably "with those of sober parents."[61] The evil effect of intemperance on the family and the home was also strongly emphasized. One ardent temperance advocate, James R. Bayley, archbishop of Newark, echoed the sentiments of the revivalists in noting that intemperance "works its worst ruin" in the family. "A drunken father or a drunken mother turn it [the family] into a hell—a place of anger and strife and misery and crime."[62] Revivalists painted scenes of the drunkard's home that were "so true and so striking that the sobs of the audience could be heard" throughout the church.[63] Temperance songs also focused on the family extolling the virtuous, temperate man; God blessed "the hand that guards, the heart that loves one's flesh and blood/ but I ban both drunken hand and heart that blasts their happiness."[64]

Another motivating force in taking the pledge was the economic benefits attached to such a decision. The intemperate man "builds his fortune on quicksand." But temperance aided in the accumulation of savings and facilitated job promotions; for the Irish "it elevates the race socially and improves their chances for the future."[65]

The emphasis on economic motivations together with the expected religious reasons for taking the pledge pointed to a basic ambiguity in revival preaching. Time and again people were told that, as far as salvation was concerned, poverty was not a bad lot. Walter Elliott comforted his audience with the following words:

> You may be a poor man—striving by wearying ceaseless toil for a poor living; you may have had little schooling and be now ignorant of what is common knowledge to your neighbor; you may in a word lack many of the comforts of this life and may feel envious sometimes to see your Protestant friends so much better off in this world's way. But there is something which you also possess which our poor friends with all their wealth cannot purchase—the true religion of Jesus Christ—a knowledge which all their books and all their colleges cannot give them; a peace of mind which all the comforts of this world cannot bestow—which can come only from the possession of the true faith.[66]

Possessing the "true religion" compensated for a lack of worldly success. For poor Catholics, "a laboring people" who "live in plain homes," a heavenly award awaited them.[67] "God wills" the abundance of poverty and only "his wisdom knows the reason why." "We also know," Father Young said in his very next breath, oblivious to the contradiction implied, "that it is a means which his providence employs to bless us, and perfect us in those virtues that fit us for heaven. He has not said in vain: Blessed are ye poor, for yours is the Kingdom of Heaven."[68] As Young said so poignantly, "this world is a riddle,"[69] but religion could give it meaning and help the poor to live with the paradox of the unjust sinner inheriting the earth. For quite predictably the sinful person was always portrayed as an individual rich in the goods of the world. But he received his just reward, not in this world, but in the next where the fires of hell would consume "his itch for money."[70] Using an appropriate metaphor the preacher reminded his audience that "the only real business you have in this world is to save your immortal souls."[71] Nothing else really mattered because the salvation of one's soul was the highest law, the supreme good; "as for the rest, though you should be reduced to the lowest condition; though you should be stripped of all your worldly possessions, all this is nothing if you arrive at length at the happy term of salvation."[72]

This gospel of acceptance of one's position in life was not unique to revival preaching. It was a message that pervaded many other educative agents in the Catholic culture. The catechism, school readers, Sunday sermons, and spiritual handbooks repeated the same message. The revival reiterated the gospel of acceptance and rendered it emotionally convincing. It made poverty sufferable by urging people to bear it joyfully or grimly, for "what does it profit a man if he gain the whole world, but suffer the loss of his soul."

Religion is interesting not only because it describes the social order, in this case the economic lot of a majority of Catholics, and gives it meaning from a transcendent perspective, but also because it shapes the social order. "It alters, often radically," wrote Clifford Geertz, "the whole landscape presented to the common sense, alters it in such a way that the moods and motivations induced by religious practice seem themselves supremely practical, the only sensible ones to adapt given the way things 'really' are."[73] Historians are in general agreement as to the way things "really" were for Catholics. Throughout the nineteenth century they occupied the bottom rungs of the economic ladder and evidenced less social mobility than Protestants and Jews.[74] But why this was so is a question that still seeks a more complete and adequate answer.

After positing several possible explanations of group differences in occupational achievement, Stephan Thernstrom, in his study of *The Other Bostonians*, reluctantly turned to "group values as a possible explanation" of such differences. In the end he concluded that "although a wide range of circumstances influenced the ability of different groups to make their way in the workaday world, differences in group culture played a significant role."[75] Ethnicity may be one way to explain the differences, but religion is also another possible explanation. To distinguish between the two is often hazardous since they are so intertwined, especially as regards German and Irish Catholics, the major ethnic groups in Catholic America during the nineteenth century. Yet, the religious values fostered in the Catholic subculture can shed light on the social status and occupational achievements of nineteenth-century Catholics. They do not totally explain their economic stagnation, any more than such variables as education, size of family, or institutional completeness do; but religion does underscore the importance of cultural values in a group's achievements, and this is an aspect of social mobility that needs more stress at a time when many historians have canonized the truth of quantifiable data. Such an analytical excursion into causation is not without its pitfalls; but the task of the historian should not be limited only to telling how it really was, but also explaining why it was thus.

To this end the religion preached at Catholic revivals does offer a measure of understanding as to why nineteenth-century Catholics were more economically retarded than other groups. The cultural values fostered at the revival stressed the gospel of acceptance. People were told to be happy with their lot; not to be embarrassed by the absence of power, wealth, and honor. To have a good trade was a sufficient sign of success; to have an "itch for money" was a sure ticket to hell. In this manner, revival religion not only rendered the inequity of the social system meaningful by

159

explaining how the poor would inherit the earth but also shaped the social order of the Catholic subculture by instilling in people a gospel of acceptance. This did not mean that Catholics were to become fatalistic and drift through life aimlessly; they had a goal to achieve, salvation, and they were to pursue it energetically. A fundamental premise in the active pursuit of salvation was that one's state in life, however humble it may be, was to be viewed positively as a stepping stone to salvation, providentially provided by God. Such a value system formulated a world view in which the value of social mobility was not a priority. Mr. Dooley, the cracker-barrel philosopher created by Finley Peter Dunne, put it very succinctly:

> No, Hinnissy, you and I, me frind, was not cut out be Provydence to be millyionaries. If ye has nawthin' but money ye'd have nawthin' but money. Ye can't ate it, sleep it, dhrink it, or carry it away with ye. Ye've got a lot iv things that McMullin hasn't got. Annybody that goes down to Mose's won't see ye'er peace iv mind hangin' in th' window as an unredeemed pledge.[76]

To make the causal connection between the gospel of acceptance cultivated at the revival and elsewhere in the Catholic culture and the persistently low occupational achievement of Catholics is not an illogical leap. The evidence gleaned from revival sermons and other agents of cultural formation also suggests that it is more than an intuitive conclusion. But additional study into Catholicism as a cultural system that shaped the actions of people and thus influenced their social order is necessary before such causal analysis can move beyond the level of inference. Still, it is noteworthy that Catholics were consistently economic-occupational underachievers at the same time that their religious value system was telling them that such under-achievement was not a bad thing. The force of a religion can be measured by its impact on the social order. If the causal connection between the gospel of acceptance and the social, economic retardation of Catholics is more than an intriguing hypothesis (and I believe it is), then religion wielded a powerful influence in shaping the social order of people who accepted and adhered to its value system.

The message of the temperance sermon, however, along with the values associated with membership in temperance societies and the taking of the pledge, did not affirm the gospel of acceptance. The ethic of the self-made man was fundamental to the temperance movement, and Catholic revival preachers upheld this value in their preaching, in promoting temperance societies, and in administering the pledge. Intemperance was a cause of poverty and correspondingly temperance became a way of improving one's position in life. Where temperance societies existed, noted John Hughes, the archbishop of New York, "prosperity has been the reward of industry, and as a matter of course more of the comforts of life are enjoyed."[77] The gospel of success, not the gospel of acceptance, was the message extolled during the revival's temperance interlude. One explanation for this is that temperance was a middle-class movement, and the preachers who enjoyed the status of the middle class were merely appealing to a certain segment of the audience. The middle-class composition of temperance societies did indicate that the appeal had its most obvious and permanent results among this constituency, but to claim that the preachers were channeling their message to one segment of the audience is hardly plausible. They wanted everyone to take the pledge, and the reward they held out to all was the promise of being "a wealthy, upright, and honored citizen."[78] This was the anomaly of revivalism: it continually propagated the gospel of acceptance, but during one major interlude it turned to the ethic of success. Why?

Intemperance was a destructive vice that wrought poverty

161

and sin; it was not sent by God, but was willfully embraced by the individual. Thus, poverty in this context was not a blessing, but a self-inflicted curse possessing no redemptive value. One could not be content with poverty caused by intemperance since it was the evil effect of sin. To be temperate, however, not only cured the vice, but it also remedied the economic and social evils which were always allied with the sin of drunkenness. Temperance was the virtuous side of the coin, and its promised rewards were just the opposite of intemperance's destructive results. The logic of the situation then made temperance and the ethic of success a plausible message, meaningful to anyone familiar with the mysterious ways in which God, and his preachers, acted. God did not draw in straight lines nor did preachers always speak a consistently logical gospel. For some paradoxes, such as the unjust sinner inheriting the earth, they could offer a transcendent explanation; other paradoxes, such as the gospel of acceptance one night and the gospel of success the following evening, were not so easily harmonized. If it works, do it, was a key principle in revivalism, and being content with one's state in life was a traditional Christian approach to the problem of poverty in the world; and there was plenty of poverty around in nineteenth-century Catholic America to justify the continual usage of this evangelical message. On the other hand, the ethic of success made the most sense when speaking about temperance. Indeed, the temperate person was not only promised salvation, the ultimate goal of all human creatures, but also earthly success. He should not seek it, but if he was temperate, it was bound to come to pass.

Another possible explanation for the intermingling of the gospel of acceptance with the gospel of success was that it reflected the influence of the host culture on an immigrant subculture. Preachers continually pointed out the materialism of the United States, where the itch for money seemed to permeate all of society. They also noted that Catholics liked this aspect of American society too much for their own good.[79] What revivalism encountered then was the dilemma of making the traditional gospel of acceptance meaningful in a society that championed the aggressive, self-made achiever. The concentration of Catholics on the lower rungs of the economic ladder made it easier to push the traditional message that the poor will eventually inherit the earth if they persevere to the end. But the American emphasis on success intruded into the Catholic culture, and in at least one area of religion, the temperance crusade, it appeared to have achieved a rather permanent place. For the moment it was a minor intrusion, but it pointed to the changing nature of religion. The motivating force behind religious decisions, in this case the temperance pledge, was becoming more secular. This was evident in the ethic of success that permeated temperance preaching; it was also present in the debate over what role God's grace was to play in facilitating the road to abstinence. At mid-century, Father Mathew had been criticized because his emphasis "was on the individual and social efforts to overcome temptation rather than on prayer and the sacraments."[80] In later decades the religious motif was less clearly focused and the main debate was over moral suasion versus legislative politics, not moral suasion versus sacramental reinforcement. The clergy did not do away with the role of religion and grace in the temperance conversion, it was merely relocated to a more remote position of importance. One Catholic bishop, John Ireland, nicely indicated what type of shift was taking place. "God never proposed to save man only by His sacraments," he stated, "God requires that we do our share." The force of example and moral suasion were in the "front round of our battlings, nevertheless we are prepared to appeal to just and fair laws. Law, we are told, never created virtue; it may be, but law assists virtue."[81]

The issue of temperance did illustrate how American and how secular Catholicism was becoming. The ethic of success and the promotion of legislative politics were typically American traits that Catholics began to promote as zealously as anyone. The increased social mobility of Catholics in the twentieth century suggests that the gospel of success, the ethic of achievement rather than of acceptance, had eventually made significant inroads in the Catholic subculture.[82] The experience of revivalism which played both tunes to the same audience indicates that this intrusion of American, Puritan values first began to surface with some degree of regularity during the closing decades of the nineteenth century when the crusade for temperance was under full sail. The revivalists did not notice the anomaly, since each ethic seemed to have its proper place; to expect them to be neatly consistent in their preaching is to ask too much of them. They were working and living at a time which witnessed the beginnings of a cultural shift in American Catholicism, and they had one foot in the old world ethic and the other in the new world gospel.

The gospel of acceptance and the ethic of success, however, did come together on one point. They both emphasized a rugged individualism. This stress on the individual was the keystone of revival religion. Its evangelical nature underscored the importance of a personal decision for Jesus, thus presenting religion chiefly as an affair between God and the individual person. The effects of the revival were primarily referred to as a conglomerate of individual victories—victory over the devil in a sacramental conversion, over Protestantism in the conversion to Catholicism, and over demon rum in the temperance pledge. The one element of reform with which the revival was identified, the temperance movement, was also a very individualistic design for social reconstruction. Here too the emphasis was on individual perfection rather than any grand overarching scheme for the reconstruction of the social order. Revival Catholics were told that "life is preparation for death" and "the only real business you have in this world is to save your immortal souls."[83] The world in which they lived and worked was always put in the same league with the devil and the choice was clear: "you must choose between God and the devil; between heaven and the sinful world."[84] Such an attitude hardly encouraged social reform.

This individualistic thrust even pushed aside from consideration the traditional concern for one's neighbor asked for in the corporal works of mercy. This was graphically illustrated in Walter Elliott's edited version of the last judgment scene depicted in the gospel of Matthew. It was personal sin, not an absence of concern, that condemned the sinner. As Elliott's Jesus said:

> You pray for pity, you who knew the true religion as well, you who neglected the sacraments, and despised my word and dishonored my church; you ask for mercy, you adulterer, and you, you drunkard, and you, you thief, you hypocrite. You had all the years of a long life, you had hundreds of warnings and examples, and now you are surprised that what I threatened you has come to pass! Depart from me ye accursed into everlasting fire.[85]

Since sin was viewed in such individual terms, holiness likewise became a personal quest. Through its ritual, preaching, and song the revival sought to make this quest emotionally convincing and rewarding. But after motivating people to follow the path of holiness, the revival did not abandon them to a sin-filled world where as spiritual orphans they would wander alone. It channeled them into "the arms of your loving mother the Holy Church" where they could find refuge during their earthly pilgrimage.[86]

Revivalism and the Community | 7

Personal conversion was only one aspect of revival religion. The spirit of evangelicalism had both an individual and a communal dimension. Jonathan Edwards underscored this point during the Great Awakening when he sought not only to renew the piety of the people, but also to strengthen the covenanted community. As adamantly as any revivalist could, Charles Finney stressed the central role of the individual in religion. But for Finney, and for others of his time, an individual's salvation was only the "beginning of religious experience, not its end."[1] Revival converts threw themselves into a variety of social movements seeking to reform and repair the fabric of the new nation. The social thrust of later nineteenth-century revivalists was considerably diminished, but they hardly limited their sights to personal conversion. They too wanted to renew the life of the church and society by reforming the individual. This emphasis on the broader impact of revivalism points to the other side of the revival experience. Revivalism did indeed stress the importance of the individual person, thereby fostering an individualistic brand of religion, but it was also oriented to the wider social arena in which people lived and worked.

Individuals do not exist in a vacuum but live, move, and have their being in communities. The community shapes their self-identity and enables them to realize their potentialities. For revival Christians this meant, at the very least, the community of believers, the church, to which they belonged; and, at the very most, the plurality of communities that shaped their social world. In speaking about the effects of revivalism it is not a question of the individual versus society, as if they were mutually exclusive, but the interaction of the two as exhibited in the revival experience and the impact that revivalism had on the community as well as on the individual.

The most obvious arena in which to examine the social impact of Catholic revivalism is the church. Revivalism did have a somewhat broader effect as it channeled a measure of its energy into the temperance movement; but its most notable impact, beyond touching the lives of countless individuals, was incorporating the converted into the church, thereby building up and consolidating the institution. Conversion was a personal experience, but one that could only be fulfilled through the sacramental life of the institution. This dimension of the conversion experience complemented the individualistic quality of Catholic revivalism. Ideally a conversion experience was but the first step of a renewed process of growth which would be nurtured by the sacramental life of the church. Catholic evangelicalism blended nurture with conversion by its insistence on the sacraments as both the fulfillment of conversion and the means to preserve and perfect this religious experience. Thus, by channeling the religion of revival Catholics into the church, it incorporated them into a community of believers and gave their spiritual consciousness a sense of identity that went beyond one's self.

The ritual of the renewal of baptismal vows, held at the close of the mission, symbolized the important place of the church in the lives of the people and its relation to their revival conversion. It was an impressive ceremony, the climax of the revival which journalists seldom failed to comment on. Invariably the church was packed with people, and all the clergy who had participated in the mission were present for this grand finale. In the sanctuary of the church stood the baptismal font, richly decorated with flowers and candles together with all the paraphernalia necessary for the sacrament of baptism. No baptism was to take place, however; the font was there merely to serve as a prop for the sermon and a reminder to the people of their first baptism into the church.

The preacher dwelt at length on the meaning of baptism and how it made them "children of God," members of his kingdom on earth, the church, and heirs to his kingdom in heaven.[2] He then reminded the people of the promise of the vows made at their infant baptism through their sponsors, how God had "covenanted with us in a great compact."[3] To underscore the holiness of that first baptism the preacher would hold up a white cloth, to remind them of "the innocence of your baptism."[4] He took it for granted that they had lost this holy innocence by breaking the vows of baptism, but the mission had reconciled them with God and restored the purity of soul symbolized by the white cloth. In confession they had privately renewed their allegiance to the divine. Now was the time to renew these vows publicly together with the other members of the community. By their sins they had given scandal to the community; by their public profession of faith they would repair the injury done to the community of the church. As Walter Elliott said, "the penitent is encouraged to begin life over again, and at this ceremony he publicly places himself on record as a newborn child of God."[5]

As part of the final stage of the revival the ritual was calculated to encourage perseverance in the people, renewed and reborn at the revival. Individually they had experienced conversion; now publicly, as members of a parish community, they were to proclaim their faith and allegiance to God and to his kingdom on earth, the church. "Born to be wanderers and outcasts on the face of the earth," the church was there to guide them "along the way of eternal life here in the world."[6] According to Father Young, "The best title of the

Christian is soldier of Jesus Christ. Why? Because there are bitter and persevering enemies to be fought, the world, the flesh, and the devil." The Christian's weapons in this struggle "are the holy sacraments." But they are more; they are also "nourishment" for the soul. They sustain the converted in the struggle and help "the germs of a new and higher life planted" in the Christian at baptism "to increase from strength to strength until we come to the perfection of the saints."[7]

This revival ritual shaped the spiritual consciousness of the people. It placed personal conversion within the context of the church and the sacraments which nurtured the converted in the quest for holiness; salvation was individual, but was sustained only through the church. For days the revival had hammered home the importance of an evangelical conversion; now, on the last night it gave this conversion a special tone by incorporating it into the community of the church to which the converted adhered. The ritual of the renewal of vows was a "plastic drama";[8] it spelled out what as Catholics they believed, but it also was a "model for the believing of it."[9] People did not stand around like spectators at the theater; they entered into the ritual by publicly affirming both their belief in God and in his church in as loud a proclamation as the preacher could elicit. To the observer it was an unusual spectacle, reminiscent of the enthusiasm seen at Protestant revivals. To the participant it was much more; it was participation in a ritual that not only symbolized his beliefs but also shaped them through his public affirmation of faith. Through this ceremony the individual left the private world of his own religious conscience and entered into the public realm of the church community where he was to find the fulfillment of his religious identity.

Even if the ritual of renewal was not included in the revival, which was sometimes the case, the mission always ended on the theme of perseverance, reminding the people that "he who perseveres to the end will be saved."[10] The erection of the mission cross underscored this point and extolled the importance of the church in the lives of the converted. The sacraments were singled out as the chosen means of perseverance and perfection with the preacher urging people to receive them frequently. A home library of books was sold at the mission, and the choice of books, principally the catechism and *The Mission Book*, clearly suggested that the life of the converted was to find its fulfillment in the church through the observance of orthodox religious practices. During the course of the revival the people had been instructed on the laws of the church; the preacher invariably invested them with divine authority, equal to the biblical commandments. The church was "the ruler and lawgiver of our souls," and outside the church salvation was not possible.[11] This insistence on the role of the church in the process of conversion broadened the individual quality of evangelical Catholicism. The evangelical thrust of the revival made conversion appear personally and emotionally convincing; the ecclesiastical dimension ensured that it would be socially meaningful.

In addition to expanding the concept of personal evangelical conversion the revival sought to promote the growth and consolidation of the Catholic community. The parish mission was a chosen agent of church renewal supported by ecclesiastical councils throughout the last half of the nineteenth century. Enjoying widespread support it served as a cementing, unifying force, not a divisive, schismatic event. In fact, the revival was often the remedy chosen to heal schism in a local community. Not infrequently Weninger was called upon to restore peace to German parishes torn apart by trustee controversies. His most noted achievement was the reconciliation of the German parish of St. Louis in Buffalo. Wracked by a prolonged trustee controversy, the parish had been closed and under interdict for

171

four years. Then, in 1855 Weninger preached a mission at St. Louis designed to heal the schism.[12] His efforts met with success, and in subsequent years priests often called upon Weninger to restore peace in a divided parish community. Other communities suffered the harmful effects of a prolonged regime of an incompetent pastor; in such instances the new pastor would schedule a revival "to mark a change from the old order to the new" by putting "new life into the people."[13] In Kensington, Connecticut, the parish had suffered through the tenure of two pastors, known for their "scandalous conduct," having been "addicted to drink." The new pastor "employed every means in his power to gain the confidence of the people, but in vain. As a last resort the bishop suggested a mission. . . ." The revival was judged a success in renewing the piety of the people and restoring their allegiance to the church.[14]

Revivals also served to help organize new parishes such as St. Paul's in Manhattan where in 1859 a mission was held "to give a start to the new congregation attending our church."[15] In the early years of the movement a revival was occasionally the time for gathering a dispersed community together with the hope that from this experience the impetus to organize a new parish would result. Most frequently, however, the revival followed the organization of a parish seeking to consolidate what had already been established.

Since it was primarily a parish event, the institutional effects of the revival were most noticeable in the local community. It not only healed schism and put new life into a fledgling community, but it also fostered the growth of established parishes by seeking to channel all religious activity into the local church. The revival desired to regulate the lives of people by pointing out the necessity of orthodox religious behavior. Regular attendance at Sunday mass and frequent reception of communion were the hallmarks of a faithful Catholic, and the revival stressed the importance of such normative behavior at every possible opportunity.

Another trademark of the loyal Catholic was the support of the church, represented in the person of the pastor. The revival underscored the central role of the pastor and told people to be obedient to his command and to financially support his work. This was a law of the church, and according to the revivalist it enjoyed divine sanction; thus, to be recalcitrant in this regard was flirting with eternal damnation. The people did not always see it in this light, however. The revivalists' repeated exaltation of the pastor and their promotion of the model of docility and obedience on the part of the faithful implied that such behavior was more an ideal than a reality.[16] Many Catholics did not evidence the docility which the revivalists encouraged, and the church was continually besieged with parish uprisings over the issue of the pastor's authority.[17] The continuance of such dissensions into the twentieth century suggests that even though some revivalists did restore parish unity, the Catholic revival was not uniformly effective in forming a docile and obedient constituency. There can be no question that this was one of its aims, but that it achieved this goal in any significant degree is much more problematic. It was more successful in putting people back on the track as regards orthodox spiritual behavior, and even this was a fleeting victory. The fear of hell was a persuasive element in promoting conversion, but most people could not make the quantum leap asked for by the clergy and acknowledge that opposition to human authority was equivalent to divine disobedience.

Orthodox behavior also included faithfully following an evangelical code of morality. This was obviously tied to an individual's personal pursuit of holiness, but the revival encouraged community supports to reinforce this personal quest. Chief among these was the parish temperance society which offered the mutual support deemed necessary to keep the pledge of total abstinence. Another aspect of this evangelical moral code was membership in secret societies. This was a hot issue both in Europe and the United States where

Catholics were forbidden to become members of select secret societies. Reflecting the mind of the official church the revivalists echoed this stricture, aiming their missiles at the Oddfellows and the Masons.[18] Another object of attack was the Fenian movement. Many Irish Americans supported the Fenian cause despite the hierarchy's outspoken opposition, and from time to time Catholic revivals attempted to destroy the power of the Fenians in a particular community.[19] Revivalists traveled to the mining towns of Pennsylvania, "declared war on the organization from the very first sermon of the mission," and announced publicly that no member of the secret society would receive confessional absolution unless he resigned his membership in the society by a written oath of renunciation.[20] The revivalist's outspoken condemnation of such societies illustrated their desire to regulate people's behavior by having them conform to the orthodox discipline of the church.

A much more positive feature of the revival was the promotion of devotional confraternities. As an instrument of institutional reform the mission seldom passed up the opportunity to press home the importance of belonging to the right kind of society, that is, one not forbidden by the church. But as an agent of religious renewal it turned its major attention to promoting societies that were more explicitly spiritual in nature. Such societies clearly served a socializing function, but their primary purpose was to foster a particular brand of piety that can best be described as devotionalism. This style of piety was not very widespread in early nineteenth-century Catholic America. The tradition of Anglo-Maryland Catholicism was still normative, and people desired "no fuss and no extremes in anything especially in religion."[21] On his visit to the United States in 1831, De Tocqueville noticed this and later wrote that "there are no Roman Catholic priests who show less taste for the minute individual observances, for the extraordinary or peculiar means of salvation, who cling more to the spirit and less to the letter of the law than the Roman Catholic priests of the United States."[22] But the devotional revolution of Roman Catholicism in the second half of the nineteenth century changed all this, and the piety of Catholics did become distinguished by "minute individual observances" and "peculiar means of salvation." Roger Aubert, the noted church historian, called this spiritual transformation the "true triumph of ultramontanism."[23] The piety of devotionalism emphasized the frequent repetition of prayers and promoted the gaining of spiritual indulgences. An active piety, it put an extreme emphasis on the ritualized performance of certain acts to the degree that they appeared almost mechanistic if not somewhat magical. It was shot through with religious sentimentality and fostered an individualistic brand of piety. A key element in this devotional revolution was the religious confraternity which promoted and nourished such popular devotions.

The major ingredients in this emerging spirituality were frequent communion, devotion to Mary, and the cult of the sacred heart. As has already been noted, the revival put a great deal of emphasis on the reception of the sacraments as both the capstone of the conversion experience and the spiritual nurture necessary to achieve "the perfection of the saints." All parish confraternities encouraged this devotional practice among their constituents. Devotion to Mary was not as central to the revival, but it did receive a great deal of attention. The books distributed at the revival, *The Mission Book* especially, promoted Marian devotions; among the religious articles for sale was the rosary. The revival generally featured the public recitation of the rosary, a ceremony which was calculated to be as much a catechetical instruction on the lives of Jesus and Mary as it was a ritual of prayer. One Paulist, Isaac Hecker, was so effective in performing this ritual that he was nicknamed "Father Mary."[24] The Dominicans in particular singled out the rosary as the most fitting devotion to Mary and encouraged the organization of the Confraternity of the Holy Rosary at their missions. The Redemptorists traditionally had a special affection for Mary, and their missions always included, "with great display," a public act of dedication to Mary. It was an elaborate ceremony replete with an array of flowers and candles, hymns, children processing through the church, and a sermon, finished off with a public dedication to Mary which expressed "the most essential qualities of a child of Mary, namely, the renunciation of all sin, having recourse to her in all danger, and placing one's self under her care morning and night."[25] Invariably the Redemptorist mission reports noted either the organization of a Marian confraternity occasioned by the revival or the increase in membership of an already established society.

Perhaps the most unique phenomenon during the second half of the century was the cult of the sacred heart. Its preeminent position in the Catholic community was such that the nineteenth century could be legitimately described as "the century of the sacred heart."[26] The roots of the cult went back beyond 1800, but only in the second half of the nineteenth century did the devotion catch on among the masses. Even as late as 1887 one Jesuit revivalist remarked that out of one thousand people he spoke to "hardly a dozen had heard of such a thing as devotion to the sacred heart."[27] But the Jesuits would change that. Indeed, all revivalists incorporated the imagery of the heart of Jesus into their preaching; it blended in very well with the evangelical appeal of the revival enabling them to paint vivid scenarios of the "bleeding heart of your murdered, crucified Savior" for the sinner to contemplate.[28] Devotion to the sacred heart encouraged a spiritual union with and affection for the physical heart of Jesus. Centering on the love of Jesus symbolized in his bleeding heart, the cult encouraged reparation for the sinful outrages committed against the divine love especially in the sacrament of the eucharist. Many revivals included such solemn acts of reparation in a very dramatic manner. But it was the Jesuits who were the most prominent advocates of the cult of the sacred heart. During their revivals it was customary to have a sermon on the sacred heart and they also used the occasion to promote the Confraternity of the Sacred Heart.[29] By 1892 the eastern Jesuit province had 110,113 people enrolled in the confraternity in parishes up and down the Atlantic coast; subsequent years witnessed a steady increase in membership.[30] The Jesuit revivalist, Francis X. Weninger, was a zealous booster of this devotion. He always preached a sermon on the sacred heart and ended his talk by enrolling people in the Heart of Jesus Confraternity; his mission book was entitled *The Sacred Heart Mission Book* and it included everything needed to deepen devotion to the suffering heart of Jesus.[31] Chiefly through the efforts of the Jesuits, devotion to the sacred heart became a staple of modern Catholic piety and the parish mission was an important agent in this development.

The parish mission also fostered other practices which were prominent in the nineteenth-century devotional revolution. Homage to the saints through the public display and application of their relics was part of the revival ritual; scapulars also were promoted and sold at the revival. Of various types and in various colors the scapular was "a badge of our love and veneration for the Mother of God."[32] Moreover, the clear implication was that those who wore the scapular not only shared in the spiritual indulgences attached to it but also enjoyed divine protection. During a Redemptorist mission in New Trier, Illinois, this point was dramatically emphasized. The steamboat, *Lady Elgin*, packed with young people and, the preacher noted, at just the moment the dancing began, collided with another ship on Lake Michigan and sank. The priests went to the lakeshore to aid in the rescue. "But what is most remarkable and wonderful in the rescue" of the few survivors encountered by the priests was that "they had almost without exception the scapular on their breasts." The preacher then noted that "when the next day the mission was continued, all Catholics without exception were so eager to get the scapulars that the supply was by far not sufficient."[33] Scapulars, however, were only a small part of the treasury of devotional articles promoted at the revival. People could purchase "medals, crucifixes, etc., all these objects of piety and devotion, together with sacred pictures, etc." and later have them blessed by the revivalists.[34] The parish mission was the superbowl of Catholic piety; the main attraction, the revival itself, was the occasion for all types of ancillary devotional promotions. Everything a pious Catholic needed to keep him or her spiritually busy was sold at the revival. Holy cards and schedule programs could be preserved as momentos of the great event; rosaries, medals, scapulars, and crucifixes could be purchased and worn as badges of an individual's religious allegiance, depicting his or her favorite holy hero. Throughout the revival liturgical extravaganzas took place and nightly fireworks burst forth from the pulpit. Just about every item in the church's devotional treasury was on public display. Scarcely anything was overlooked to promote the cause of religion, and the people loved it. As entertainment the revival rivaled the theater; as a religious experience there was nothing else like it.

The panoply of devotions promoted at the revival reflected the striking shift in popular piety from the early decades of the nineteenth century. Most of these devotional practices had a long tradition in the church, but during the late eighteenth and early nineteenth centuries they had lain dormant. The triumph of ultramontanism and its Italian style of piety resurrected many of these practices and discovered new ones. Though they were very individualistic in nature, it is essential to remember that the resource center of such piety was the local church and in particular the parish confraternities. The church sanctioned a myriad of devotions to Mary, to the eucharist, and to the sacred heart and garnished them with rich spiritual indulgences. By promoting these devotions the revival was educating the people in correct and accepted religious behavior. It spelled out a discipline of piety to which right living and correct praying Catholics should conform. In this manner it was helping to consolidate the church by shaping the religious behavior of people, insuring that such behavior would be orthodox.

The confraternities which grew up around these devotional practices were looked upon as "giving stability to the good effected" at the revival.[35] They "conserved the fruits of the mission" and according to Walworth were "invaluable for forming virtuous habits."[36] Moreover, as Walworth went on to say, such "sodalities are the life of my parish."[37] This remark of a revivalist turned pastor underscored the point that the devotionalism promoted by the revival was funneled into the parish. In doing this the revival necessarily had a major impact on the spiritual vitality of parochial life. The "flying visit" of the revivalist toned up the body religious, but it did not end there. Conversion was but the first step; sacramental nurture and the practice of devotional piety were also deemed necessary to sustain and perfect conversion. The most appropriate place to perform these rituals was in the parish church where public devotions to Mary, the eucharist, and the sacred heart frequently took place, and the most powerful influence in fostering these devotions was the parish confraternity, very often founded during a Catholic revival meeting.

Another feature of the mission which elicited support for the institutional church was its emphasis on the education of children and in particular its enthusiastic support for the parochial school. Parents were reminded of their responsibility to provide for the religious education of their children. Basically this duty was fulfilled both in the home and through the church. Family prayers were encouraged: parents were to see that their children read the right books and had good, God-fearing companions. They were also to provide for their children's religious training by sending them to catechism classes where they could properly prepare for first communion.[38] But the crusade for parochial schools which gained momentum during the middle decades of the nineteenth century added another ingredient to the revivalist's message. This was the urgent necessity to support and promote the cause of the parish school. Because of the dissension in the church on the necessity of such schools, the revivalists' preaching often assumed a very apologetical tone.[39] Generally the apologia for parochial schools was incorporated into the sermon on the duties of parents, but occasionally it was singled out with a special sermon on the benefits of Catholic education. The whipping boy was the public school, *"eine moralische pest,"* according to Weninger,[40] which weakened the loyalty of children to their church by omitting religion from education and even worse, in the case of the Germans, by encouraging them to become American—a trait which for Weninger, a zealous Germanophile, was second only to Godlessness.[41] Another target of the preacher's wrath was those Catholics who were lukewarm in their support of the parochial school. Prior to the decree of the Third Plenary Council of Baltimore on the necessity of parochial schools such opposition was quite vocal and public. The Redemptorists encountered it in New York where Father Edward McGlynn had won a large following of priests and people to his dissenting views on the necessity of parochial schools.[42] Further south in Augusta, Georgia, the Redemptorist insistence on the parochial school "stirred up some resentment among the mothers of the parish."[43] The Jesuits met similar opposition in Boston, long a retarded region in the development of parochial schools, where, one revivalist noted, such opposition was "not confined to one city or town," but was "too common in these parts."[44] Despite such occasional opposition, the revivalists reflected the majority opinion of the clergy and the hierarchy and insisted on the support of Catholic schools "no matter how great the burden."[45] Nor was their preaching ineffectual. Their persuasive powers often resulted in an increase in the parish school population which the mission chronicles proudly reported.[46] If a school did not exist, the revival was often the occasion to promote its establishment.

In a more tangible manner the revival also featured collections for the maintenance of the parish. When a new altar was needed, the basket was passed; when debts for the church or the school were still outstanding, a collection took place. The revival left no stone unturned in promoting the welfare of the parish.

Personal conversion was completed through the sacraments of the church; parish schisms were healed; pastors were invested with godlike authority; orthodox religious behavior, centered around a new devotional piety, was promoted; and the organization of parish confraternities took place. In these ways the parish felt the impact of the revival. Throughout the nineteenth century the parish was becoming the vital center of all pastoral activity and the Catholic revival meeting reinforced this trend not only by renewing the piety of the people but also by channeling this experience into the parish community, thereby invigorating the life of the institution as well as the lives of individual Catholics.

Seen in this light revivalism was more than just a religious phenomenon. It was a social movement which strived for the collective conversion of American Catholics. It played a major role in the organizing process of the church on the local and regional level by gathering people together and shaping their religious consciousness in such a manner that it was able to realize its potentialities only within the context of the local church.[47] During the middle decades of the century the church was undergoing a critical period of transformation. It was a transitional period when the church moved out of its earlier missionary condition and sought to gather together the thousands of immigrants who were coming to America in hopes of a better life. Rather than create something new, the church reverted to old familiar forms which had been the trademark of Catholicism ever since the days of the Catholic reform period in the sixteenth and seventeenth centuries. One of these old forms was the ritual of revivalism. As an agent of the institution it helped in the organizing process of an immigrant church whose roots, only recently transplanted to a new environment, were still fragile and in need of continued sustenance. With each new wave of immigrants the revival reappeared as a central component in the organizing process of the church. Later, as people settled into American society and established their communities, the revival became a "maintenance mechanism" of the total institutional system, seeking to preserve the religion of the people according to the discipline of orthodox behavior.[48] At every stage of the process of growth then, from the early years of organization to the later years of consolidation, the revival was on the scene shaping and maintaining the religion of the people so that the institution could take root and grow in its new environment.

Viewing revivalism as an organizing movement also helps to explain how it aided the immigrants in coping with their new social situation. It did this mainly by helping them acquire a sense of belonging, an identification with a community in a society where the opportunities for such identification were severely limited for foreign-born Catholics. Like the ethnic parish which it served, revivalism strengthened the sense of group consciousness among Catholics and facilitated their adjustment to the New World. Weninger repeatedly commented on this aspect of revivalism, noting that the parish mission "served to create a closer union among the Germans."⁴⁹ A pastor in Louisiana remarked that the "greatest good of these missions is a general movement of return to the Bon Dieu" and the establishment of a Catholic society, "*imprimé à toute une société Catholique*," as he put it.⁵⁰ Other priests frequently noted that as a result of the revival Catholics had become a "united people."⁵¹

The revival was a time when Catholics from all walks of life could come together and unite under the banner of religion. It offered something to everyone. One could receive the sacrament, another could join a society or take the pledge, and another could just sit back and enjoy the free entertainment of a fiery preacher hurling thunderbolts at sinners and saloon keepers. There was a variety of options available to the spectator, and they ranged from the more demanding to the least demanding. One could approach it in a serious highminded way; another could view it as a pleasant form of entertainment. As both a religious experience and a form of recreation the revival brought Catholics together in a public gathering where they could profess their faith in a visible way and share the sense of a common heritage.

The planting of the mission cross outside the church, a frequent practice in small towns, was one revival ritual in which Catholics enthusiastically demonstrated their common heritage. All segments of the community were represented in the procession to the site of the cross; a band and singing choir enlivened the march; banners of the parish confraternities lined the procession; and people joined in song honoring the cross. In a small Ohio town they gave out three cheers "for the honor of the cross." An observer noted that the people had abandoned their shyness and did not fear to exhibit themselves as Catholics. He called the occasion "Catholic Independence Day," and the description was appropriate, since these Catholics were celebrating their religious independence from the rest of American society.⁵²

They were a distinct subculture, and the mission helped to underline this fact, seeking to bind them together as Catholics and give them a sense of identity in a new, sometimes unfriendly, environment.

Like most Americans, Catholics were very mobile, but wherever they went they could almost always find a parish revival. For a people on the move it was a point of identification, a common experience that they could share with new neighbors. The preachers might even be the same ones that performed in the old parish and in a strange neighborhood, perhaps the only familiar face. Catholics in Chicago shared common values and norms with their counterparts in New York, and the revival, like the parish, enabled the mobile to experience the familiar amidst the unfamiliar.

There was a double edge to the revival experience. Its evangelical thrust altered the lives of individuals in an emotionally convincing manner; its social impact transformed the church by organizing and strengthening the community of believers. Not everyone bought the total package. Confraternities attracted only a minor portion of the revival audience, and for nominal Catholics revivalism was often their only encounter with organized religion. But the proliferation of Catholic revivals and their popular support among large numbers of Catholics indicated that revivalism exercised a major influence in the development of American Catholicism on both the popular and institutional level. By shaping the spiritual consciousness of people it helped to mould the cultural values of the Catholic community, and it thereby provides a clue to why Catholics behaved in the manner that they did.

Revivalism—American and Catholic | 8

In 1868 James Parton wrote two articles in *The Atlantic Monthly* on "Our Roman Catholic Brethren." Parton had visited St. Stephen's Church in New York one Sunday morning and began his first article by describing for his readers what went on inside a Catholic church. His description of the Catholic mass was true to form. People were huddled in the pews, silently praying, kneeling, and bowing as they followed the actions of the priest at the altar. The atmosphere was shrouded in awesome mystery; a reverent and "complete silence" prevailed, only occasionally broken by the tinkle of a bell or "a low, eager whisper of prayer." No sermon was given. "The priest uttered not an audible word," as Parton put it. The mass quickly ended as silently and ceremoniously as it had begun with two altar boys escorting the priest from the altar. To Parton the Sunday mass was an impressive ritual with the quiet devotion and ceremonial "etiquette" of the people being particularly edifying.[1]

Such was the impression that many Americans had of Catholic piety. What attracted their attention was the religious drama of the mass, an elaborate ritual enriched by such Romish practices as candles, incense, and vestments. Even the language of the mass, Latin, added an aura of mystery; it was a sacred medium which presumably only God and the priest could understand. For Parton the Catholic mass was an edifying experience. For other Protestants, however, it smacked of superstition, or even worse, of magic. Too much emphasis was placed on right ritual and elaborate ceremony and too little attention was given to preaching the gospel of Jesus, beckoning sinners to conversion. If the Sunday mass was the only encounter a person had with Catholic piety, the criticism would have been understandable. This was precisely the problem, however. Most nineteenth-century Protestant Americans, when they commented on Catholic piety, thought only of the mass, the rosary, or devotion to the saints—Romish practices which the Reformation had done away with. Likewise most historical accounts of Catholicism, when they speak of Catholic piety, limit themselves to the mass and the institutional administration of the sacraments. Indeed, these are the principal sources of Catholic piety and very rich ones as well, but they are not all that the church had to offer the people.

Catholicism was and still is a very ritually oriented religion, but at certain moments in its history the spirit of evangelicalism complemented and even overshadowed the piety of ritual. This experiential strain of religion has always been present in Catholic piety. Francis of Assisi underscored the importance of experiential religion, as did Teresa of Avila, Ignatius of Loyola, and Alphonsus de Liguori. They called people to reform and repent, and all of them emphasized the importance of personal conversion. In time the fires of enthusiasm would cool off, and evangelical piety would once again be overshadowed by the religion of ritual until that moment when the spirit of renewal rekindled the need for a call to conversion and repentance.

This was the situation in the United States during the middle decades of the nineteenth century. The early part of the century was a time when ritual overshadowed evangelicalism in American Catholic piety, but the widespread neglect of religion and the competitive spirit of the American religious environment demanded something more than ritual and ceremony. People had to be converted to religion before they could practice it. The key to the renewal of piety was the Catholic revival. It had been tried and tested in Europe and found successful; it was ideally suited for the religious climate of the United States and the immigration of European preachers skilled in revival preaching furnished the manpower necessary to make it go. With the emergence of the Catholic revival the piety of Catholics underwent a significant transformation. The experiential dimension of religion moved to the forefront, and evangelicalism overshadowed ritualism. It was a new variety of religious experience as far as Catholic America was concerned, and its widespread and prolonged popularity indicated that the spirit of evangelicalism was becoming a major current in the mainstream of Catholic piety.

By the end of the century the revival meeting was one of the dominant features of Catholic life. The 1906 Census on Religious Bodies pointed this out by describing these "evangelistic or revival services" as the major activity of the "home missionary work of the church."[2] As a means of evangelization the Catholic revival gathered together the people of the parish and offered them a memorable religious experience; it channeled their piety into the church, thereby strengthening the vitality of the institution; and it reinforced the devotional revolution taking place in Roman Catholicism and made religion as much a personal experience of conversion as it was the right performance of ritualized ceremonies. Evangelicalism had made its mark on the community, and any historical view which omits this aspect of Catholic life tells only a part of the story.

The invincible presence of Catholic revivalism and its unique offering of saving grace bore many resemblances to the revivalistic religion that permeated Protestant America. Both religious movements traced their origins back to seventeenth- and eighteenth-century Europe when the spirit of religious renewal swept through Protestant and Catholic churches alike. From this religious awakening emerged Continental Pietism, English Methodism, and Catholic Evangelicalism. Ronald Knox, in his study *Enthusiasm*, acknowledged this similarity when he described the Jesuit mission preacher Paul Segneri as the John Wesley of seventeenth-century Italy.[3] Other historians of religion in modern Europe have made similar comparisons between the parish mission and Protestant revivalism.[4] In nineteenth-century America and the comparisons between Catholic and Protestant revivalism were equally striking, but historians have generally overlooked them. Yet, the similarities were there. Given the common heritage of these two phenomena in the religious awakening of modern Europe such resemblances were not unexpected. It should be emphasized, however, that Catholics were not imitating American Protestants any more than John Wesley was copying Paul Segneri. They were adopting a European form of the pastoral ministry that fitted in very well with the American environment.

In comparing Protestant and Catholic revivalism, however, it must be clearly emphasized that the Protestant version, unlike the parish mission movement, underwent significant and substantial changes from the days of Jonathan Edwards to Dwight Moody. Most important in this transformation was the erosion of the Calvinist theological system which highlighted the sovereignty of God and the emergence of a more Arminian approach to religion which focused on the role of human choice in the salvation process. Nor was Protestant revivalism so homogeneous that a simple description can do justice to a phenomenon that was indeed very complex. There were many varieties in the Protestant evangelical tradition, a point that was most evident in the late nineteenth century when this tradition began to split up, with various strains of evangelicalism becoming institutionalized in a variety of new denominations. Acknowledging the complexity of Protestant revivalism, however, does not preclude a comparison between two different expressions of a common tradition. Certain aspects of Protestant revivalism were characteristic of the movement as a whole, and these major points of consensus resembled certain traits found in Catholic revivalism.

A most obvious similarity was that both movements fostered a new type of ministry—the itinerant revivalist. Revivalistic religion called for a special brand of preaching and a special breed of person. They were specialists in their work, more skilled in rekindling the fires of religion than the ordinary preacher. Singled out by the community, they took to the road and traveled across the countryside moving from town to city and back again, an itinerant "spiritual masseur" periodically called upon "to tone up the body religious."[5] At every stop large crowds of people turned out to hear the gospel preached with power and persuasion. Eventually the lone itinerant was replaced by a large group of preachers who traveled about as a team so that they could more effectively minister to the needs of increasingly larger crowds. Catholic revivalists focused their attention on a particular parish locale. In the city this meant a specific neighborhood, while in the rural town a single parish almost always represented the entirety of the town's Catholic population. Protestant revivalists also worked the parish network, but people like Finney and Moody conducted citywide revivals that cut across parish and denominational lines. Occasionally Catholic preachers would conduct a citywide revival, but the normal pattern was a parish mission limited to the members of a specific congregation.

In time revivalism adopted certain new techniques. Finney's new measures initially created a storm of protest, but they soon became an accepted feature for many revivalists. Moody underscored the importance of music, and both men realized the necessity of promotional publicity in booming up the revival. Handbooks on revivalism, to instruct aspiring evangelists, also became quite commonplace. The emphasis on technique was also evident among Catholic revivalists. Handbooks spelled this out in great detail, instructing the preacher on not only what to preach, but how he could do this most effectively. Certain rituals, certainly "new measures" for Catholic America in the 1850s, were recommended, but like Finney's innovations, the use of these rituals was a sensitive issue, and they had to be carried out with discretion. Catholics also realized the importance of music at a revival, but it never reached the level of popularity and excellence that it achieved among Protestants.

Such external similarities led many nineteenth-century observers to note the likeness between a parish mission and a Protestant revival. James Parton, in his article on Catholics, commented on this resemblance, stating that Catholics were adopting "Protestant plans and expedients ... putting American machinery into the ancient ark."[6] In 1826 the *U.S. Catholic Miscellany* described what a mission was for its Catholic readers, noting that in "this country it will be better understood by comparing it to a camp meeting."[7] When the Redemptorists went to Emmitsburg, Maryland, in 1855, their purpose was "to get up a revival." They were so successful that the Protestants in town "had to resort to similar means in self-defense," but only the Catholics were said to have gained real benefit "by their revival."[8] A journalist in Penn Yan, New York, summed it up best when in describing a Paulist mission, he noted that "the work of religious revival is by no means confined to the Protestant denominations."[9]

In addition to external similarities, other, more theological likenesses existed. Both movements put a strong emphasis on the conversion experience. This was primarily a change of heart that ushered in a new life of grace. How this was sustained and what it actually meant theologically not only set Catholics apart from Protestants, but was even interpreted differently within the Protestant evangelical tradition. Yet the fundamental emphasis on conversion was a common ingredient in revivalistic religion. What the preacher meant by this differed, depending on his denominational affiliation, but the kernel of the message was basically the same for a Finney or a Weninger. This becomes clearer when the experiential element is added to conversion. Conversion necessarily aimed at the heart of the penitent sinner and very often resulted in an emotional, religious catharsis. It was a personal decision, heightened emotionally by a sense of urgency coming from the preacher's platform. To produce a change of heart, not a change of opinion, as Finney said, was the key to revivalistic preaching.[10] This was a basic point that united the Protestant evangelical tradition and an essential quality in Catholic revivalism as well.

Ethically, both Protestant and Catholic revival crusades fostered a rigorous moral code. Drinking, dancing, gambling, and a number of other forms of entertainment and recreation were condemned by both Catholic and Protestant preachers. Very often priests and ministers joined forces in a common crusade against demon rum, the saloon, or the dance hall. Though they were not typically American themes, they constituted the dominant social morality abroad in the United States during the second half of the nineteenth century. In supporting this morality Catholics demonstrated that they too had a strain of Puritanism in their blood. This social ethic encouraged a gospel of thrift, hard work, and rugged individualism, or what has classically been labeled the gospel of success. This too was a part of the Catholic culture fostered at the parish mission.

Socially, the emphasis on personal religion and a rigorous, individual moral code overshadowed any attempt at a reconstruction of the social order. Even though such individualism did not preclude the possibility of social reform, as was evident in the Finney era of revivalism, still the dominant strain in Protestant revivalism encouraged an individual gospel, not a social gospel. Catholic revivalism clearly moved in this direction. The world, the flesh, and the devil were partners in the kingdom of evil, and personal salvation was keyed to a world hereafter.

As far as the institution was concerned, Catholic revivalism clearly channeled the enthusiasm of revivalistic religion into the local church. It awakened the piety of the people, fostered the devotional revolution taking place in Roman Catholicism, and ultimately strengthened the institution. How permanent and long-lasting this was on a personal level can be seriously questioned, but without a doubt revivalism did have a substantial impact in establishing the parish as the center of Catholic piety and thus the vital organ of the institutional church. Protestant revivalism also reinvigorated the spiritual health of the local congregation and increased the number of churchgoers, even though such increase may have been modest and temporary. Protestant revivalism was also a powerful social movement that organized thousands of people into small church communities and formed a consensus that was so widespread throughout the nation that to understand American evangelicalism is, as William McLoughlin put it, "to understand the whole temper of American life in the nineteenth century."[11] To understand Catholicism during the same period it is also necessary to comprehend the pervasive and powerful force of Catholic revivalism. It left an imprint on the community that shaped the piety of the people and the growth of the institution. This influence persisted well into the twentieth century and helps to explain why Catholics thought and acted the way they did.

During the 1950s Catholic intellectuals began to assess the historical record of American Catholicism. The evaluation was primarily centered on the intellectual poverty of the community and the reasons for this backwardness. From this public discussion emerged an intensive and prolonged debate on what made Catholics think and act the way they did.

The basic thesis was that intellectually, Catholics, despite their large numbers, had made little or no contribution to the intellectual and cultural life of the nation. Though a few people dissented, most commentators agreed that Catholic America was an intellectual wasteland.[12]

Recent historical investigations have helped to explain more thoroughly the reasons for this state of affairs.[13] In the late nineteenth and early twentieth centuries there was an emerging intellectual culture in Catholic America, but the condemnation of Americanism in 1899 and of Modernism in 1907 effectively cut short any possible growth of this movement. These developments, together with the manifest and latent cultural patterns of American Catholicism, succeeded in stifling any significant intellectual achievements in the community. Only recently, within the last generation, has this situation changed, and today Catholics are generally recognized for their contributions to the intellectual and cultural life of the nation.

In seeking an explanation for the intellectual backwardness of Catholics it is necessary to consider the influence of revivalism. This certainly was not the single reason for such low achievement, but the pervasive presence of revivalistic religion did help to form the cultural and intellectual world of masses of people and in the process it reinforced the tendency to deemphasize the intellectual virtues. Revivalism fostered a religion of the heart, and this emphasis undercut the role of reason in a person's orientation toward God. The revivalists aimed their message to the affections of the people, seeking to elicit an emotional, personal conversion. Their sermons were not doctrinal expositions; they had no time for that. They wanted to massage the hearts of their audience, using vivid, sentimental imagery to elicit an equally moving, heartfelt conversion. Such an approach was not necessarily anti-intellectual. Indeed, the great preachers were educated men, intellectuals in the community. Moreover, the revival always included doctrinal instruction in its schedule. But these instructions were clearly secondary to the more conspicuous attention given to the evangelical summons that came forth from the preacher's platform every evening. When the preacher stood before the people, he knew and was continually advised that his sermons had to be plain moral exhortations, "mission harangues, not cathedral sermons." This emphasis subordinated the importance of intellectual virtues to a more nonrational approach to God. Moreover, it was a thin line that divided anti-intellectualism from such intellectual subordination.

Another aspect of Catholic culture that found support in revivalistic religion was the tendency to divorce the sacred from the secular. For Catholics "the life of man in the world," in the words of Thomas O'Dea, "has no interior relation to the spiritual development of the human person."[14] As a result learning for learning's sake becomes an eccentric posture, and "the call of the intellectual life falls like seed upon stony ground."[15] Revivalism with its stress on the world hereafter was just another cultural manifestation of Catholicism's tendency to downplay the importance of human fulfillment in the secular world. This obviously undermined the meaningfulness of intellectual pursuits, but it also goes a long way toward explaining why Catholics lagged behind in the area of social action and in the pursuit of social justice. Indeed, Catholics could boast of a John Ryan, "the Right Reverend New Dealer," and of a tradition of concern for the working man and woman in its support of labor. But people like John Ryan were few and far between, and the concern for labor was most visible only when it coincided with the goals of the institution. If necessary, clerics could be used as strikebreakers, and labor priests were most often lonely prophets in a community that saw little relationship between the affairs of this world and the world hereafter. A people shaped by the piety of evangelicalism were more concerned with the personal pursuit of holiness, not the reconstruction of the social order.

In following the interpretation offered by O'Dea in 1958, the concept of moralism, or the tendency to see the world "as a place of moral danger" and life "as a series of moral problems," was also endemic to the Catholic culture.[16] The Catholic revival certainly reinforced this attitude. Its rigorous moral code not only interpreted sin in strict individualistic terms, but it also viewed life as a continuous moral battle. Ethical legalism emerged from this way of thinking, with the letter of the law having more force than the spirit of the law. James T. Farrell captured this trait as it pertained to human sexuality in his classic, *Studs Lonigan,* and there was no better illustration of this than the mission sermon of the fictional Father Shannon.[17] The Legion of Decency, the birth control campaign, and most recently the anti-abortion crusade reflected this inclination of both the institution and the people to view life as a series of moral problems. The only social issues worth challenging were personal moral problems, and this clearly was the message of the Catholic revivalist. Subsequent events suggest that the people learned this lesson well.

There was another aspect of Catholic revivalism that shaped the culture of Catholics in both the nineteenth and twentieth centuries. These were the symbols of piety evoked by the preacher and the support the revival gave to the devotional transformation of modern Catholicism. The cross, the crucified savior and his bleeding, wounded heart injected a strong dose of romantic sentimentality into the piety of the people. The revival also fostered a galaxy of devotions, and this stress on an active piety, along with the strain of romanticism, persisted well into the twentieth century. If, as one historian claimed, this devotional transformation represented the true triumph of ultramontanism in northern Europe, the same may be said for American

Catholicism.[18] The twentieth century did see the increasing Romanization of the church in the United States, but this has been attributed more to the increasing centralization of the church in Rome and the close link between episcopal appointments and loyalty to the Vatican. Not discounting these factors, the devotional transformation that emphasized the institution as the indispensable fountain of grace and stressed the ritualized performance of certain approved devotions in order to gain God's favor tended to make religion more dependent on the church, thereby fostering a loyalty that was spiritually meaningful as well as institutionally desirable.

Like most religious denominations Catholicism has always had a tendency towards clericalism. But the authoritarian structure of Catholicism and the unique sacramental quality attached to the clerical state has made such a tendency a prominent trait in the Catholic culture. It tended to "give the priest-role a monopoly with respect" to intellectual pursuits, thus limiting the sphere of intellectual activity.[19] Coupled with this was a strong dose of authoritarianism which vested in the clergy seemingly infallible wisdom in all areas of life. Popularly these qualities have been expressed in the phrase that the proper role of the laity is to "pay, pray, and obey." The Catholic revival strengthened this mentality by singling out the important and authoritative role of the pastor. When the revival began, the pastor invested the revivalists in the preacher's stole, signifying not only a transfer of power and authority, but where such authority rested. At the close of a revival the preacher invariably promoted the cause of the local pastor by reminding people of their obligation to heed his command and be docile subjects. Moreover, the Catholic revival could not take place without the priest. He was the only person allowed to preach the gospel and administer the sacraments, without his participation conversion could never be ratified sacramentally. This not only had its effect on the intellectual culture of Catholics, but equally significant it limited the sphere of lay activity in other areas of church life. Whether by design or default, the clergy monopolized church affairs and the revival served to underscore this point. At times the laity may have won some battles in this area, but they never won the war over the issue of the clerical monopoly of power.

Recent scholarship has pointed out the important role of the neighborhood parish in the development of American Catholicism. The Catholic revival clearly illustrated this. As an organizing force it strengthened the parish community; as a spiritual agent it not only awakened the piety of the people, but channeled this renewed enthusiasm into the local church and encouraged the formation of parish confraternities. It promoted the loyalty of the people to the institution by focusing their attention on something most people could identify with, the church in the neighborhood. As Andrew Greeley observed, "institutional Catholicism in the United States prospered as long as it did because it provided self-definition and social location for the immigrants, their children, and their grandchildren; and it did so precisely through the institution of the neighborhood parish."[20] The Catholic revival was an important agent in shaping this "self-definition and social location." This self definition was also closely associated with a separatist mentality that set Catholics off from the rest of society. The parish was a religious and ethnic fortress within which Catholics could gather, secure from the hostility of a Protestant culture that appeared to threaten them on all sides. Insofar as the revival made people more loyal to the parish, it also strengthened this defensive, minority complex.

In analyzing some of the traits of twentieth-century Catholicism from the historical perspective of revivalistic religion, there is one development that bears a striking resemblance to this nineteenth-century phenomenon. This is the charismatic movement that has swept through Catholic America during the 1970s with the speed and enthusiasm of a classic religious revival. Clearly no explicit, historical connection exists between the two movements. The charismatic movement can best be explained historically as a Catholic appropriation of the spirit of pentecostal religion—thus, the name Catholic Pentecostals, which was the label adopted by the movement in the 1960s but subsequently abandoned for the preferred term, charismatic. Historically, Protestant pentecostalism came out of the revivalistic tradition of Methodism, as did the holiness movement which preceded and spawned twentieth-century pentecostalism. Although the historical connections between Protestant revivalism and pentecostalism are evident, no such link existed between the clerically dominated parish mission movement and the lay-inspired Catholic charismatic revival. Yet enough similarities do exist to justify a comparison and to posit the thesis that the contemporary pentecostal revival is another manifestation of the latent experiential strain of religion that has been present in Roman Catholicism and periodically has emerged to become, if not a dominant, certainly a very powerful motif in the community. Moreover, both these phenomena can be legitimately located in the current of evangelical religion which flowed through both Catholic and Protestant churches. From this perspective Catholic pentecostalism can be seen as a modern-day version of Catholic revivalism, obviously different but not totally disconnected. It is a twentieth-century expression of Catholic evangelicalism.

A major difference between the two movements is their principal symbols of piety. Revivalists focused on the cross and the crucified savior whose heart bore the wounds of mankind's sins. The pentecostals focus on the symbol of the Holy Spirit and the charismatic gifts which the Spirit bestows on the Christian. Jesus is obviously an important figure for the pentecostals, but the principal symbol of piety is the Spirit of God, not the Son of God. In pentecostalism the laity play a very prominent role, whereas in the parish mission movement the priest was the dominant actor. Other differences could be pointed out as well, such as the central role of the parish in revivalism and its contingent presence in pentecostalism, the millenarianism of pentecostalism, and its predominantly middle-class constituency. The decreased importance of confession and of many traditional devotional practices are also points of divergence from the Catholic revival movement, which was predominantly a lower-class phenomenon that stressed the necessity of confession and promoted a very active devotionalism.[21] Such differences can largely be explained by the influence of twentieth-century pentecostalism as well as by the cultural and religious transformation which took place as Catholicism moved from the era of the post-Tridentine church to the age of post-Vatican II religion.

Despite such differences, revivalism and pentecostalism converge on several important points. A major likeness is the emphasis placed on the conversion experience. For charismatic Catholics the "pentecostal experience is essentially a change of heart, a religious *metanoia*, a conversion experience."[22] A spiritual conversion is essential to charismatic spirituality; a goal not achieved by all perhaps, but an experience which all desire and actively seek. A key to this conversion is the experiencing of it, since conversion is, essentially, an experiential phenomenon. For charismatics Christianity is "above all, a religion of the heart."[23] The power of God is to be experienced, felt in one's bones, in one's body, above all in one's heart. As was true of Catholic evangelicalism, pentecostalism fosters a religion of the heart, not of the head. This does not necessarily mean that pentecostalism is anti-intellectual, but for many the emphasis placed on a heartfelt religion is so central to their spirituality that it tends to obscure the role of the intellectual virtues in the pursuit of holiness. As a result, doctrine or theological instruction occupies a secondary place in the charismatic movement. The subjective experience of religion rather than the intellectual understanding of it is pentecostalism's most conspicuous trait. This is especially evident in the emphasis given to the charismatic gift of tongues, which is a nonrational experience manifested in an unintelligible language. As was true of Catholic revivalism, however, many of the leaders of the charismatic movement are highly educated individuals, but their piety flows from the heart, not from the head. Obviously this is a legitimate religious experience, but it has been more associated with Protestant evangelicalism than with Roman Catholicism. The charismatics have once again reminded people that Catholicism can be evangelical as well as sacramental; that piety is as important as ritual when it comes to the expression of religion.

Flowing from this emphasis on heartfelt religion is the conspicuous presence of emotionalism. Predictably, the charismatics downplay the role of emotion. The conversion experience is "not necessarily dramatic or emotional," notes a handbook on charismatic spirituality.[24] But later on, the author urges his readers "to be fervent in their piety, Christ will expect no less."[25] Evangelical religion has always had a problem dealing with the emotional fervor of its adherents. Jonathan Edwards downplayed the necessity of emotional enthusiasm, Charles Finney counseled against it, and Catholics have always found it difficult to deal with religious enthusiasm. But a religion of the heart lends itself to such fervent, enthusiastic piety. In pentecostalism, moreover, "the person who demonstrates the most enthusiasm is often considered the member who is most 'Spirit-filled.'"[26] Spokesmen for the movement claim such emotion is not necessary, but of its nature pentecostalism elicits a heartfelt emotional response. For nineteenth-century revival

Catholics, the emotions were manifested principally in sorrowful, tearful expressions brought on by the fear and trembling of a sinner confronted with the image of an angry God. In pentecostalism they are generally more positive, more joyful expressions of a personal experience of the presence of God's Spirit.

Coming out of the evangelical tradition, Catholic pentecostalism manifests a trait closely identified with this religious movement—individualism. Catholic charismatics have exhibited a visible concern for one another and most frequently express their religion in a community setting. But as was true of eighteenth-century revivalism especially, the concern for community is based on the premise that the experience of religion remains a very personal affair between God and the individual. Although it is usually in the midst of the local charismatic community "that an individual is drawn into the charismatic experience," the critical point is the personal experience of the Spirit.[27]

Like its nineteenth-century counterpart, pentecostalism is a Catholic version of evangelicalism which is linked with the sacramental life of the church. Yet, in pentecostalism the sacraments are not so prominent and essential as they were with revival Catholics. For the charismatics the sacraments are not the fulfillment of the conversion experience, but the nurture necessary to sustain a charismatic spirituality. This is especially true of the eucharist, whereas confession appears to be of considerably less importance. For revival Catholics confession was essential to conversion, without it there was no conversion; not so with the pentecostals.

The individualism of the Catholic charismatic movement is perhaps best illustrated by the absence of a concern for involvement in social action. As Joseph Fichter noted in his study of Catholic pentecostalism, "the charismatic movement tends to withdraw its members from the struggle for social justice and to blunt their zeal for social reform."[28] Like

201

revival Catholics the pentecostals have concentrated their energies on the individual pursuit of salvation. Theirs is an individual gospel, not a social gospel. Their most important ministry is to praise God, and everything else pales before this concern.

The gift of healing is also prominent in the pentecostal movement. The sick are gathered together and prayed over in the hope of a miraculous cure. The belief in miraculous cures has long been a part of the Catholic tradition, but pentecostalism has greatly stressed this miraculous gift and made it a prominent part of the total charismatic experience. Healings also took place at Catholic revivals though they were never as integral to the revival experience as they are to the pentecostal experience. For revival Catholics, healing was a sacramental miracle; for pentecostals, it is a miraculous gift of the Spirit. Yet, both movements are similar in that they included this aspect of the miraculous.

Naturally similarities are to be expected in any version of the Catholic religious experience. For purposes of historical analysis, however, what binds these two movements together is more significant than what separates them. Both pentecostalism and revivalism are examples of sustained efforts to renew the piety of the people; they are attempts at evangelization which have fostered a special brand of piety, a religion that emphasizes the work of God in the hearts of individuals. It was evident in nineteenth-century revivalism, and it has emerged again with twentieth-century Catholic pentecostalism.

The revival did indeed foster a new religious experience for Catholic Americans. A century later a similar phenomenon has occurred with the emergence of the pentecostal prayer meeting. In both instances there has been a striking resemblance to the evangelical current of religion in American Protestantism. Such a resemblance underlines the popularity and the pervasiveness of evangelicalism in the American character. Individualism has long been a trait of the American people. Rugged or refined, it has characterized the nation in its social, political, and economic history. Evangelicalism suggests that individualism is also a major trait in American religious history in both the Protestant and Catholic phases of this story. The free church tradition and the principle of voluntarism have encouraged this development by stressing the importance of persuasion. During the nineteenth century the revival technique became the most widespread manifestation of this concern for persuasion. Through the revival, evangelicalism became a national religion which united the American people more than has been previously imagined. Catholics and Protestants alike enjoyed the soul-stirring, heart-warming quality of evangelical religion.

Catholic evangelicalism, like its Protestant counterpart, was never totally consistent. It fostered a religion of the heart, a very personal religious experience. At the same time it directed this piety into the community of the church and made salvation outside the church appear impossible. It fostered an evangelical piety, but it also stressed the importance of ritual by ratifying conversion through the sacraments. It was rooted in the tradition of Roman Catholicism, but it strongly resembled the evangelical tradition of American Protestant revivalism. Some of the revivalists, Hecker and Elliott, were leading Catholic liberals; others, Weninger and Wissel, the Jesuits and Redemptorists, were supporters of conservative Catholicism. Never consistent, it was always complex. Catholics were indeed Roman in their tradition, ritualistic in their devotion, and eternally bound to the church. But revivalism has demonstrated that Catholics were nurtured in a piety that was also strikingly American, fiercely evangelical, and deeply individualistic. Any historical view which omits this dimension of Catholic life tells but part of the story.

Notes |

1. Charles G. Finney, *Memoirs* (New York: A. S. Barnes and Co., 1876), pp. 367–68.
2. This conclusion is based on material contained in Ellen H. Walworth, *Life Sketches of Father Walworth* 2d ed. (Albany: J. B. Lyon Co., 1907). Briefly put, Chancellor W—— is the title often used for Walworth's father, who was chancellor of the state of New York. The younger Walworth was a lawyer, did enter the Catholic church, became a priest, and was in London in 1850 preaching parish missions as a newly ordained Redemptorist priest. He continued this ministry for more than a decade after his return to the U. S. in 1851. Timothy L. Smith, in reading the *Memoirs*, came across this passage and provided me with the initial link between Finney and Walworth. Having read the passage, it was clear to me that the person referred to by Finney was Father Walworth. My thanks to Professor Smith for bringing this information about Finney and his lawyer convert to my attention. My hunch was subsequently confirmed by an examination of the manuscript edition of Finney's *Memoirs* located at Oberlin College. My thanks to William Bigglestone and Mary E. Cowles of the Oberlin College Library for assisting me in confirming this point of information about Finney and Walworth.
3. Joseph H. Fichter, S. J., *Dynamics of a City Church*, vol. 1, *Southern Parish* (Chicago: University of Chicago Press, 1951), pp. 211–29.
4. For the variety of evangelical religion and how it can be referred to in a limited, doctrinaire manner as well as a more interdenominational understanding see David F. Wells and John D. Woodbridge, eds., *The Evangelicals* (Nashville: Abingdon Press,

1975); see also Timothy L. Smith, "The Postfundamentalist Party," *The Christian Century* 93, no. 4 (February 1976): 125–27, for a critique of this book and an appeal for a more ecumenical understanding of evangelicalism.

NOTES TO CHAPTER 1

1. R. Aubert, J. Beckmann, P. Corish, and R. Lill, *Die Kirche in der Gegenwart*, Erster Halbband: *Die Kirche zwischen Revolution und Restauration*, vol. 6 of *Handbuch der Kirchengeschichte*, ed. H. Jedin et al. (Freiburg: Herder, 1971), pp. 106–107 and 210.
2. Joseph Prost, C.SS.R., "Founding the Redemptorist Congregation in the U.S.A., 1832–1843," *Social Justice Review* 64, no. 4 (July–August 1971): 130. These memoirs, which appeared in nineteen installments in vols. 64–66, offer a good illustration of the European missionary mentality toward the U.S. and a rich commentary on Catholic life at the time.
3. Ibid.
4. Edward F. Sorin, "Chronicles of Notre Dame du Lac," mss., p. 513. (This chronicle is available in the archives of the University of Notre Dame. I want to thank Thomas J. Schlereth for making his personal copy available to me.)
5. Ibid., p. 3.
6. Prost, "Founding . . . ," *Social Justice Review* 66, no. 2 (May 1973): 66.
7. Sorin, "Chronicles," pp. 14 and 16.
8. R. Aubert et al. *Die Kirche in der Gegenwart*, 1: 107.
9. Edwin Scott Gaustad, *Historical Atlas of Religion in America* (New York: Harper and Row, 1962), p. 43.
10. Prost, "Founding . . . ," *Social Justice Review* 64, no. 10 (February 1972): 379.
11. Quoted in Dan Herr and Joel Wells, eds., *Through Other Eyes: Some Impressions of American Catholicism by Foreign Visitors from*

1777 to the Present (Westminster, Md.: Newman Press, 1965), p. 15.

12. Msgr. Whitfield, Archbishop of Baltimore, to Society for Propagation of the Faith, February 16, 1832, *Annales de L'Association de la Propagation de la Foi* 5, no. 30 (October 1832): 717; hereafter cited as *Annales*.

13. John Dubois, "The Diocese of New York in 1830," *Historical Records and Studies*, 5 (November 1907): 218.

14. Martin J. Becker, "A History of Catholic Life in the Diocese of Albany 1609–1864" (Ph.D. dissertation, Fordham University, 1973), p. 73.

15. Msgr. Fenwick, Bishop of Boston, to Society for Propagation of the Faith, May 16, 1831, *Annales* 5, no. 28 (April 1832): 432–40.

16. M. Byrne to Society for Propagation of the Faith, *Annales* 4, no. 24 (April 1831): 713–14.

17. Thomas D. Clark, *Frontier America* (New York: Scribner, 1959), pp. 290 and 292.

18. "Bishop Flaget's Report of the Diocese of Bardstown to Pius VII, April 10, 1815," *Catholic Historical Review* 1, no. 3 (October 1915): 313.

19. T[homas] T. McAvoy, "Bishop Bruté's Report to Rome in 1836," *Catholic Historical Review* 29, no. 2 (July 1943): 187–88.

20. Sorin, "Chronicles," pp. 37, 330–31.

21. Ibid., p. 331.

22. John Gilmary Shea, *The History of the Catholic Church in the United States*, 4 vols. (New York: J. G. Shea, 1886–92), 3: 620.

23. Richard C. Wade, *The Urban Frontier* (Chicago: University of Chicago Press, 1964), p. 263.

24. Prost, "Founding . . . ," *Social Justice Review* 64, no. 11 (March 1972): 421.

25. Wade, *The Urban Frontier*, p. 262.

26. John Rothensteiner, *History of the Archdiocese of St. Louis*, 2 vols. (St. Louis, 1928), 1: 581–85, 730–35, 798.

27. Roger Baudier, *The Catholic Church in Louisiana* (New Orleans: A. W. Hyatt, 1939), pp. 317 and 323.

28. McAvoy, "Bishop Bruté's Report to Rome," p. 223.
29. M. Blanc to M. Abbé Boue, August 8, 1830, *Annales* 4, no. 24 (April 1831): 668.
30. *Annales* 4, no. 19 (January 1830): 72.
31. M. Abbé J. Massi à M. Etienne, Jan. 18, 1831, *Annales* 5, no. 29 (July 1832): 605.
32. *Annales* 4, no. 24 (April 1831): 651.
33. McAvoy, "Bishop Bruté's Report to Rome," p. 224.
34. *Annales* 8, no. 45 (March 1836): 340.
35. R. Aubert et al., *Die Kirche in der Gegenwart*, 1:650–54.
36. Thomas T. McAvoy, C.S.C., *A History of the Catholic Church in the United States* (Notre Dame: University of Notre Dame Press, 1969), pp. 124–25.
37. Gerald Shaughnessy, *Has the Immigrant Kept the Faith?* (New York: Macmillan, 1925), p. 262.
38. Robert Baird, *Religion in America* (a critical abridgment with an introduction by Henry Warner Bowden) (New York: Harper and Row, 1970), p. 190.
39. Perry Miller, *The Life of the Mind in America from the Revolution to the Civil War* (New York: Harcourt, Brace and World, 1965), p. 7.
40. Walter Brownlow Posey, *Frontier Mission* (Lexington: University of Kentucky Press, 1966), pp. 33–34.
41. Martin J. Spalding, *Sketches of the Early Catholic Missions of Kentucky* (Louisville: B.J. Webb and Brother, 1844), p. 104; see also Samuel Mazzuchelli, O.P., *The Memoirs of Father Samuel Mazzuchelli, O.P.* (Chicago: The Priory Press, 1967), pp. 174–76, 288, for a similar evaluation.
42. Orestes Brownson, "Protestant Revivals and Catholic Retreats," *Brownson's Quarterly Review* 3, no. 11 (July 1858): pp. 294ff.
43. Winthrop S. Hudson, "How American is Religion in America?" in *Reinterpretation in American Church History*, ed. Jerald C. Brauer (Chicago: University of Chicago Press, 1968), p. 156.

44. M. Van Delft, C.SS.R., *La Mission Paroissiale: Pratique et Théorie*, trans. Fr. Van Groenendael (Paris: Lethielleux, 1964), p. 44. This is an excellent study of the parish mission in Europe.

45. Ibid., p. 47.

46. Quoted in Van Delft, *La Mission Paroissiale*, p. 51.

47. Ibid., p. 84.

48. Ibid., p. 92.

49. Roger Aubert, *Le Pontificat de Pie IX* (Paris: Bloud and Gay, 1963), p. 144.

50. Élisabeth Germain, *Parler du Salut? Aux Origines d'une mentalité religieuse* (Paris: Beauchesne et ses fils, 1967), pp. 23 and 61. See also Ernest Sevrin, *Les Missions religieuses en France sous la Restauration 1815–1830*, 2 vols. (Paris: 1948–59).

51. Germain, *Parler du Salut?*, p. 23; Erwin Gatz, *Rheinische Volksmission im 19. Jahrhundert* (Dusseldorf: Verlag L. Schwann, 1963), p. 16.

52. Spalding, *Sketches*, pp. 219–220; see also John M. David, *A Spiritual Retreat of Eight Days*, ed. M. J. Spalding (Louisville: Webb and Levering, 1864).

53. Francis X. Curran, S.J., *The Return of the Jesuits* (Chicago: Loyola University Press, 1966), pp. 17–18; also John V. Mentag, S.J., "Catholic Spiritual Revivals: Parish Missions in the Midwest to 1865" (Ph.D. dissertation, Loyola University [Chicago], 1957), p. 17.

54. L.-J. Rogier, G. DeBertier De Sauvigny, and J. Hajjar, *Siècle des Luminières, révolutions, restauration*, vol. 4 of *Nouvelle Histoire de L'Église*, ed. L.-J. Rogier, R. Aubert and M. D. Knowles (Paris, n.d.), p. 310.

55. Mentag, "Catholic Spiritual Revivals," pp. 17–20.

56. Spalding, *Sketches*, pp. 288–300.

57. Mentag, "Catholic Spiritual Revivals," p. 23.

58. *Decreta Conciliorum Provincialium et Plenarii Baltimorensium* (Baltimore: Apud Joannem Murphy et Socios, 1853), p. 11, no. 22. This assessment is based on the use of *exercitiis* in the decree. I believe that this is a reference not to mission work in general,

but to the "exercises" (i.e., missions) given by the priest while on mission.

59. John H. Lamont, *History of the Archdiocese of Cincinnati 1821–1921* (New York: Frederick Pustet Company, 1921), p. 120.

60. The 1837 Pastoral Letter of the Third Provincial Council of Baltimore cited in Peter Guilday, *The National Pastorals of the American Hierarchy* (Washington, D. C.: National Catholic Welfare Council, 1923), p. 113. This letter went on at length about the negligence of Catholics in the practice of their religion.

61. John F. Byrne, C.SS.R., *The Redemptorist Centenaries* (Philadelphia: The Dolphin Press, 1932), p. 261.

62. Joseph Wuest, C.SS.R., *Annales Congregationis SS. Redemptoris Provinciae Americae*, 5 vols. (vols. 1–3: Ilchester, Md., 1888–99; vols. 4–5: Boston, 1914–24), 1: 239.

63. Curran, *The Return of the Jesuits*, p. 69.

64. Van Delft, *La Mission Paroissiale*, p. 93; see also Robert G. North, S.J., *The General Who Rebuilt the Jesuits* (Milwaukee: The Bruce Publishing Co., 1944).

65. *The Metropolitan Catholic Almanac and Laity's Directory 1850* (Baltimore: Fielding Lucas, 1849), p. 226; Mentag, "Catholic Spiritual Revivals," pp. 47–60.

66. Francis X. Weninger, S.J., *Erinnerungen aus Meinem Leben in Europa und Amerika durch achtzig Yahrs 1805 bis 1885* (Columbus, Ohio, 1886) [p. 22 of the English translation of this autobiography]. A copy of the rare German-language original is available in the St. Louis University Library. A typewritten English translation, which I used, was kindly provided to me by Rev. Henry H. Regnet, S.J., former librarian at St. Louis University.

67. Gilbert J. Garraghan, S.J., *The Jesuits of the Middle United States*, 3 vols. (New York: America Press, 1938), 2: 54.

68. *The Metropolitan Catholic Almanac, 1850*, p. 227. This total of thirty-six missions from 1832–49 is the estimated number given by Wuest, *Annales*, 1: 445–46; 2: 476–77.

69. Mentag, "Catholic Spiritual Revivals," pp. 26–71.

70. Weninger, *Erinnerungen* [English translation], p. 16.
71. Quoted in Edward F. X. McSweeny, *The Story of the Mountain*, 2 vols. (Emmitsburg, Md.: The Weekly Chronicle, 1911), 1: 418. See Emmet Larkin, "The Devotional Revolution in Ireland," *American Historical Review*, 77, no. 3 (June 1972): 625–52 for the religious situation in Ireland; and Jay P. Dolan, *The Immigrant Church* (Baltimore: Johns Hopkins University Press, 1975), pp. 83–85 for the German situation.
72. *The Metropolitan Catholic Almanac, 1850*, pp. 234–35.
73. Sidney E. Mead, "The Rise of the Evangelical Conception of the Ministry in America," in *The Ministry in Historical Perspective*, ed. H. Richard Niebuhr and Daniel D. Williams (New York: Harper & Row, 1956), p. 208.
74. Ibid., p. 223.
75. *The Metropolitan Catholic Almanac, 1850*, p. 235.

NOTES TO CHAPTER 2

1. See Jay P. Dolan, "A Critical Period in American Catholicism," *Review of Politics* 35, no. 4 (October 1973): 523–36.
2. Philip Schaff, *America: A Sketch of Its Political, Social and Religious Character*, ed. Perry Miller (Cambridge, Mass.: Harvard University Press, 1961), p. 183.
3. Gaustad, *Historical Atlas*, pp. 52 and 108–110; Shaughnessy, *Has the Immigrant Kept the Faith?* pp. 125, 134, 145; by decade, the percentage of population increase was: 1830–40, 108%; 1840–50, 142%; 1850–60, 93%.
4. Ibid., pp. 262 and 189.
5. *Report on the Statistics of Churches in the United States at the Eleventh Census, 1890* (Washington, D. C., 1894), pp. xxvii and 92.
6. David Ward, *Cities and Immigrants* (New York: Oxford University Press, 1971), pp. 63–64.
7. Ibid., p. 75.

8. Stephan Thernstrom, *The Other Bostonians* (Cambridge, Mass.: Harvard University Press, 1973), p. 155.
9. Harold J. Abramson, *Ethnic Diversity in Catholic America* (New York: John Wiley and Sons, 1973), p. 39.
10. See Dolan, *The Immigrant Church*; and Josef Barton, *Peasants and Strangers* (Cambridge, Mass.: Harvard University Press, 1975).
11. *The Metropolitan Catholic Almanac, 1850*, p. 233 and *The Metropolitan Catholic Almanac and Laity's Directory, 1860* (Baltimore: John Murphy and Co., 1859), p. 266.
12. Ibid.; the early years, 1790–1830, obviously recorded a relatively higher growth when the church grew from one diocese in 1790 to eleven by 1830.
13. *Report on the Statistics of Churches, 1890*, pp. xxi–xxii.
14. Rogier, De Bertier, De Sauvigny, and Hajjar, *Siécle des Luminières*, pp. 385–86.
15. Ibid., p. 386.
16. Eugenio Corecco, *La Formazione della Chiesa Cattolica negli Stati Uniti D'America attraverso l'attività sinodale* (Brescia: Morcelliana, 1970), p. 26 and table in Appendix. 'Major councils' technically means plenary (national) and provincial (regional), see pp. 235–40 in Corecco.
17. Ibid., p. 26.
18. *Decreta Conciliorum Provincialium et Plenarii Baltimorensium*, p. 8, no. 10 (1829 council); p. 19, no. 44 (1837 council); and p. 31, no. 80 (1852 council).
19. Thomas W. Spalding, *Martin John Spalding: American Churchman* (Washington, D.C.: Catholic University of America Press, 1973), pp. 229–30.
20. Kenneth Scott Latourette, *The Nineteenth Century in Europe: Background and the Roman Catholic Phase* (Grand Rapids: Zondervan Publishing House, 1969), p. 370.
21. Aubert, *Le Pontificat de Pie IX*, p. 461.
22. See Larkin, "The Devotional Revolution," especially pp. 644–45 and 648, for one example of how the devotional revolution took on an ultramontane flavor.

23. Aubert, *Le Pontificat de Pie IX*, p. 461.
24. Latourette, *The Nineteenth Century in Europe*, p. 353.
25. Aubert, *Le Pontificat de Pie IX*, p. 453.
26. J. D. Mansi, *Sacrorum Conciliorum Nova et Amplissima Collectio*, 53 vols. (Paris, 1901–27), 43, col. 86; Gatz, *Rheinische Volksmission*, p. 68.
27. Ibid., pp. 133–34, 163–74.
28. Y.-M. Hilaire, "Les Missions intérieures face à la déchristianisation pendant la second moitié du XIXe Siècle dans la région du nord," *Revue du Nord* (Lille), (January 1964), pp. 51–52; Paul Huot-Pleuroux, *La Vie Chrétienne dans le Doubs et la Haute-Saône de 1860 a 1900* (Paris: Université de Paris, 1966), p. 30.
29. *Acta et Decreta Sacrorum Conciliorum Recentiorum. Collectio Lacensis* (Freiburg: Herder, 1875), 3, col. 1353 (Pastoral Letter of the Third Provincial Council of Westminster, 1859); also Aubert et al., *Die Kirche in der Gegenwart*, 1: 552–53.
30. Archives of the Archdiocese of New York, Copy of letter of Bishop John Hughes to Society for the Propagation of the Faith, January 23, 1845.
31. *United States Catholic Miscellany*, February 14, 1857, quoted in Wuest, *Annales*, 3, pt. 1: 387.
32. Archives of the University of Notre Dame (hereafter AUND), Copy of letter of Orestes Brownson to Isaac Hecker, New York, August 5, 1857. I want to thank Joseph Gower and Rev. Richard Leliaert for making available to me their collection of the Hecker-Brownson correspondence.
33. AUND, Isaac Hecker to Orestes Brownson, Richmond, Va., April 12, 1856.
34. AUND, Isaac Hecker to Orestes Brownson, New York, July 29, 1851.
35. George Ruland, C.SS.R., to seminarians, Baltimore, February 4, 1856, quoted in Wuest, *Annales*, 3, pt. 1: 381.
36. Timothy L. Smith, *Revivalism and Social Reform* (New York: Harper and Row, 1965), p. 7.

37. Orestes Brownson, "Mission of America," *Brownson's Quarterly Review* 1, no. 4 (October 1856): 435, 431, 425.

38. AUND, Isaac Hecker to Orestes Brownson, New York, July 29, 1851.

39. AUND, Bishop John Hughes to the Society for the Propagation of the Faith, Paris, February 5, 1845, f. 104.

40. Brownson, "Protestant Revivals and Catholic Retreats," p. 305.

41. Ibid., p. 289.

42. Quoted in Vincent Holden, *The Yankee Paul* (Milwaukee: Bruce Publishing Co., 1958), p. 161.

43. Michael J. Curley, C.SS.R., *Cheerful Ascetic: The Life of Francis Xavier Seelos, C.SS.R.* (New Orleans, 1969), p. 260.

44. The figure was calculated from Wuest, *Annales*, vols. 1–5.

45. Mentag, "Catholic Spiritual Revivals," p. 288; Weninger's missions are described in Mentag, pp. 71ff., and were also listed in Weninger's autobiography. The midwest region comprised the states of Ohio, Indiana, Michigan, Illinois, and Wisconsin.

46. Holden, *The Yankee Paul*, pp. 152–65.

47. Wuest, *Annales*, 2: 136.

48. Archives of the Paulist Fathers (hereafter APF) Mission Chronicles (hereafter MC), 1: 3.

49. *The Mission Book: A Manual of Instructions and Prayers Adapted to Preserve the Fruits of the Mission*, 2nd ed. (New York: D. and J. Sadlier, 1859), p. 5.

50. Wuest, *Annales*, 4, pt. 1: 200–205; *Acts of the Second Provincial Chapter of the Province of St. Paul of the Cross 1866* (West Hoboken, N.J.: St. Michael's Passionist Monastery Press, 1901), pp. 24–25. My thanks to Rev. Clement Buckley, C.P., for making available copies of this material.

51. *Acta et Decreta Sacrorum Conciliorum*, 3, col. 210, no. 9.

52. Brownson, "Protestant Revivals and Catholic Retreats," p. 320.

53. Frederick W. Faber, "Catholic Home Missions," in *The Lives of Father Paul Segneri, S.J., Father Peter Pinamonti, S.J., and Ven.*

John de Britto, S.J. (New York: Edward Dunigan and Brother, 1851), p. 18.

54. Smith, *Revivalism and Social Reform*, p. 45.
55. Dolan, *The Immigrant Church*, pp. 56–57.
56. *American Celt*, August 11, 1855.
57. Archives of the Archdiocese of New York, Diary of Rev. Richard L. Burtsell, March 27, 1865.
58. AUND, Copy of letter of Orestes Brownson to Isaac Hecker, June 25, 1845.
59. Brownson, "Protestant Revivals and Catholic Retreats," p. 307.
60. Mentag, "Catholic Spiritual Revivals," p. 288.
61. Cassian J. Yuhaus, C.P., *Compelled to Speak* (Westminster, Md.: Newman Press, 1967), p. 235.
62. Ibid., p. 319.
63. Quoted in Holden, *The Yankee Paul*, p. 187. This book discusses the founding of the Paulists.
64. Archives of the Archdiocese of New York, Diary of Rev. Richard L. Burtsell, November 24, 1867.
65. APF, MC, 1: 43.
66. Walter Elliott, *The Life of Father Hecker*, 4th ed. (New York: The Columbus Press, 1898), p. 326.
67. These figures were calculated from Wuest, *Annales*, vols. 1–5, and from the Paulist Mission Chronicles in APF.
68. This figure was arrived at from statistics given in annual volumes of *Woodstock Letters*.
69. This figure was obtained from Weninger's autobiography, *Erinnerungen* (English translation).
70. Urban is defined as a place numbering 8,000 or more inhabitants.
71. *Report on the Statistics of Churches, 1890*, pp. 39 and 91–115.
72. Mentag, "Catholic Spiritual Revivals," pp. 28–29; *Seven Hundredth Anniversary of the Order of Preachers* (n.p.: The Rosary Press, 1916), pp. 94–95.

73. "Notes on Retreats and Missions," *Woodstock Letters* 5 (1876): 48; "Nebraska," *Woodstock Letters* 15 (1886): 75–76.
74. Michael J. Curley, C.SS.R., *The Provincial Story* (New York: The Redemptorist Fathers, 1963), p. 178.
75. Joseph Wissel, *The Redemptorist on the American Missions* (New York: John Ross and Son, 1875). The 1875 edition appeared in an expanded three-volume edition in 1886 and a third edition was reprinted in 1920.
76. F. X. Weninger, *Pratische Winke für Missionäre zur Abhaltung der Missionen* (Cincinnati, 1885).
77. Yuhaus, *Compelled to Speak*, pp. 253–54.
78. Mentag, "Catholic Spiritual Revivals," p. 124; Spalding, *Martin J. Spalding*, pp. 194–237.
79. AUND, Archdiocese of Baltimore, Administration of Archbishop Martin J. Spalding, Box 39 A-D-4, "Animadversiones Theologorum Septimae Congregationis," pp. 42–43.
80. *Acta et Decreta Sacrorum Conciliorum*, 3, col. 530, no. 487.
81. Ibid., col. 526, no. 473; Van Delft, *La Mission Paroissiale*, pp. 98–99.
82. Pastoral Letter of Edgar P. Wadhams, Bishop of Ogdensburg, 1874, quoted in Sister Mary Christine Taylor, "A History of the Foundations of Catholicism in Northern New York" (Ph.D. dissertation, St. Louis University, Department of History, 1967), p. 277.
83. Stephen Byrne, *Irish Emigration to the United States* (New York: The Catholic Publication Society, 1873), p. 49.
84. Philip Newton, "The Roman Catholic Parish Mission Movement in the United States, 1875–1885" (seminar paper, University of Notre Dame, 1975).
85. Weninger, *Erinnerungen* [English translation, p. 381].
86. James A. McVann, "The Beginnings of the Paulist Apostolate to Non-Catholics" (S.T.L. dissertation, Catholic University of America, 1932), pp. 40–41.
87. Walter Elliott, "The Missionary Outlook in the United States," *Catholic World* 57, no. 342 (September 1893): 758.

88. *The Missionary* 1, no. 1 (March 1896): 2; see also McVann, "The Beginnings of the Paulist Apostolate," pp. 50–51.

89. Alexander Doyle, "The Outlook With A Retrospect," *The Winchester Conference* (New York, 1905), pp. xiv–xv.

90. See Walter Elliott, *Non-Catholic Missions* (New York: The Catholic Book Exchange, 1895) where the program of the non-Catholic mission is outlined.

91. APF, MC, 6: 318ff.

92. *The Missionary* 14 (April 1909): n.p.

93. McVann, "The Beginnings of the Paulist Apostolate," p. 59.

94. Faber, "Catholic Home Missions," p. 21.

95. The pertinent statistics were published in the *Woodstock Letters* annually.

96. Garraghan, *The Jesuits in the Middle United States*, 2: 51.

97. Yuhaus, *Compelled to Speak*, pp. 297–98.

98. Archives of the Archdiocese of San Francisco, *Relatio Archidioecesis Sancti Francisci Facta Sacrae Congregational de Propaganda Fide 1899*, p. 3 where the Catholic population of San Francisco is estimated at 180,000; and "Statistics, 1901," of the archdiocese, where only an estimated 79,000 Catholics are counted in the parish censuses.

99. "An Apostolate Church in the City," *The Winchester Conference* (New York, 1901), pp. 50–51.

100. See chapter 5, "Revival Catholics," below, for this assessment.

101. Archives of Archdiocese of San Francisco, "Spiritual Census 1937," pp. 3–5, for data to indicate that only 42 percent of the Catholic population attended Sunday mass; also François Houtart, "A Sociological Study of the Evolution of the American Catholics," *Sociaal Kompass*, January/April 1955, pp. 189–216, for similar patterns in other cities in the twentieth century.

102. "Hints on Giving Missions," *Woodstock Letters* 31 (1902): 418.

NOTES TO CHAPTER 3

1. This scene was reconstructed from information given in Walter Elliott, *Non-Catholic Missions* pp. 62–65, and from other promotional literature pertinent to the revival available in the Paulist Archives, along with the Mission Chronicles of the Paulists.
2. APF, *To the People of St. Paul's Parish*, leaflet (1873), pp. 1–2.
3. APF, "Sermon Book of Walter Elliott," Sermon on Delay.
4. APF, *To the People of St. Paul's Parish*, p. 4.
5. APF, MC, 2: 65; other religious orders followed the same practice of home visitation prior to a revival. Cf. Wuest, *Annales*, 3, pt. 1: 294.
6. *The Mission Book*, p. 5.
7. Faber, "Catholic Home Missions," p. 21.
8. Garraghan, *The Jesuits of the Middle United States* 2: 62; see also, Weninger, *Praktische Winke*, for Weninger's detailed instructions.
9. Wuest, *Annales*, 3, pt. 1: 344.
10. See *Synodus Dioecesana Syracusana Prima, 1887* (New York, 1887), ch. 42; also *Synodus Dioecesana Buffalensis Decima Septima, 1871* (Buffalo, 1871), ch. 11; APF, MC, 3: 69. All agreed that missions should occur at regular intervals, but the time lapse did vary from as little as a three-year interval to as much as a ten-year interval; see also Van Delft, *La Mission Paroissiale*, p. 118.
11. Wuest, *Annales*, 3, pt. 1; 194–95.
12. APF, MC, 2: 182; also Wuest, *Annales*, 5, pt. 2; 75–76.
13. APF, MC, 5: 57.
14. APF, MC, 2: 352.
15. APF, MC, 4: 159 and 233.
16. APF, MC, 2: 74.
17. George Paré, *The Catholic Church in Detroit 1701–1888* (Detroit: The Gabriel Richard Press, 1951), pp. 567ff.
18. APF, MC, 2: 186–87.

19. Wuest, *Annales*, 5, pt. 2: 235.
20. APF, MC, 1: 238.
21. APF, MC, 5: 107–108.
22. Wuest, *Annales*, 3, pt. 1: 344.
23. Newton, "The Roman Catholic Parish Mission."
24. Mentag, "Catholic Spiritual Revivals," pp. 242–45.
25. Calculated from *Woodstock Letters* 20 (1891).
26. The principal sources for the collective study were, for Damen: Joseph P. Conroy, S.J., *Arnold Damen, S.J.* (New York: Benziger Bros., 1930) and "Father Arnold Damen," *Woodstock Letters* 19 (1890): 214–32; for Elliott: McVann, "The Beginnings of the Paulist Apostolate," pp. 40–42, Joseph McSorley, *Father Hecker and His Friends* (St. Louis: B. Herder Book Co. 1952), pp. 237–53; for Maguire: "Father Bernard A. Maguire," *Woodstock Letters* 26 (1887): 3–10; for Seelos: Curley, *Cheerful Ascetic*; for Walworth: Ellen H. Walworth, *Life Sketches of Father Walworth* (Albany: J. B. Lyon Co., 1907), Walter Elliott, "Father Walworth: A Character Sketch," *Catholic World* 73, no. 435 (June 1901): 320–37; for Weninger: "Father Francis Xavier Weninger," *Woodstock Letters* 18 (1889): 43–68, "Fr. Francis Xavier Weninger, S.J.," *Central Blatt and Social Justice*, 20 (1927–28): 38–39, 135–37, 178–80, 250–51, 287–88; Weninger, *Erinnerungen*; for Wissel: "The Reverend Joseph C. Wissel, C.SS.R., Redemptorist Missionary," *Central Blatt and Social Justice* 20 (1927–28): 284–86, 358–59, 394–95; 21 (1928–29): 52–53, 88–89, 131–34, 177–79, 249–50; for Young: APF, Walter Elliott, "Rev. Alfred Young," ms., "Rev. Alfred Young, C.S.P.," *Catholic World* 71, no. 422 (May 1900): 257–64.
27. Maur. De Meulemeester, *Histoire Sommaire de la Congrégation de T.S. Rédempteur* (Louvain, 1950), p. 158.
28. Curley, *Cheerful Ascetic*, p. 35 passim.
29. "The Reverend Joseph C. Wissel," *Central Blatt and Social Justice* 20, no. 12 (March 1928): 394.
30. Mentag, "Catholic Spiritual Revivals," p. 245; where he states that the average age of mission preachers in the midwest area was thirty-seven years when they began their revival ministry.

31. Wissel, *The Redemptorist*, p. 48 (all references to this work are for the 1886 edition, vol. 1, subtitled: *Missions*, unless otherwise noted). The other two volumes of the 1886 and 1920 editions were subtitled: *Renewals*, vol. 2, and *Retreats*, vol. 3.
32. Walworth, *Life Sketches*, p. 41.
33. Ibid., p. 104.
34. APF, Baker Papers, Letter of Chessie (Morse) to her sister, April 15, 1853.
35. Walworth, *Life Sketches*, p. 125.
36. Ibid., p. 129.
37. John F. Byrne, C.SS.R., *The Glories of Mary in Boston* (Boston: Mission Church Press, 1921), p. 538.
38. "The Reverend Joseph C. Wissel," *Central Blatt and Social Justice* 21, no. 6 (September 1928): 179.
39. Wuest, *Annales*, 4, pt. 1: 202–203.
40. Curley, *Cheerful Ascetic*, p. 254.
41. "The Reverend Joseph C. Wissel," *Central Blatt and Social Justice* 21, no. 8 (November 1928): 249; Wissel, *The Redemptorist*, p. 43.
42. Ibid., pp. 72 and 50.
43. Archives of the Archdiocese of New York, Diary of Rev. Richard L. Burtsell, November 18, 1867.
44. *The Winchester Conference* (New York, 1901), pp. 47 and 44.
45. McSorley, *Father Hecker and His Friends*, pp. 241–42.
46. McVann, "The Beginnings of the Paulist Apostolate," ch. 6.
47. APF, Elliott, "Rev. Alfred Young."
48. *Katholische Kirchenzeitung*, June 21, 1860.
49. Conroy, *Arnold Damen*, p. 230 passim.
50. Quoted in Mentag, "Catholic Spiritual Revivals," p. 235.
51. Ibid., p. 136; and Conroy, *Arnold Damen*, p. 266.
52. Ibid., p. 272.
53. "Father Bernard Maguire," *Woodstock Letters*, p. 9.
54. Wissel, *The Redemptorist*, p. 27.
55. APF, MC, 3: 18.
56. Wissel, *The Redemptorist*, p. 27.

57. Cf. Wissel, *The Redemptorist*, pp. 31ff.; APF, Mission Chronicles; Yuhaus, *Compelled to Speak*, p. 259; "Missionary Labors," *Woodstock Letters* 13 (1884): 62; Wuest, *Annales*, 4, pt. 2; 402–8 passim, for the schedules of the missions.

58. Wissel, *The Redemptorist*, p. 39.

59. APF, MC, 1: 266–67, and also Wissel, *The Redemptorist*, pp. 98ff.

60. Ibid., pp. 57–58.

61. Wuest, *Annales*, 4, pt. 2: 406.

62. Wissel, *The Redemptorist*, pp. 111–117 and Weninger, *Die Heilige Mission* (Cincinnati, 1885), pp. 419–529.

63. Wissel, *The Redemptorist*, p. 543.

64. "Hints on Giving Missions," p. 419.

65. *The Winchester Conference* (New York, 1901), p. 47.

66. Walter Elliott, *A Manual of Missions* (Washington, D.C.: The Apostolic Mission House, 1922), p. 73.

67. "Hints on Giving Missions," p. 421.

68. P. Hitz, C.SS.R., *To Preach the Gospel*, trans. Rosemary Sheed (New York: Sheed and Ward, 1963), pp. 113ff.; Sevrin, *Les Missions Religieuses*, 1: 134 and Germain, *Parler du Salut?*, p. 24 come to the same conclusion.

69. Hitz, *To Preach the Gospel*, p. 113.

70. Ibid., p. 106.

71. APF, MC, 1: 237.

72. "Hints on Giving Missions," pp. 419 and 422; see also Mentag, "Catholic Spiritual Revivals," p. 251 and "Missionary Labors," *Woodstock Letters*, 20 (1891): 436, for other descriptions of Jesuit missions.

73. Wissel, *The Redemptorist*, p. 62.

74. Hitz, *To Preach the Gospel*, p. 119.

75. Wissel, *The Redemptorist*, p. 157.

76. Yuhaus, *Compelled to Speak*, p. 244.

77. Wissel, *The Redemptorist*, p. 158.

78. Weninger, *Praktische Winke*, pp. 13–36.

79. Ibid., p. 123.

80. AUND, Isaac Hecker to Orestes Brownson, May 15, 1851.
81. Wissel, *The Redemptorist*, pp. 51 and 157.
82. Yuhaus, *Compelled to Speak*, pp. 243–44.
83. Ibid., p. 244.
84. Wuest, *Annales*, 4, pt. 1: 204.
85. Ibid., pt. 2: 301 and Wissel, *The Redemptorist*, pp. 62–63.
86. APF, MC, 2: 10.
87. See Frederick William Faber, *Hymns* (Baltimore: John Murphy and Co., 1880), and Alfred Young, *The Catholic Hymnal* (New York: The Catholic Publication Society Co., 1884).
88. APF, MC, 4: 73.
89. "The Work of Our Missionaries," *Woodstock Letters*, 25 (1896): 290.
90. Faber, *Hymns*, p. 351.
91. Wissel, *The Redemptorist*, p. 26; see also Wuest, *Annales*, 4, pt. 1: 23, and 2, pt. 1: 387.
92. *Daily Herald*, March 15, 1861.
93. AUND, Archdiocese of Baltimore, Administration of Archbishop Spalding, 39-A-D-4, "Animadversiones . . . " pp. 42–43; *Decreta. Concilium Plenarium Baltimorense Secundum*, p. 156 (a copy of this edition of the preliminary decrees of the 1866 council was provided by Mr. Anthony Zito of the archives of Catholic University of America Library); *Acta et Decreta Sacrorum Conciliorum*, 3, col. 526, no. 476.
94. See Yuhaus, *Compelled to Speak*, p. 249; Mentag, "Catholic Spiritual Revivals," p. 130.
95. Yuhaus, *Compelled to Speak*, pp. 270–71; Wuest, *Annales*, 4, pt. 1: 223.
96. Garraghan, *The Jesuits in the Middle United States*, 2: 63–64; Mentag, "Catholic Spiritual Revivals," p. 236; and Conroy, *Arnold Damen*, pp. 275–83.
97. Wuest, *Annales*, 4, pt. 1: 24 and 16.
98. John Tracy Ellis, *The Life of James Cardinal Gibbons*, 2 vols. (Milwaukee: Bruce Publishing Co., 1952), 1: 151.

99. These were Faber's essay, "Catholic Home Missions," and Brownson's essay, "Protestant Revivals and Catholic Retreats."
100. Brownson, "Protestant Revivals and Catholic Retreats," p. 289.
101. Ibid., p. 314.
102. Ibid., pp. 303 and 314.
103. Faber, "Catholic Home Missions," p. 52.
104. Wuest, *Annales*, 2:470. For an indication of this opposition see John Talbot Smith, *The Catholic Church in New York*, 2 vols. (New York, 1908), 1: 202.
105. Wuest, *Annales*, 4, pt. 2: 405–6.
106. *Sacramento Bee*, April 7, 1875.
107. Mentag, "Catholic Spiritual Revivals," p. 171.
108. "Missions at Arlington and Lexington," *Woodstock Letters* 4 (1875): 173.

NOTES TO CHAPTER 4

1. Jonathan Edwards, *The Great Awakening*, ed. C. C. Goen, vol. 4 of *The Works of Jonathan Edwards*, ed. John E. Smith (New Haven: Yale University Press, 1972), p. 2.
2. Paulus Scharpff, *History of Evangelism*, trans. Helga Bender Henry (Grand Rapids, Mich.: William B. Eerdmans Publishing Co., 1966), pp. 3ff., for a brief background to the modern history of evangelism.
3. Smith, *Revivalism and Social Reform*, for a delineation of the evangelical strain in various denominations; Dieter Voll, in his study, *Catholic Evangelicalism*, trans. Veronica Ruffer (London: The Free Press, 1963), has demonstrated how evangelicalism shaped nineteenth-century English Anglicanism.
4. Scharpff, *History of Evangelism*, p. 3.

5. Wuest, *Annales*, 5, pt. 2: 75; "Father Weninger on the Pacific Coast," *Woodstock Letters* 2 (1873): 32.
6. This was the assessment of C. Loring Brace in *The Dangerous Classes of New York and Twenty Years' Work among Them* (New York: Wynkoop and Hallenback, 1872), pp. 154–55.
7. John Talbot Smith, *Our Seminaries* (New York, 1896), p. 122; see Robert F. McNamara, *Catholic Sunday Preaching: The American Guidelines 1791–1975* (Washington, D.C.: Word of God Institute, 1975) for a discussion of the nature of the Sunday sermon.
8. Curley, *Cheerful Ascetic*, p. 252.
9. APF, "Mission Sermons of Alfred Young," Delay of Penance.
10. Weninger, *Erinnerungen* [English translation, p. 368].
11. Wissel, *The Redemptorist* (1875 edition), p. 117. This sermon summarized the Catholic theology of conversion.
12. APF, "Mission Sermons of Clarence Walworth," Necessity of Penance and Sacrilegious Communion.
13. Archives of the Baltimore Province of the Redemptorists, (hereafter ABPR), "Mission Sermons of Elias F. Schauer," Delay of Conversion.
14. APF, Young Sermons, Delay of Penance.
15. Ibid.
16. Wissel, *The Redemptorist*, p. 210.
17. Weninger, *Die Heilige Mission*, p. 346.
18. Ibid.
19. Wuest, *Annales*, 4, pt. 1: 9; and 2: 143.
20. APF, Elliott Sermons, On Life and Death of a Sinner.
21. APF, Walworth Sermons, The Doctrine of Eternal Punishment.
22. APF, Elliott Sermons, Hell.
23. Ibid.
24. Faber, *Hymns*, p. 352.
25. Wissel, *The Redemptorist*, (1875 edition), pp. 82–83.
26. APF, Walworth Sermons, Opening.
27. See Wissel, *The Redemptorist*, pp. 47–48 for emphasis placed on

the conversion of the heart; also, APF, Elliott's and Young's sermons on delay of conversion for the same emphasis.

28. Faber, *Hymns*, p. 351.
29. APF, Young Sermons, The Mercy of God.
30. APF, Walworth Sermons, Necessity of Contrition.
31. *Hymns for the Year* (London: Burns, Oates and Co. n.d.), p. 282.
32. Young, *The Catholic Hymnal*, p. 95.
33. Faber, *Hymns*, p. 353.
34. Ibid., p. 425.
35. Weninger, *Die Heilige Mission*, p. 119.
36. Ibid., p. 121; see also pp. 52–53 for another such example.
37. APF, Elliott Sermons, General Judgment.
38. Ibid.
39. APF, Young Sermons, The Last Judgment.
40. ABPR, "Sermon Book of Joseph R. Wissel, Jr.," Mortal Sin. This was the nephew of Joseph C. Wissel, the foremost Redemptorist mission preacher.
41. APF, Young Sermons, Hell; ABPR, "Mission Sermons of Joseph Kautz," *Occasio Proxima*.
42. APF, Elliott Sermons, Hell.
43. *Freeman's Journal*, March 24, 1877.
44. Ibid., Nov. 25, 1876.
45. Weninger, *Die Heilige Mission*, p. 126.
46. Wissel, *The Redemptorist*, p. 2.
47. APF, Walworth Sermons, Renewal of Vows.
48. Weninger, *Die Heilige Mission*, p. 349.
49. APF, Walworth Sermons, Value of the Soul.
50. APF, Young Sermons, Delay of Penance; see Voll, *Catholic Evangelicalism*, for the important role of the sacraments in evangelical Anglicanism.
51. Faber, *Hymns*, p. 352.
52. Young, *The Catholic Hymnal*, p. 95.
53. Weninger, *Die Heilige Mission*, p. 440; see also APF, Elliott

Sermon Book, Instructions on Penance and Examination of Conscience.

54. APF, Elliott, Examination of Conscience.
55. Wissel, *The Redemptorist*, pp. 133–34.
56. APF, Elliott Sermons, Sacrament of Penance; see also, Brownson, "Protestant Revivals and Catholic Retreats," for a similar assessment.
57. Hitz, *To Preach the Gospel*, p. 121.
58. Wuest, *Annales*, 5, pt. 2: 76.
59. APF, Elliott Sermons, Delay of Conversion.
60. APF, Walworth Sermons, Necessity of Penance.
61. APF, Elliott Sermons, Delay of Conversion.
62. Ibid., Renewal of Vows; see also Faber, *Hymns*, p. 351.
63. Wissel, *The Redemptorist*, p. 57.
64. APF, Elliott Sermons, Intemperance.
65. ABPR, Wissel, Jr., Sermons, Drunkenness.
66. Wissel, *The Redemptorist*, p. 83.
67. Ibid., p. 84.
68. APF, Walworth Sermons, Judgment.
69. Ibid.
70. Wuest, *Annales*, 5, pt. 2: 240.
71. Ibid., 4, pt. 2: 176.
72. Ibid., 4, pt. 1: 411.
73. APF, Elliott Sermons, Occasions of Sin; ABPR, Kautz Sermons, Occasions of Sin.
74. APF, Walworth Sermons, Opening.
75. "Hints on Giving Missions," p. 419.
76. APF, Walworth Sermons, Opening.
77. "The Missionary and His Topics," *The Winchester Conference* (New York, 1901), p. 47.
78. Ibid., p. 44. This was the opinion of Alexander Doyle, a Paulist colleague of Elliott.
79. Ibid., p. 47.
80. Germain, *Parler du Salut?*, p. 70, comes to the same conclusion about nineteenth-century mission preaching in France.

NOTES TO CHAPTER 5

1. Brownson, "Protestant Revivals and Catholic Retreats," p. 289.
2. *Freeman's Journal*, September 18, 1875.
3. APF, MC, 2: 23.
4. Wuest, *Annales*, 3, pt. 2: 109; APF, MC, 2: 34.
5. Wuest, *Annales*, 5, pt. 2: 102.
6. Ibid., 5, pt. 2: 87.
7. Ibid., 5, pt. 2: 225–26.
8. "Missions in Charles County, Maryland," *Woodstock Letters* 11 (1882): 112. The Paulists had similar experiences in Washington, D.C., APF, MC, 2: 162.
9. *Acta et Decreta Sacrorum Conciliorum Recentiorum*, col. 530, no. 487.
10. *Acta et Decreta Concilii Plenarii Baltimorensis Tertii 1884* (Baltimore: Typis Joannis Murphy et Sociorum, 1886), p. 133, no. 238.
11. Weninger, *Erinnerungen*, for the mission activities of Weninger.
12. Quoted in William G. McLoughlin, *Modern Revivalism* (New York: The Ronald Press Co., 1959), p. 166.
13. A. F. Hewit, *Sermons of the Rev. Francis A. Baker, C.S.P. with a Memoir of His Life*, 6th ed. (New York: The Catholic Publication House, 1865), p. 122.
14. APF, MC, 3: 69 and MC, 2: 426; *Metropolitan Record*, December 26, 1863.
15. APF, MC, 3: 69.
16. For the Paulists see chapter 2, table 1, showing that New York City had close to 37 percent of all the Paulist revivals; for Chicago, see Geiermann, *Annals of the St. Louis Province of the Congregation of the Most Holy Redeemer*, 1: 19 passim.
17. *Metropolitan Record*, July 25, 1859.
18. *Report of the Council of Hygiene and Public Health of the Citizens Association of New York* (New York, 1865), p. 303.

19. Figures for 1890 were calculated from *New York State Assembly: Report of the Tenement House Committee, 1894* (Albany, 1895), p. 272; figures for 1900 were calculated from *First Report of the Tenement House Department of the City of New York* (New York, 1903), 2: 28.

20. *Report of the Tenement House Committee*, p. 273.

21. Canon Peter L. Benoit, "Diary of a Trip to America," Archives of the Josephite Fathers, p. 319.

22. *Calendar*, December 1893, p. 7. This was the parish newsletter.

23. The information for 1900 was given in *First Report of the Tenement House Dept.*, 2: 28 and 92–97. This report included a block-by-block study of New York based on the 1900 manuscript census schedules.

24. Oral interview with Rev. James A. McVann, Paulist priest and former resident of the neighborhood, February 27, 1974.

25. Elliott, *The Life of Hecker*, p. 326; James A. McVann, manuscript history of the Paulists. My thanks to Father McVann for letting me read this manuscript.

26. Figures were calculated from parish confirmation registers in 1891, 1895, and 1898.

27. *Report of the Council of Hygiene*, p. 303.

28. AUND, *Scritture Riferite nei Congressi: America Centrale*, vol. 19, letter 1841, Rev. Isaac Hecker to Prefect of Propaganda Fide, June 26, 1861.

29. Figures were calculated from parish registers which listed parents' place of birth.

30. APF, MC, 2: 363.

31. Ibid., 3: 126.

32. Ibid., 3: 297.

33. *U.S. Census 1880: Social Statistics of Cities*, pp. 562–63; James Ford et al., *Slums and Housing: With Special Reference to New York City* (Cambridge, Mass.: Harvard University Press, 1936), 1: 165.

34. *Souvenir of St. Paul's Sunday School* (New York, 1891), p. 3.
35. Kate H. Claghorn, "The Foreign Immigrant in New York City," *Reports of the Industrial Commission on Immigration and Education* (Washington, D.C., 1901), 15: 486.
36. A. E. Costello, *Our Police Protectors* (New York, 1885), p. 386.
37. Ibid., p. 380.
38. See table 2, above; also *First Report of Tenement House Dept.*, 2: 28.
39. Figures calculated from parish baptismal registers.
40. U.S. Census 1890. John S. Billings, *Vital Statistics of New York City and Brooklyn* (Washington, D.C., 1894), pp. 236–37.
41. *First Report of the Tenement House Dept.*, 2: 28 and 92–97. This source provided the information for the block map of the parish.
42. Oral interview, Rev. James A. McVann, February 27, 1974.
43. Thernstrom, *The Other Bostonians*, p. 77.
44. Thernstrom discusses these problems in *The Other Bostonians*, pp. 269–70 and 284–85.
45. Ibid., pp. 283–88; Peter R. Knights, *The Plain People of Boston, 1830–1860* (New York: Oxford University Press, 1971), pp. 133–39.
46. This conclusion is based on a reading of several sources, notably Claghorn, "The Foreign Immigrant and Russell Sage Foundation," and *West Side Studies* (New York, 1912).
47. APF, Young Sermons, Heaven; see also Elliott Sermons, Third Commandment; and Weninger, *Die Heilige Mission*, p. 32.
48. ABPR, Kautz Sermons, Instructions for Young Men.
49. APF, Elliott Sermons, Duties of Parents.
50. ABPR, Kautz Sermons, Salvation.
51. Newspaper account from Utica, N.Y., recorded in Wuest, *Annales*, 3, pt. 1: 344, and Sacramento *Daily Record*, April 5, 1875.
52. *Calendar*, December 1893, p. 7; *Federation* 1 (June 1902), appendix, p. 81.
53. This calculation was based on the percentage of New York

City's population nineteen years old and under, 38 percent, in 1890 and 1900. Figures were given in *U.S. Census 1890, Population*, pt. II, 126 and *U.S. Census 1900, Population*, pt. II, 138.

54. "Labors of Father Maguire and Companions," *Woodstock Letters* 9 (1880): 228–29.

55. "The Work of Our Missionaries," *Woodstock Letters* 31 (1902): 117.

56. APF, MC, 2: 363.

57. Holden, *The Yankee Paul*, p. 187.

58. McVann, manuscript history of Paulists, ch. 2. From 1858 to 1958 there were 358 Paulist priests ordained and only 31 were converts; however, up to 1872, the members of the community were all converts.

59. APF, calculated from MC, 6: 318ff.

60. The number of converts were listed in the Mission Chronicles. Their names and prior affiliation were given in the register of converts.

61. There were 1675 converts from 1860–1900 and the sample numbered 337. Episcopalian: 34% of the sample; no affiliation: 24%; Lutheran: 13%; Presbyterian: 10%; Methodist: 5%; Baptist: 5%; Jewish: 1%; and other: 8%.

62. Paul Kleppner, *The Cross of Culture* (New York: Free Press, 1970), p. 73.

NOTES TO CHAPTER 6

1. Clifford Geertz, *The Interpretation of Cultures* (New York: Basic Books, 1973), p. 97 passim, for a discussion of moods and motivations in religion.

2. See Appendix, below, p. 241.

3. Garraghan, *The Jesuits in the Middle United States*, 2: 91–92; Geiermann, *Annals of the St. Louis Province of the Congregation of the Most Holy Redeemer*, 1: 193 and 492.

4. Garraghan, *The Jesuits in the Middle United States*, 2: 92–93.
5. This conclusion was based primarily on an examination of the registers of St. Paul's parish. A more cursory examination of parish registers in New York City and in San Francisco reflected the pattern of St. Paul's. See also Wuest, *Annales*, 4, pt. 2: 117; 4, pt. 2: 38; 5, pt. 1: 208.
6. Wissel, *The Redemptorist*, vol. 2 *Renewals*, pp. 2–4.
7. *Conspectus Laborum Apostolicorum Congregationis SS. Redemptoris* (Ilchester, Md., 1893), pp. 110–112; APF, MC, 6: 318ff.
8. Garraghan, *The Jesuits in the Middle United States*, 2: 98.
9. See Yuhaus, *Compelled to Speak*, p. 319, where the Passionists listed 350 converts from 1856–66.
10. Weninger, *Praktische Winke*, pp. 137–68; also *Freeman's Journal*, February 24, 1877.
11. Weninger, *Die Heilige Mission*, p. 568.
12. Congregation of the Holy Cross, Provincial Archives, Notre Dame, Ind., Minutes, Minor Chapter, Notre Dame Foundation, Minute Book, p. 51, December 9, 1892. (My thanks to Thomas J. Schlereth for bringing this to my attention.) See also Yuhaus, *Compelled to Speak*, p. 88.
13. Ellis, *The Life of James Cardinal Gibbons*, 1: 28; also APF, MC, 2: 128 for evidence of the vocational decision of a Christian Brother. Alexander Doyle, the Paulist, stated that he decided to enter the priesthood after hearing the Paulists preach a mission in California in 1875.
14. A study of the *Freeman's Journal* from 1875 to 1885 came up with only one incident of a healing experience; see Newton, "The Roman Catholic Parish Mission Movement."
15. Yuhaus, *Compelled to Speak*, pp. 264–65, also p. 267, note 26 for other reported cures.
16. *Freeman's Journal*, October 7, 1876.
17. Quoted in Yuhaus, *Compelled to Speak*, p. 266.
18. See "Missionary Labors," *Woodstock Letters* 20 (1891): 437–38 for reference to the Jesuit practice of blessing the sick.
19. Weninger *Die Heilige Mission*, p. 593; see also Weninger, *Erin-*

nerungen [English translation, pp. 142, 269 passim] for references to the ceremony of the sick.

20. Francis X. Weninger, "Account of the Miracles Admitted by the Congregation of Rites for the Canonisation of St. Peter Claver," *Woodstock Letters* 17 (1888): 106. Peter Claver (1581–1654) worked with Negro slaves in South America. Called the Apostle of the Negroes, he was canonized by the Roman Catholic church in 1888. He was a hero of Weninger who zealously promoted the cause of the apostolate among Negroes in the United States.

21. Garraghan, *The Jesuits in the Middle United States*, 2: 65, note 28.

22. For a study of the Catholic temperance movement in general, see Joan Bland, *Hibernian Crusade* (Washington, D.C.: Catholic University of America Press, 1951).

23. Wissel, *The Redemptorist*, p. 80.

24. Ibid., p. 81.

25. Weninger, *Die Heilige Mission*, p. 446.

26. Francis X. Weninger, *Conférences Originales, Courtes et Pratiques*, 2 vols. (Paris: Delhomme et Briguet, n.d.), 1: 56.

27. APF, MC, 6: 318ff.

28. APF, Elliott Sermons, Drunkenness.

29. APF, MC, 3: 243.

30. See Appendix, below, p. 241. These percentages at St. Paul's were representative of the ratio of pledges to adult revival participants at Paulist missions across the country.

31. APF, MC, 2: 52.

32. Brian Harrison, *Drink and the Victorians* (London: Faber, 1971).

33. Quoted in Andrew M. Greeley, *That Most Distressful Nation: The Taming of the American Irish* (Chicago: Quadrangle Books, 1972), p. 131.

34. APF, MC, 2: 363 and 3: 18.

35. Wuest, *Annales*, 5, pt. 2: 467.

36. Rev. Alexander P. Doyle, "The Attitude of the Roman

Catholic Church toward Temperance Reform," *Federation* 2 (March 1903): 34.

37. *Report of the Police Department of the City of New York 1885*, p. 51; ibid., *1894*, p. 76.

38. Gerald Kurland, *Seth Low: The Reformer in an Urban and Industrial Age* (New York: Twayne, 1971) discusses this investigation and the Sunday closing law.

39. Rev. Walter Laidlaw, "The Distribution of Homes, Churches, Settlements and Saloons in Greater New York," *Federation* 2 (March 1903): 44.

40. Joseph R. Gusfield, *Symbolic Crusade: Status Politics and the American Temperance Movement* (Urbana, Ill.: University of Illinois Press, 1963), pp. 101 and 132; from 1911–1915 the annual average per capita consumption of alcohol of people over 14 years of age was 2.56 gallons.

41. APF, Elliott Sermons, Occasions of Sin.

42. Doyle, "The Attitude of the Roman Catholic Church," p. 35.

43. Quoted in Greeley, *That Most Distressful Nation*, p. 142.

44. "Address of the Right Rev. Bishop Bayley of New Jersey before the State Total Abstinence Union, November 28, 1871," *The Temperance Circular*, no. 1, p. 2.

45. John Ireland, *The Catholic Church and the Saloon* (Buffalo: Catholic Truth Society, 1894), p. 1.

46. Pastoral Letter of the Third Plenary Council of Baltimore 1884, quoted in Bland, *Hibernian Crusade*, p. 123.

47. APF, MC, 3: 201.

48. APF, MC, 2: 442; letter from member of St. Francis Parish to Rev. Elliott, March 12, 1882.

49. Jon M. Kingsdale, "The Poor Man's Club: Social Functions of the Urban-Working Class Saloon," *American Quarterly* 25 (October 1973): 474 and 480.

50. Ireland, *Catholic Church and the Saloon*, p. 7.

51. Quoted in Ronald M. Benson, "American Workers and Temperance Reform" (Ph.D. dissertation, University of Notre

Dame, 1974), p. 114; see chapter 4 of this dissertation for an excellent study of the saloon and the workingman's culture.

52. "Address of Bishop Bayley," p. 4.
53. APF, *Silver Jubilee Pamphlet of St. Paul's Temperance Guild, 1873–1898*, p. 19; APF, Elliott Sermons, Drunkenness.
54. APF, *Silver Jubilee Pamphlet*, pp. 5 and 17.
55. Members were listed in the jubilee pamphlet and located in the City Directory; 73 of 132 (55%) were located.
56. Harrison, *Drink and the Victorians*, pp. 152 and 222; Gusfield, *Symbolic Crusade*, pp. 80–81 and 130.
57. Ibid., p. 5 and Harrison, *Drink and the Victorians*, p. 150.
58. APF, *Silver Jubilee Pamphlet*, pp. 11 and 25.
59. Ibid., p. 51.
60. Kinsdale, "The Poor Man's Club," p. 487.
61. *Why I am a Total Abstainer* (New York, 1892), p. 1; and APF, Elliott Sermons, Drunkenness.
62. "Address of Bishop Bayley," p. 2.
63. *Freeman's Journal*, December 21, 1878.
64. *Temperance Truth* 3, no. 12 (August 1896): n.p.
65. APF, Elliott Sermons, Drunkenness; APF, Temperance Pledge Card.
66. APF, Elliott Sermons, Renewal of Vows.
67. Ibid., Third Commandment.
68. APF, Young Sermons, Heaven.
69. Ibid.
70. APF, Elliott Sermons, Life and Death of a Sinner.
71. ABPR, Wissel, Jr., Sermons, Salvation.
72. William Gahan, O.S.A., *Sermons and Moral Discourses for all the Sundays and Principal Festivals of the Year, on the Most Important Truths and Maxims of the Gospel* (Dublin, 1846). This book of sermons was very popular in the United States.
73. Geertz, *The Interpretation of Cultures*, p. 122.
74. Thernstrom, *The Other Bostonians*, pp. 145–175 in particular, is the best treatment of the issue; Thomas Kessner, *The Golden Door: Italian and Jewish Immigrant Mobility in New York City*

1880–1915 (New York: Oxford University Press, 1977) also shows the higher rate of social mobility among the Jews in comparison with the Italians.

75. Ibid., pp. 168 and 175.
76. Quoted in Moses Rischin, ed., *The American Gospel of Success* (Chicago: Quadrangle Books, 1965), p. 191.
77. Lawrence Kehoe, ed., *Complete Works of the Most Rev. John Hughes, D.D.*, 2 vols. (New York, 1865), 1: 438.
78. APF, Young Sermons, Occasions of Sin.
79. Weninger is the best example of this attitude; see *Die Heilige Mission*, pp. 32–38 passim.
80. Bland, *Hibernian Crusade*, p. 37.
81. Ibid., p. 118.
82. For evidence of increased social/occupational mobility among post-World War II Catholics see Andrew M. Greeley and Peter H. Rossi, *The Education of American Catholics* (New York: Aldine, 1966) and Andrew M. Greeley, *Religion and Careers* (New York: Sheed and Ward, 1963). A more recent update is Andrew M. Greeley, *Ethnicity, Denomination, and Inequality* (Beverly Hills, Calif.: Sage Publications, 1976). The gospel of success was not the sole reason for such mobility, but it is a cultural ingredient that together with other variables may help to explain this shift.
83. APF, Elliott Sermons, Death; ABPR, Wissel, Jr., Sermons, Salvation.
84. Ibid., Close of the Mission.
85. APF, Elliott Sermons, General Judgment.
86. Ibid., Renewal of Vows.

NOTES TO CHAPTER 7

1. T. Scott Miyakawa, *Protestants and Pioneers* (Chicago: University of Chicago Press, 1964), p. 172.
2. APF, Young Sermons, Close of the Mission.

3. APF, Elliott Sermons, Renewal of the Vows of Baptism.
4. APF, Walworth Sermons, Renewal of Vows.
5. Elliott, *A Manual of Missions*, p. 125.
6. APF, Elliott Sermons, Renewal of the Vows of Baptism.
7. APF, Young Sermons, Close of the Mission.
8. Geertz, *The Interpretation of Cultures*, p. 114.
9. Ibid.
10. This was the inscription on all mission crosses erected by Weninger.
11. APF, Young Sermons, The Laws of the Church, where Young clearly envelops the laws of the church with the same authority and binding obligation as the ten commandments.
12. Curran, *The Return of the Jesuits*, pp. 109–16; for other incidents of Weninger's efforts at peacemaking see Mentag, "Catholic Spiritual Revivals," pp. 283ff.; for the Redemptorists, see Wuest, *Annales*, 2: 233 and 270.
13. APF, MC, 4: 158–59.
14. Ibid., 3: 38.
15. Ibid., 1: 238.
16. Ibid., 4: 64.
17. One account that illustrates such contention is Victor Greene, *For God and Country* (Madison: The State Historical Society of Wisconsin, 1975).
18. Wuest, *Annales*, 2: 358 and 4, pt. 2: 294; see also Fergus MacDonald, *The Catholic Church and the Secret Societies in the United States* (New York: U.S. Catholic Historical Society, 1946).
19. Wuest, *Annales*, 5, pt. 1: 14.
20. Rev. Andrew Skeabeck, C.SS.R., "Most Rev. William Gross: Missionary Bishop of the South," *Records of the American Catholic Historical Society of Philadelphia* 66, no. 1 (March 1955): 47.
21. APF, MC, 2: 382.
22. Alexis de Tocqueville, *Democracy in America*, 2 vols. (New York: Vintage Books, 1945), 2: 28.
23. Aubert, *Le Pontificat de Pie IX*, p. 461.

24. Holden, *The Yankee Paul*, p. 163.
25. Wissel, *The Redemptorist*, pp. 151–54.
26. Aubert, *Le Pontificat de Pie IX*, p. 465.
27. "Missionary Labors," *Woodstock Letters* 16 (1887): 234.
28. APF, Young Sermons, Necessity of Penance.
29. "Hints on Giving Missions," p. 420 and "Missionary Labors," *Woodstock Letters* 7 (1878): 30.
30. "Appendix," *Woodstock Letters* 21 (1892). Each annual volume recorded the number of members in the confraternity.
31. F. X. Weninger, *Herz Jesu Missionbuch* (New York: Benziger Bros., 1976). This was copyrighted by Weninger in 1849 and, in his autobiography, *Erinnerungen* [p. 509], he states that it was issued in over one hundred editions in the English, German, French, and Bohemian languages. In 1882 Benziger put out the fortieth American edition of this book.
32. *The Mission Book*, p. 109; see Yuhaus, *Compelled to Speak*, p. 250 for the Passionist promotion of the black scapular of the passion and a corresponding confraternity.
33. Wuest, *Annales*, 4, pt. 1: 411–13.
34. Ibid., 4, pt. 2: 406.
35. APF, MC, 3: 19.
36. Wuest, *Annales*, 5, pt. 1: 209; Walworth, *Life Sketches of Father Walworth*, p. 207.
37. Ibid.
38. APF, Elliott Sermons, Duties of Parents.
39. Wissel, *The Redemptorist*, p. 505.
40. Weninger, *Praktische Winke*, p. 196.
41. Weninger, *Erinnerungen* [English translation, pp. 364–65].
42. Skeabeck, "Most Rev. William Gross," *Records of the American Catholic Historical Society of Philadelphia* 65, no. 3 (September 1954): 150 and 156.
43. Ibid., 65, no. 4 (December 1954): 221.
44. "Missions Given by Father Maguire and His Companions," *Woodstock Letters* 7 (1878): 37.
45. APF, MC, 2: 132.

46. "Missions Given by Father Maguire and His Companions," p. 37.
47. For a discussion of revivalism as an organizing force, see Donald Matthews, "The Second Great Awakening as an Organizing Process 1780–1830," *American Quarterly* 21 (Spring 1969): 23–43.
48. This is the phrase used by Victor Turner in *Dramas, Fields, and Metaphors* (Ithaca: Cornell University Press, 1974), p. 228 where he discusses the function of pilgrimages. His analysis of the pilgrimage does offer some suggestive parallels with revivalism.
49. Weninger, *Erinnerungen* [English translation, p. 376].
50. Wuest, *Annales*, 5, pt. 2: 332.
51. Ibid.
52. Ibid., 4, pt. 1: 14–15.

NOTES TO CHAPTER 8

1. James Parton, "Our Roman Catholic Brethren," *The Atlantic Monthly* 21, no. 126 (April 1868): 432–34.
2. *Religious Bodies: 1906* (Washington, D.C., 1910), 2: 606.
3. R. A. Knox, *Enthusiasm* (Oxford: Clarendon Press, 1950), p. 304.
4. See Jean Delumeau, *Le Catholicisme entre Luther et Voltaire* (Paris: Presses Universitaires de France, 1971), p. 274, and Rogier, De Bertier, De Sauvigny, and Hajjar, *Siècle des Luminières Revolutions Restauration*, pp. 325 and 354.
5. McLoughlin, *Modern Revivalism*, p. 160.
6. Parton, "Our Roman Catholic Brethren" (May 1868), p. 559. In this second of two articles Parton does refer briefly to the Catholic revival.
7. *United States Catholic Miscellany*, August 19, 1826.
8. AUND, Letter of David Whelan to John B. Purcell, Mount St.

Mary's, Emmitsburg, Md., February 2, 1855. My thanks to Philip Gleason for bringing this reference and several other similar ones to my attention.

9. *Penn Yan Chronicle*, February 1, 1876.

10. Charles Grandison Finney, *Lectures on Revivals of Religion*, ed. William G. McLoughlin (Cambridge: The Belknap Press, Harvard University Press, 1960), p. 50.

11. William G. McLoughlin, ed., *The American Evangelicals 1800–1900* (New York: Harper & Row, 1968), p. 26.

12. A brief resumé of this debate is given in Thomas F. O'Dea, *American Catholic Dilemma* (New York: Sheed and Ward, 1958), pp. 3–17.

13. See Michael V. Gannon, "Before and After Modernism: The Intellectual Isolation of the American Priest," *The Catholic Priest in the United States: Historical Investigations*, ed., John Tracy Ellis (Collegeville, Minn.: St. John's University Press, 1971), pp. 293–383.

14. O'Dea, *American Catholic Dilemma*, p. 156.

15. Ibid., p. 157.

16. Ibid., p. 160.

17. James T. Farrell, *Studs Lonigan* (New York: New American Library, 1965), pp. 408–28.

18. Aubert, *Le Pontificat de Pie IX*, p. 461.

19. O'Dea, *American Catholic Dilemma*, p. 160.

20. Andrew M. Greeley, "Catholicism in America: Two Hundred Years and Counting," *The Critic* 34, no. 4 (Summer 1976): 42.

21. Joseph H. Fichter, *The Catholic Cult of the Paraclete* (New York: Sheed and Ward, 1975), pp. 44–45 and 70–72 for a discussion of these characteristics in Catholic pentecostalism.

22. Fichter, *The Catholic Cult*, p. 60.

23. James E. Byrne, *Living in the Spirit: A Handbook on Catholic Charismatic Christianity* (New York: Paulist Press, 1975), pp. 49 and 17.

24. Ibid., p. 43 and 27.

25. Ibid., p. 81.
26. Fichter, *The Catholic Cult*, p. 47.
27. Byrne, *Living in the Spirit*, p. 142.
28. Fichter, *The Catholic Cult*, p. 92.

Appendix |

DATE	PARISH POPULATION*	MISSION ATTENDANCE†	TEMPERANCE PLEDGES	DURATION OF MISSION
1859		725 adults		1 week
		75 children		
1860	5,096			
1873		5500		2 weeks
				5 days-children
1875	12,416			
1878		6200		3 weeks
1879		2900 female		1 week
		2450 male		1 week
		400 children		
1882		1645 m. female		1 week
		1791 s. female		1 week
		1321 m. male		1 week
		1768 s. male		1 week
		150 children		
1885	20,484	6450 adults		1 week-male
		500 children		1 week-female
				3 days-children
1888		4375 female	2561	1 week
		3021 male		1 week
		1000 children		
1891		2840 m. female	3000	1 week
		3610 s. female		1 week
		2250 m. male		1 week
		2300 s. male		1 week
		650 children		
1895	27,170	2200 m. female	1600	1 week
		3300 s. female		1 week
		2100 m. male		1 week
		2100 s. male		1 week
		800 children		
1898		3450 m. female	2750	1 week
		3700 s. female		1 week
		2400 m. male		1 week
		2600 s. male		1 week
		700 children		
1900	25,606			

*Figures based on information in Table 1.

†Figures were based on number of confessions or communions at the mission; m. = married, s. = single. Information was given in the Paulist Mission Chronicles.

Index |

243